DOONESBURY.COM'S

DOONESBURY.COM'S

DISPATCHES FROM TROOPS IN IRAQ AND AFGHANISTAN

Introduction by G. B. Trudeau

Edited by David Stanford,
Duty Officer, *Doonesbury* Town Hall

**Andrews McMeel
Publishing, LLC**
Kansas City

07 08 09 10 11 RR2 10 9 8 7 6 5 4 3 2 1

Library of Congress Cataloging-in-Publication Data

Doonesbury.com's the sandbox : dispatches from troops in Iraq and Afghanistan / edited by David Stanford; introd. by G. B. Trudeau. —1st ed.
    p. cm.
    ISBN-13: 978-0-7407-6945-0
    ISBN-10: 0-7407-6945-6
    1. Iraq War, 2003—Personal narratives, American. 2. Afghan War, 2001—Personal narratives, American. 3. Soldiers—United States—Blogs. 4. United States—Armed Forces—Biography. 5. United States—History, Military—21st century—Sources. I. Stanford, David. II. Trudeau, G. B., 1948–

    DS79.76.D665 2007
    956.7044'34092273—dc22   2007021334

www.andrewsmcmeel.com

COVER PHOTO CREDITS
Cover photo © 2007 Chad Hunt, chadhuntphotography.com
    PFC William Tyler Pinson at the Korengal Outpost (the KOP), in
    Afghanistan, November 2006. Hometown: Chattanooga, Tennessee
Cover sunset photo: Courtesy of U.S. Army
Jingle truck photo: "Danny" Ernest D. Anderson, SFC(R)NCOIC, Recruiting
    Assistance Team, Kabul, Afghanistan
Night vision photo: Terry Wade, courtesy of U.S. Army
Oasis photo: LT Carl Goforth, desertflier.blogspot.com
Book cover design: George Corsillo/Design Monsters
All other photos and text are the exclusive property of their individual creators.
    Used by permission. All rights reserved.

ATTENTION: SCHOOLS AND BUSINESSES
Andrews McMeel books are available at quantity discounts with bulk purchase for educational, business, or sales promotional use. For information, please write to: Special Sales Department, Andrews McMeel Publishing, LLC, 4520 Main Street, Kansas City, Missouri 64111.

CONTENTS

CONTENTS

EDITOR'S NOTE

In the summer of 2006, almost two and a half years after *Doonesbury* character B.D. was wounded in Iraq, Garry Trudeau asked me what I thought about adding a military blog to our 11-year-old Doonesbury. com Web site. By that point the milblog phenomenon was well under way, with several thousand already on the Web, but there was the sense that the readership was largely limited to family, friends, and a few fellow bloggers. It seemed like we might be able to help serve as a link to a more general audience—to people without a direct personal connection to anyone deployed—and thereby help focus public awareness on our troops.

We also thought that there were probably deployed service members who didn't want to take on the burden of creating and maintaining their own blogs, but who would welcome a forum in which to write about their experiences.

Six weeks before it would appear in the newspapers, Garry wrote a Sunday *Doonesbury* strip in which the character Ray Hightower—B.D.'s companion in Gulf War I and Iraq—introduced *The Sandbox*, urging service members to report on the war so readers back home could stay informed. Once that strip went into production, we were committed to the project and spent weeks writing to milbloggers, asking if we could republish particular posts on *The Sandbox*, so that there would be something to read on the site when it went live. This "priming of the pump" put us in touch with a wonderfully diverse group of writers.

On October 8, 2006, the Sunday strip ran and *The Sandbox* was launched, with this top-of-the-page greeting:

Welcome to The Sandbox, *our command-wide milblog, featuring comments, anecdotes, and observations from service members currently deployed to Iraq and Afghanistan. This is GWOT-lit's forward position, offering those in-country a chance to share their experiences and reflections with the rest of us. The Sandbox's focus is not on policy and partisanship, but on the unclassified details of deployment—the everyday, the extraordinary, the wonderful, the messed-up, the absurd.*

We immediately began to receive new material from deployed troops, but we also continued to post pieces from the bloggers we were already in touch with—and we kept discovering other good writers as we explored our way through the ever-changing milblog realm. So *The Sandbox* was initially, and continues to be, a mix of content—some written for the site, some sent to us from other sites, some requested by us from other sites.

We had assumed we would be receiving brief posts, perhaps expecting that deployed troops would be writing in haste during rare spare moments. We were stunned by the volume of high-quality writing that came in—epic, detailed accounts of complex and grueling missions; thoughtful meditations; moving epiphanies; historical perspectives; and humorous vignettes. Many of our posters were clearly not only service members who were writing, but writers who were serving. After weeks of putting up several posts a day, some of them thousands of words long, Garry remarked that we seemed to have created the war's first literary journal.

In this first *Sandbox* collection there is a tremendous range of subject and tone. Both the Iraq and Afghanistan theaters are represented, as are spouses at home, returned vets, and caregivers. Each *Sandbox* writer adds something to our understanding of the vast undertakings in which we are engaged. There is a glossary at the end of the book to help readers traverse the acronym-heavy portions of the wordscape. When it comes to abbreviating rank, each branch of the military adheres to its own tradition. Although the Army, the

Navy, the Air Force, and the Marines are all represented in this book, *The Sandbox* utilizes a unifying hybrid system.

This book is but a sampling from the rich archive of *The Sandbox*, an ongoing, open-ended online project that by now includes hundreds of posts, photos, and videos—all still available at gocomics .typepad.com/the_sandbox. On the site you can read more posts by the writers represented here, as well as contributions from those who have joined us since this volume was put together. You can post comments and write to many of the posters directly. I hope that other deployed service members will write to us and lend their voices to *The Sandbox*.

I would like to thank my colleagues at AMU and uclick for their support, especially tech guru Carl Ferrara, who showed me the Way of the Blog; our book editor, Erin Friedrich, for her passion for the project; Christi Hoffman for her production care; and Shelly Barkes and Jennifer Collet for getting the word out. Thanks also to early readers John and Betty Stanford for their encouragement and feedback; Karen Sublette for her helpful editorial suggestions; designer George Corsillo for his artistry; and Garry Trudeau for having yet another damn good idea.

To the *Sandbox* posters with whom I have had the pleasure of working and corresponding: Thank you for your service, your openness, and your creativity, and for entrusting me with your words.

David Stanford, Duty Officer,
Doonesbury Town Hall
themanagement@doonesbury.com

INTRODUCTION

BY G. B. TRUDEAU

For six years now, the country has had a common story: the tragedy of 9/11—a shared experience of immense narrative power.

At first it was too big, too overwhelming, to process; veteran news anchors were struck dumb on the air. What had happened was quite literally the unspeakable. But it didn't take long for journalists to rejoin their instincts and race to tell the story of a lifetime, and in so doing help the rest of us begin the long, painful process of making sense of a calamity beyond imagination.

Bearing witness has always been vital to society's well-being. Without the healing spell of stories, we would live in chaos. Ever since our miserable species huddled together in small groups on the savannah, there's been a storyteller around the fire, the one who reminded all the others of who they were and where they came from. Ancient bards were indispensable in ameliorating the unceasing struggle for survival by making it seem less arbitrary.

Not much has changed since then. *The Sandbox* isn't all that different from a warrior's campfire, albeit one that welcomes thousands to pull up a log. Five days a week for the last year, our contributors have logged in with fresh, intimate reports of life down range. The military calls these contemporaneous debriefings "hot wash," a kind of actionable nonfiction. From an unsettling catalog of the various sounds of incoming projectiles, to an accounting of conscience following a raid on a civilian home, to an aching meditation on the night sky above a desert outpost—these highly personal narratives get at the soldier's reality in gritty, granular detail—and with an insightfulness that often eludes even the most skilled media embeds.

These are stories told from the inside out—and as such, each bears the particular emotional coloration of its author at a particular moment in time. There is no mistaking the fear or the boredom or the irony in the voices here assembled—not much flat, detached mil-speak in evidence. Sometimes posting within hours of a hostile action, sometimes writing during a soul-deadening stretch of inactivity, the *Sandbox* posters reach out to us in a way that combatants never have—in real time, and often before the raw feelings behind the posts have been pinned down and smoothed out.

When PBS's remarkable series on the Civil War debuted some years back, many viewers commented on the uncommon beauty of the letters written by soldiers in the field. Could today's warriors possibly be that eloquent? Well, yes. As this book confirms, each era has its singular chroniclers, men and women trapped in extraordinarily stressful circumstances who somehow discover within themselves the need and capacity to make art from it. Thanks to David Stanford's tireless scouting sorties to the hundreds of milblogs that have sprung up in the last four years, *The Sandbox* has managed to bring together and showcase some of the very best of these young writers. We are deeply grateful for their participation, and it is our hope that readers new to them will be as moved, informed, and yes, entertained, by their work as we have been.

THE SEARCH

NAME: **1LT ADAM TIFFEN**
STATIONED IN: **IRAQ**
MILBLOG URL: **THEREPLACEMENTS.BLOGSPOT.COM**

She is handsome, rather than beautiful. Her black dress covers her from head to toe, with only her face showing under a black head scarf. Still, her open, expressive face is attractive in a motherly way, as she smiles and looks down at her curly-haired baby, the child's fist crammed firmly into his mouth. Sitting on the woven carpets in the bare room are her other children. A slender girl with her back against the white plastered wall, perhaps 14 years of age and wearing a red dress, smiles shyly up at me. The third child, a young boy, sits quietly beside his mother, his dark eyebrows and pale skin forming a striking contrast. Children's books and white notepads filled with children's drawings are scattered on the carpets that line the floor of the room.

We have come to raid their house.

Standing in the room with the mother and children, I feel slightly foolish as I post a young, serious soldier with a squad automatic weapon to guard them. He is to prevent them from getting up and moving around the house while my soldiers conduct their search. For both their safety and ours, I can take no chances.

Turning to the boy, I have my interpreter ask him where the family's weapon is. Throwing a quick glance at his mother, he gets up and walks into his parents' bedroom. There, behind a curtain covering an opening into a cupboard, is a well-maintained AK-47 and a 40-round banana-clip magazine. Each household in Iraq is allowed to have a single AK-47 and one clip of ammunition. Reaching into the cupboard I take out the weapon. It takes only a second to remove the magazine, clear the chamber, and place the weapon back on safe. One less thing to worry about.

"Are there any more weapons in the house?"

"No," he says, and shakes his head.

"All right, go back in the room with your mother."

Walking into the hallway, I stop next to my squad leader and give him the go-ahead to begin searching the house. He moves up to the top floor and out onto the balcony with his search team.

Turning, I survey the house. As houses in Iraq go, this is a relatively nice one. The small refrigerator and freezer in the hallway appear to be new, and the house is neat and well kept. As in all Iraqi houses, almost none of the rooms have furniture, just mats and rugs on the floor for family members to sit on.

In the kitchen, what is left of the afternoon meal is sitting on a large metal platter. Cut cucumbers, white rice, and what looks like curried beans are each sitting separately in small metal bowls on the platter. When the family eats, they place the platter on the ground between them and scoop the food out of the communal dishes with their hands. My stomach gives a little flutter. The food is covered in a crawling mass of flies.

Walking up the staircase to the roof, I come across a growing pile of electric cables and copper wires. The squad leader and one of his men are collecting the spools from a corner of the rooftop and placing them into a pile for removal. These are the kinds of materials used to manufacture and detonate IEDs. This is exactly what we are looking for.

From the rooftop I can see my soldiers securing the perimeter of the house. To the north and east, armored HMMWVs are staged, giving the gunners good sectors of fire. In the event that we are fired upon while conducting our search, the gunners will be able to return fire and suppress the enemy. In the distance, to the west, looking out over no-man's-land and past the mosque, I can see the rooftop and gun positions of the Alamo. We are just a stone's throw from home.

Walking back down the stairs and out of the intense heat, I reenter the room with the mother and her children. Behind her, a color television sits on top of a large cupboard, an Arabic soap opera loudly and emotionally playing out on the screen. I notice that the outfits and hairstyles look like something straight out of the 1960s.

The woman is looking at me expectantly, her dark eyes smiling as she plays with her child. She asks me something in Arabic, and the girl behind her giggles.

"What did she say?"

"She wants to know if you want to take a picture with the baby."

Caught off guard, I smile briefly down at her pleasant face, but then my smile begins to fade. The woman does not know that we have arrested her husband on suspicion of being an insurgent. He is currently out in one of the vehicles awaiting transport to a holding facility. With a sinking feeling, I try to shut out my emotions. I know that what we are doing is going to be bringing a lot of pain and suffering to this friendly, motherly woman and her delightful children. I tell myself that it is part of the job. Still, I don't have to like it.

My squad leader appears behind me and beckons me back into the hallway. "We've completed the search. We found a mess of wires and cables and a couple of boxes of documents."

"All right, good work. Go ahead and move everything into the back of my HMMWV. I'll go talk with the CO and let him know the search is complete." I walk outside into the heat. In one of the vehicles, my commander sits talking on the radio. He is coordinating events with another platoon searching a different house just down the road. The captain looks at me through a sheen of sweat on his bright red face.

"OK, good work. Bring him inside and let him get some toiletries and a change of clothing."

I walk back to a second HMMWV and open the back door. There is the woman's husband, his hands bound behind his back, and a pair of dark goggles covering his eyes. Surprisingly, he is an older man, his salt-and-pepper hair and mustache accenting a strong, stern face. The soldier guarding him is sitting beside him.

"Take him out of those cuffs and remove the blindfold. She doesn't need to see him like that. Oh, and when you guard him inside the house, try not to look like that is what you are doing." The soldier nods. This is going to be emotional enough.

The man rubs his wrists as he steps out of the vehicle, briefly stretching his legs. On his face, I can see that he is steeling himself to face his family under these circumstances. It is a struggle for him to keep his face emotionless while he walks toward his home. Following behind him, I can see him square his shoulders and muster his dignity.

As I let him lead me into the house, I can see his wife on the floor, no longer smiling, as she looks at her husband with shock and concern all over her face. Trembling, she turns to me and starts asking me questions in Arabic. "What has he done? Where are you taking him?" Clasping her hands together she is almost pleading with me.

"Ma'am, we are just taking him over to our base to ask him some questions about a few matters that need clearing up."

"How long will he be gone? Can he be back tonight?" The pain in her voice is obvious. She is terrified for her family and for her husband. The soldiers have come to take him away, and for all she knows, she may never see him again. My heart is in my mouth.

"Ma'am, I am afraid that this is not possible. You should expect him to be gone for a few days at least."

She glances down at her children and then looks at her husband. He speaks to her in Arabic, and she moves into the bedroom to pack some belongings for him. With a nod, I send a soldier in after her to keep watch.

The man asks permission to gather a few papers that he wants to take with him. He walks over to the cupboard and under the watchful eyes of his guard gathers what he needs.

Within a few minutes, his wife enters the room clutching a plastic bag filled with clothing and a towel. She looks at her husband as if she wants to say something, and then she turns back to me as he is getting ready to leave the room.

"She wants to know if she can keep the AK-47."

"Tell her that she can. Each household can keep a weapon for their own protection."

She looks relieved, and then she continues hesitantly. Her hands are clasped together as if in prayer. "What will I do? How long will he be gone? I cannot stay here alone. It is dangerous here. Please bring him back tonight. If you do not, where will I go? Who will protect us?"

Behind her, I can see that her daughter has tears in her eyes. I turn away from their stricken faces. Glancing at the soldier behind me, I can tell that this is as difficult for him as it is for me. In a quiet voice, I give instructions to the private standing behind her husband.

"All right, take him back out to the vehicle, and let's get ready to go. Let the CO know that we are done here."

Accompanied by the subdued young soldier, the man leaves the room and walks outside without so much as glancing at his wife or his children.

"Ma'am, do you have family you can go and stay with? Is there someone you can live with until all of this is resolved?"

She thinks a moment and then replies: "Yes, my husband's family lives in Baghdad. I could take the children and go there." I nod my head and attempt to look encouraging.

"I recommend you do that. I honestly don't know how long your husband will be gone."

She looks at my face as if trying to read something, and then she glances down at her children and clutches at her infant's chubby little hand. Turning away, I address the other soldiers still left in the room.

"All right, let's get moving. Go ahead outside and mount up. Let's get out of here."

As the soldiers file out, I turn and place her AK-47 on the ground and ask her not to pick it up until we have left. Then, after all of the soldiers have left the room, I stop in the doorway and turn back.

"Steve, tell her that if she chooses to stay here, I will patrol near the house and check in on her from time to time to see if she and the children are OK. Also tell her that if she leaves and goes to Baghdad, I will try to stop by and make sure the house is OK."

She listens and then nods her head quietly.

It is the least that I can do.

ALARM CLOCK

NAME: **SGT ROY BATTY**
STATIONED IN: **BAGHDAD, IRAQ**
HOMETOWN: **YELLOW SPRINGS, OHIO**

The ocean is deep, shadowed dark, full of the keening whispers of whale song and the lunar musing of the tide. I swim mindlessly in the liquid womb of its embrace, the half-felt shadows of distant sharks sliding over the sun-dappled pillars of light above, undulating. Life is safe, unseen but body felt, blood warm, and thick with the musk of sleep, and I clutch at it, slowly, like a sleeping infant at his mother's breast. The blind comfort of nipple dreams.

Noise, deep, sharp, more felt than heard. The wooden barracks thrums twice, buckling and then springing back into place. I am thrown from my bed, the stuffed animals that my wife keeps sending me flying wildly, eyes bulging and felt paws flailing, into the tiny space I call home. I don't know if the local detonation of high explosives actually flings you around, or if it is some incredibly fast autonomic response sparked from the recesses of your reptilian brain, but it is impossible to lie still when it happens.

Clearly, this is Rustimayah, and we are under yet another mortar/rocket attack. The good thing about being in the Army in Iraq is that you are always in uniform, even when asleep, which means that one can usually run to the bunker without having to suffer the embarrassment of public nudity and the subsequent hilarity among your comrades in arms. Unless one runs straight into the camouflage poncho strung across your four square feet of living space, falls down, and flails on the ground like a stunned porpoise in a fishing net.

Which is exactly what I did.

Extricating myself from the eager folds of my plastic curtain, I sheepishly realized that this was not Rustimayah, but our four-star accommodations at FOB Shield, and since there were no follow-up explosions, we were not getting mortared. Must be a VBIED—a car bomb. A big one.

In any case, I was awake, and there was no sense in going outside unprepared. I grabbed a can of Starbucks DoubleShot and a pack of Camels and wandered out to find out what the hell was going on.

The dusty patio in front of our dilapidated barracks was full of the usual flares of post-blast cigarettes and the hasty stories of perturbed soldiers. All of the civilians had frozen in place and stared, but, fresh from the joys of Camp Rusty, our MPs had collectively done the 360 spin-in-place and headed for the nearest bunker. A thin mushroom cloud, drab and brown with atomized sand and smoke, rose from the western side of the perimeter.

There was a lot of talk about what it might have been. Some of the officers authoritatively announced that it was an IED, down on Route Wild. Others, NCOs like me, were sure it was a VBIED. It looked to be like it was in the market area two blocks from us, the same place that was hit by three simultaneous VBIEDs just a few days ago. Either way, it was huge—somehow this single blast was louder than those three. We watched the smoke cloud to be sure. If it was just an IED, it would quickly dissipate. If it was a car bomb, it would smolder and burn for some time.

Over the wall, there was a sprinkled crackle of gunfire, along with the distant wailing of police and ambulance sirens. I wondered for a minute if this was a coordinated attack, until someone noted that the IPs were clearing traffic in their normal way, by shooting at the cars. That's not an exaggeration; that really is how the police clear traffic here—by shooting at you. It sounded as if every cop in Baghdad was making his way to the scene, which probably wasn't far from the truth.

The mushroom cloud slowly faded in the chilled blue of the early morning sky, a burnt offering sent back to Allah as it was intended. It was gradually replaced with thin streams of jet-black smoke, trickling up from the secondary fires in the square. Yep, I was right. A VBIED. Trapped by the early morning convection layer, the smoke hugged the dull brown skyline of the city, spreading slowly southward like ink in a glass of water. I watched the vapor with curious distaste; it seemed more fluid than smoke—black, thick, viscous. Evil, as if it was imbued with everything that is wrong with this country—hatred, petroleum, and the smell of burning human fat.

After a bit, people wandered off to continue doing whatever they had been up to before the Big Boom. Guys trudged by with towels and ditty bags, headed for the shower. Squads, headed out on mission, went back to their trucks to tinker with their obstinate mounts. IPLO civilians drifted off to the chow hall for breakfast. The rest of us stood and drank our coffee and sucked on our cigarettes, watching the smoke, quietly.

It's interesting to watch people trying to be normal in the aftermath of a fundamentally disturbing event. A few blocks away, corpses were littering the blackened asphalt of a city square, burning. Ambulance crews would be arriving and trying to find the wounded among the debris and the dead. But not us. It was someone else's job, and there really wasn't anything to do here but carry on with the mundane details of the still alive. So, we all walked around and fiddled with our gear or stood and tried to make small talk through clenched jaws; but all the voices were a little too loud or a little too quiet, and the people walking by tended to look down at the gravel a little too intently, with the occasional anxious glance toward the shrouded sky or the perimeter wall that seemed just a little too close.

After a bit, Fish and some of the other guys went inside to see if they could find out what happened, via the Internet. Astonishingly, only 20 minutes or so after it happened, the attack was already on Yahoo. The blast was in Tayaran Square, not in the market area as I had guessed, but about a block west of it. The square is right in front of one of the bridges to the Green Zone, and I had driven through it and across that bridge only yesterday. Now Yahoo was saying that 23 people had been killed and a hundred or so wounded. The number would be sure to rise.

Eventually, I have to go off in search of gainful employment. We have a critical "distro" run to make, shuttling administrative papers from one FOB to another. As we are gearing up and preparing to leave, there are a couple more explosions, which eventually turn out to be pyromaniac EOD teams blowing up suspicious banana boxes out on the highway. Getting dressed and squaring away the truck to roll out of the gate is a curious exercise, in light of this morning's reveille. It's all down to a set routine now, and I hold to the sequence faithfully, as if that act of contrition will somehow save me from swerving too close to the wrong white and orange taxi cab. I strap on my $70 WileyX assault gloves and slip on my Peltor headphones in the solemn hope that they will fend off the combined demons of Wahhabism and plastique.

Through group consensus, we decide to go against the usual tactic of driving at a stately 15 mph along our route and instead careen at high speed through our chores, scattering civilian vehicles as we go. I feel protected and comfortable in my high-speed gear amid the bolted-on armor of the HMMWV, although I know it is an illusion. We do whatever we can to help protect ourselves, but in the end, if it is your time to go, then you're going. I notice myself absentmindedly swearing, out loud, at the local drivers as we pass them.

At the Rustimayah PX, I score another case of DoubleShot and reluctantly buy a pirated Xbox from the kaffiyeh'd bandit at the base hospital store. My old game finally collapsed in a dusty corner of the barracks a week ago, its mouth cracked open permanently, another victim of the choking Iraqi sand. The new one is all sleek and plastic wrapped, boasting a bootleg chip that plays every kind of VCD known to mankind, including, inexplicably, ancient Sega Genesis games. Maybe there is a remote clan of Genesis-enthralled bedouin tribesmen out there in the wasteland somewhere, snapping these things up as fast as they are churned out. All I know is that this new beast bellows wailing Arabic music at me every time I turn the damn thing on. Oh well. As long as I can play Need for Speed, I'll be OK.

There's nothing like pulling out into Baghdad traffic with your trunk full of expensive and newly purchased toys to make you pray extra hard not to get hit by an IED. Never mind losing your legs; it would really suck if that carton of real Camels, case of overpriced espresso, and new Xbox got shredded by an Iranian land mine.

Eventually we complete our tour of east side Baghdad FOBs and return to our pleasure palace at Shield. Yahoo, still light-years ahead of the military intelligence reservists across the street, coughs up the latest details on this morning's bombing. Seems that some Sunni dude rolled up to the square in his pickup truck and got together a crowd of guys with promises of a full day's pay for some odd jobs. Apparently this particular place is a known gathering spot for day laborers, mostly Shia men, looking for work. Once the scumbag had a good number of folks around him, boom, he blew himself and everyone around him up. Killed 63 people and wounded over 200.

Take a minute to think about that one. Ya' know, sitting here in front of your computer, catching up on your favorite blog, it's fairly easy to go, "OK, makes a sort of sense." But can you actually imagine it? I mean really visualize it, doing it? Not as the plot of some dumb-ass Tom Clancy book or Hollywood's next blockbuster movie. For real.

Driving to work with a pickup full of artillery shells and propane tanks rolling around in the truck bed behind you. A detonator in your pocket. Waking up, getting out of bed, knowing that you are going to kill yourself this morning, along with a whole shitload of other human beings. Oh, and not a military convoy, not a checkpoint or some general or a vital headquarters, or anything important like that. Just a bunch of ordinary Joes, looking for a couple of bucks sweeping out somebody's garage. And then actually doing it.

Baghdad averages three car bombs a day.

One other interesting thing about yesterday. It's 8 P.M. or so, I am sitting outside, smoking a cigarette with my friend Phil. Phil is sipping on his ritual Coors beer. He has one every night, after chow. It doesn't actually have any alcohol in it, since such immoral things are disallowed in George W.'s puritan militia, along with pornography, sex, and tight-fitting civilian clothes. Or any civilian clothes, for that matter. Phil just drinks it because it helps him to remember home. That, and the hope that someone at KBR will screw up and let a real one through the supply channels.

So we're sitting there, enjoying the crisp dusk, when every single person in the Greater Baghdad Metropolitan Area with a machine gun starts shooting. Seriously . . . every single one. The sky is full of tracers. It looks like CNN footage from the opening of the first Gulf War, only not in shiny night-vision green. Black sky, red tracers. Badadadadada. We sit there, a Camel hanging off my lip, a beer can halfway to Phil's mouth, agape at the sheer volume of metal suddenly appearing in the night sky in front of us.

Presently the FOB loudspeaker system cranks up and the Marine 1SG who runs the camp comes on, telling "All Hands" that the shooting is not a mass uprising against the infidels, as we all suspected, but celebratory gunfire due to a soccer game. Everyone not on mission has to get indoors, and everyone who has to be outside has to be in full battle rattle. Phil and I reluctantly move to the wooden double doors of the barracks, where we stand and watch the spectacle.

It seems that the Iraqi national soccer team is doing pretty well for itself at the Asia Games in Doha, and the locals are simply showing their appreciation for its latest success. Baghdad style, fo' shizzle.

Phil and I are standing there, talking about how stupid it is to get everyone indoors. It's not like our flimsy plywood barracks is going to protect us or anything. Still, we want to watch the fireworks and don't want to go to the trouble of putting our gear on, so we just stand in the doorway and sip our beer and puff on our smokes and feel cool.

Suddenly there is a sharp CLANG! between our feet and a puff of dust in front of us. We both jump and spin back inside the barracks, shocked for a second, and then laugh. Not one, but two rounds have hit right by us. Our feet were only eight or nine inches apart, and one round impacted between them. Once the shooting dies down, we go out to investigate and pry an AK-47 slug out of the metal grate in front of the door. One of our soldiers finds a PKC round in the sand a couple of feet farther out. I'm not going to bitch about the FOB safety rules anymore.

You gotta love a city that wakes you up with a car bomb and puts you to bed with machine-gun fire—for fun. Easing into the blue womb of my bed, I glance at my German cell phone, the one I use as an alarm clock, sitting on the plywood table. Do I really need to set it for tomorrow's wake-up?

MAIL BECOMES PARAMOUNT

NAME: **CAPT LEE KELLEY**

STATIONED IN: **IRAQ**

HOMETOWN: **SALT LAKE CITY, UTAH**

MILBLOG URL: **WORDSMITHATWAR.BLOG-CITY.COM**

When you're in Iraq, mail becomes paramount.

No longer do you grab the stuff in your mailbox with the monotony that consumes after years and years of junk mail and coupons you'll never use. The walk to the mailbox is not a mechanical part of your day anymore. No more is your mail a constant trickle of companies reminding you that you owe them money. Mail becomes a miniature Christmas, a small token or package or gift from a magical land far away that now seems kind of fuzzy in your memory, like Santa and his reindeer through the glass of a child's globe that has just been shaken and presents you with a snowy winterscape. A quickening of the spirit occurs when you receive a letter or package from your friends and family back in the United States. It must be how one would feel receiving a message in a bottle after being shipwrecked on an island for years. This simile may be a stretch, but you get my drift.

Whether you are a true patriot and you bleed red, white, and blue, or you are simply here because duty came knocking at your door and you have some honor and some pride in what you do, it feels really good to receive thoughts and prayers from all of you back home.

You may be cooking one of us some homemade brownies this morning in a snug little town in the Blue Ridge Mountains of North Carolina, as you sip your Colombian coffee and enjoy watching the fog rise up off the slopes through your window, thinking about your son or daughter who is deployed in the Middle East.

You may send a photo of yourself snowboarding at the Canyons in Park City, Utah, and write, "I missed you on the lift tonight," or some other inside joke in black marker right across the mountainous scene in the background to your friend in Iraq.

You may be retired. You may be a veteran or a veteran of a foreign war. You may have been sitting in your living room just today writing a letter of appreciation on your favorite stationery and licking the seal and sending it to one of your grandchildren over here.

You may be a guy in Detroit who recently sent one of my sergeants some new boots and a carton of smokes. He signed up on operationac.com to "sponsor" a soldier deployed overseas.

You may be a child writing a letter in first period to a soldier from your hometown. We love the flags that you draw us in crayon or magic marker, coloring so carefully inside the lines. And we enjoy the intelligent letters you send us, wondering what it is like over here and if we are scared.

Whoever you are, and regardless of your political interests or your feelings about the military, or war, or violence, or our commander in chief, or Iraq, or Muslims, or the current stock market trends, we appreciate your support. Regardless of your favorite color, your skin color, the type of car you drive, your age, the college you went to, your lack of education, or your bad attitude toward teenagers and video games, we still thank you.

Because we are you. We are the American people, temporarily displaced for a spell in the Middle East. We exemplify virtually every race, class, profession, and opinion that you do over there across the pond. We're just fighting right now, that's all. We've been pulled away from "normal" life to serve our country as millions have done for America in past conflicts. Some of us believe in the political machines that nudge entire nations into war, and some of us just believe in ourselves and each other and doing the duty we raised our hand and swore to do.

CRANKY OLD PEOPLE

NAME: **DOC IN THE BOX**
STATIONED IN: **IRAQ**
HOMETOWN: **PRESCOTT, ARIZONA**
MILBLOG URL: **DOCINTHEBOX.BLOGSPOT.COM**

After three trips out here you start to notice trends—what works and the people who make a difference. There's always someone who goes beyond what is expected of them, doing things that aren't asked, and has that shining moment when they're so pissed or some subject irks them so much that they just have to fix it.

There's a guy in our squadron who worked construction for the decade prior to joining the Marines in his late thirties on an age waiver. He came out here and witnessed the shoddy work that his fellow Marines had done—primitive benches, shelves that weren't level, lean-tos covering the smoking areas—in some cases I've seen better construction on a tree house. Hidden behind his mild-mannered bifocals, SGT Elka started building a deep resentment for all of the crap that these amateurs had built and were displaying proudly.

My own pet peeve was the crappy bookshelves that were up. People who lived in shanties would have made better bookshelves then the ones we were using. So one of our first projects was to make some new ones, and I planned to use them to put everything in order. (One of our officers was also getting miffed by all of the books lying around and was requesting marshmallows in care packages for the book burning, so we had to work quickly.)

Then SGT Elka started in on making these octagon picnic tables and putting park benches all over. As usual, no good deed goes unpunished, and the command started putting in requests, too. Soon we had a phone booth built with its own AC unit. COs from other units would come by and start talking about wanting such things at their units. (And—egad!—having their books put in order!! Glad I'm going home soon. Have you ever had to go through several thousand books that have been through a couple of years' worth of dust storms? Very messy!)

It's not the people who do well on their day jobs who make the mark that everyone remembers; it's those cranky old men who get pissed off by the status quo and do something about it. I know those bookshelves and picnic tables will be around for a long time after we're gone.

FORGOTTEN

NAME: **FC1 (SW) ANTHONY McCLOSKEY (Tadpole)**
STATIONED IN: **AFGHANISTAN**
MILBLOG URL: **ARMYSAILOR.COM**

While I was home on leave recently, all the talk on every news channel was about the 10-year-old murder case of a little girl; hardly any mention of the war at all. When there is mention of the war, it's almost always of Iraq. Many people seem to have forgotten about Afghanistan altogether. Many of us over here feel like the forgotten bastard stepchildren of war. We get the leftover equipment and very little recognition.

Now don't get me wrong, we don't do what we do for the recognition. I recently got into a bit of a tiff with one of my officers over here. I was expressing the fact that I don't really agree with most of what we are doing here, and I definitely don't agree with our methodology. In my opinion it's wasteful and not very productive. Basically, like all things run by the government, I feel this operation is being run poorly at best. So he asked me why I was over here then. I think I surprised him with my answer.

I am not here because I have to be. I am not here because of orders or a contractual obligation or anything of the sort. I am here to support my comrades in arms. I am here to support the man next to me. I am here to help relieve the burden of a soldier. I am here so that a man with a wife and kids can spend a little more time at home with his family. Few others seem to understand that.

What I don't understand is why so many Americans are so apathetic about this whole situation. I really feel like most people look at this war as little more than a television event. How many have ever taken the time to stop and think about what we go through every day over here? The bullets, rockets, and IEDs are not the hard part. The hard part is knowing that life goes on back at home.

(By the way, I am a U.S. Navy sailor serving with a U.S. Army Special Operations unit. Some people are not aware that the Navy is contributing a large portion of the effort on the ground, and that we march into combat, side by side with our Army brethren.)

MY FIRST ADVENTURE

NAME: **MAJ DAVE TUKDARIAN (Yambo)**
HOME STATE: **FLORIDA**
STATIONED IN: **AFGHANISTAN**

I am back from my first adventure, down to Kandahar, a lovely place in the southern desert with daytime temps around 130°F. The breeze feels like a hair dryer. Plus we're carrying 80 pounds of helmet, weapons, vest, and ammunition. A real joy. At times this feels like another training event, but then something strange happens, like you reach into your pack and pull out a grenade.

After a hot and crowded C-130 flight, we convoy out to the Afghan Army camp. I am there to evaluate the communications for the Afghan corps. In the general's office there are handshakes and chai tea all around. The job I did in Japan really prepared me for talking through translators. It is a metered conversation that has to be direct, with simple words and no slang. Not as easy as you think. Try it sometime.

Then we're off to inspect the brigade's communication center, which is right next to the Afghan mess hall, the building with the goat pen. As we are talking communication, the smell starts to get to me. "What is that? Did the sewer back up?" "What's a sewer? We just throw everything in a pit out back by the mess hall." Thankfully the inspection is nearing an end, just in time for lunch. Hey, I saw a Burger King at Kandahar airfield! What? Our inspection includes eating with the Afghans in their mess hall. All eyes turn to the three Americans as we walk in. There is a tub of water in the middle of the room, and a cook is rinsing dishes then putting them back on the stack to use again.

Since we are guests, we sit down and a platoon of soldiers starts shoveling trays of food at us. Fresh plums and dates; so far so good. Then a soldier comes out with a sour goat milk yogurt lumpy drink.

I focus intently on talking to the interpreter so I don't have to refuse the offer. My brothers in arms are not so lucky. A major with the look of Opie Taylor graciously accepts the beverage, and all eyes are upon him as he takes a sip. And gags. A source of great amusement to the Afghans, to say the least. Our other guy has gone slowly, so he could see Opie's reaction, and in the commotion he deftly hides his glass under the table. Smart man.

Time for the food—a plate of rice and a bowl of some kind of stewed meat and red beans. Out of the corner of my eye I am watching the interpreter and doing what he does. Don't use your left hand; they consider that unclean. So here I am with a plate of flat bread, rice, and meat. Uh, where is the silverware? There is none. Grab the bread, scoop the rice, and tear off a piece of meat. Oh well. When in Rome . . .

I feel like an infant again; there is rice everywhere. I'm getting about half of everything into my mouth. The rest goes on the Afghan Army corps communication officer. After a while, he asks if I want to use a fork. He issues a quick command and the Afghan soldiers around the table scatter to search for one, and one is found. It looks like it has been used as a gardening tool. A quick wipe and some bending to straighten it out. Voila! Good as new. A nice gesture.

Finally, it's time to leave the mess hall. Hey, where did the goats go? I don't want to know.

It's time to train. I see a computer in the corner of the operations center. At least I think it's a computer. It's covered by a sheet, with flowers on top. Does anyone know how to use a computer? Only the major. Would anyone like to learn? Their eyes light up, and they immediately start thanking me. Three hours later they can turn on the machine and play solitaire. It's a start.

Time to leave. More handshakes and tea, and it's off to the airport. Our U.S. Air Force airplane never shows up. Gotta love those Air Force guys. For them, an order is optional. We wait for the next flight, then pile onto another C-130 and are about to take off when the plane turns around and shuts down. Never a good sign. There is a bit of discussion, and we are told we have to reconfigure for other passengers and cargo. Pull everything off the plane and stand by as three guys looking like something out of *Road Warrior* drive up and park their truck in the plane. We reload our baggage, and it's off again.

The road warriors never leave their truck. We land, and they drive off into the night. I don't want to know.

Now it's time for us to drive cross-country to go to a meeting. I see a few sights that make me think. The first is a Russian Army jeep with an inscription on the door: "The assistance of Russia to Afghanistan." My first thought is, "Gee, thanks. Like you haven't done enough already."

Second is a scene that sums up this entire experience. In the foreground is a fence with a land mine sign. Beyond it, poppies grow wild, and in the middle of the field is a destroyed Russian tank. In the background is a snow-covered mountain.

All over this country there are people working donkey carts, wheelbarrows, trucks; people building and trying to survive. I don't feel so bad about being here. These people want to succeed; they just need our help.

At the end of our journey, we meet with the U.S. commander in Afghanistan, in a room so rank-heavy that captains are making copies and getting coffee. And just think, this is only the first week! Tomorrow it's off to Mazar-e Sharif to do the entire process all over again. Note to self: Bring lunch.

A HARD PLACE TO BE

NAME: **SSG GLENN YEAGER**
STATIONED IN: **AFGHANISTAN**
HOMETOWN: **SANDY, OREGON**

It sucks that the Afghan National Army is being targeted only because they're standing up for their country and what they believe is right, and we're being targeted only because we're here trying to help the ANA stand up for their country and what they think is right. What does the enemy want? Well, they want to be free to roam the country and do what they do best: terrorize. As far as the civilians in this country, some support us and try to help us out by giving us intelligence on what's going on. Others either turn a blind eye to what the enemy is doing, or they're too scared to do anything but help the enemy, whether they support them or not.

It's a hard place to be, Afghanistan. It's not like wars we've fought in the past, wars when you knew who the enemy was, where they were, and knew how to hit them. Now, you can't tell who's who, where they're hiding—or when you do know where they're hiding, it's a place we're not allowed to hit. It's frustrating to all of us.

Some people back home either don't support us being here or maybe just don't understand. Others do support us, no matter what the reason. That's what we have to rely on to keep us going, knowing that there are people back home that are behind us, each in their own special way—whether they send words of comfort and support, wave the American flag proudly, send care packages, or just keep us in their thoughts and prayers. We as soldiers appreciate those people. And, as far as the other people, the ones who see it their own way and the way they want to ... well, we're still proud to wear the uniform for them, too.

Generations before us have come together in times of war and hostility. Those were times when the entire nation stood behind their military. We were a different nation back then. Here's something to think about as I close this: What would they think of how this country is now? One thing is for sure, they would still support the troops. Because none of us would be here today if it wasn't for our military men and women, who are over here just doing their jobs. A job they volunteered for. It's not something that deserves disrespect or a cold shoulder.

When you hear of a soldier dying, either here or in Iraq (or anywhere for that matter), bow your head and think of the family of that soldier. And then remember them always. Remember the soldiers, both home and abroad, no matter what they're doing. Never forget them.

NOT MY GRANDFATHER'S WAR

NAME: **SGT STEVEN KANE**
STATIONED IN: **IRAQ**
HOMETOWN: **OMAHA, NEBRASKA**
MILBLOG URL: **SACKINIRAQ.BLOGSPOT.COM**

This is not my grandfather's war.

One of my grandfathers was in a naval ship steaming toward Japan as part of the ground invasion force when WWII ended. He was saved from forcibly liberating the country by the decision to drop two atomic bombs. My other grandfather was a Navy corpsman who was decorated for defending his Marine platoon during an ambush in the Korean War. He treated his wounded comrades while simultaneously defending their position against an ongoing attack, as most of the leathernecks in his unit were too badly injured to fire a weapon. They awoke in the morning surrounded by their own wounded and piles of enemy dead.

I wondered aloud the other day what my grandfathers would think about this war.

What would they think about the 50 pounds of body armor that we wear, when they wore not much more than a steel pot? About our only being allowed to move tactically in armored vehicles, when they had forced marches of large groups of soldiers? About fewer casualties in four years of fighting than in some single days of WWII fighting? About wearing a reflective belt at night on a forward operating base? About Baskin-Robbins in the DFAC, daily phone calls home, e-mail and Internet access, when they didn't eat for days upon days and the best they could hope for was a three-month-old letter from home? About two-man, air-conditioned rooms, air-conditioned offices, and air-conditioned Humvees, when they slept in the mud? About two-week leave back to the States in the middle of our one-year tour? About the four duffel bags of gear that I've been issued, when they often had boots with holes in them or no cold-weather gear in the middle of the European winter?

I think that my grandfathers would understand the advancements that our military has made in the last 50 to 60 years.

I think they would even understand the constant complaining by soldiers who have living conditions infinitely better than they could have dreamed. After all, it is every soldier's right to complain about the hand they've been dealt, while at the same time sacrificing countless nights away from their spouse and kids, missing irreplaceable births of children and deaths of parents, sacrifices that even for a staff NCO like myself are greater than most at home can fathom. All for an idea that is America.

All for the same reason my grandfathers fought.

All for freedom.

HERE IN BAGHDAD

NAME: **SGT AITCH**

STATIONED IN: **IRAQ**

HOME STATE: **PENNSYLVANIA**

I had been pulled for an OP here in Baghdad. So I grab a private, my favorite private, and tell him to throw on his gear and leave those books behind.

College was a terror. I went from Protestant and a believer to well-read and subversive. Let's break the mold, son. Let's enlist and have things to write about.

So here I am, educated and enlisted, an infantry sergeant enamored with the violence. And to promote, among other things, the development of a good private, I suggest reading lists. I steer these buggers away from pulp and pop and more toward explorations of the dark night of the soul, hoping, somehow, to get these dudes to realize the enormity of their present baptism in world affairs. So this private, the one throwing on his gear and leaving behind the books, is my little project. A social service product, a kid with no home, a kid who tags along on leave; this is the kid I pick for everything. I hammer his genitals into the wall. I want to make him my son and me his father. I want him to trust me.

So we go out, we infil, we lay there on the gun, we whisper and conduct our hourly radio checks. And this kid, this little bugger once soft and pink and now 20 years older than he was last year, this kid who read my list of books, gobbled my list of books, this kid says, "Sarn, we have to personify something, don't we?"

"Kid, we are human beings. We have the luxury of *being* the metaphor."

He thinks a second, shoots an azimuth at a cluster of people there in the haze, adjusts a few million pounds of gear; he says, "Nah, Sarn, I used to have the luxury."

God bless you, Mr. Palahniuk.

And this kid, this little hero, is about one month from returning home to a country that will fear him, to girls who will desire him. He'll get his miniature round of applause at Atlanta airport, the USO will give him a razor and can of shaving cream and will thank him, impersonally, for being present in another debacle. And sooner or later, this kid, hopefully, will thank God for his involvement in the deterioration of Baghdad, the crumbling of American foreign policy, seeing bodies turned to burger, watching a tracer round from his weapon burn a hole through a man's neck, the reading of books, the performance of thousands of push-ups, the lack of sleep, the dust in his lungs; hopefully he'll thank God for this devastation.

I know I do. It has brought us away from the luxury of the metaphor. And this rarely happens in my world. And yours. He is exponentially disconnected from nuclear America. And now, a dog of war, now, having read the books and pulled the trigger, having bowed down to the violence, away from celebrity magazines and bad music, away from social formulae, this kid is as fatalistic as he needs to be, being what we in uniform have become.

THE "WHO HAS IT WORSE" GAME

NAME: **C. MALONEY**
HUSBAND: **DEPLOYED ON FLOAT . . . SOMEWHERE**
HOMETOWN: **SEATTLE, WASHINGTON**
MILBLOG URL: **CORPSDJOUR.BLOGSPOT.COM**

Between deployed Marines/soldiers and their spouses, it's easy to play the "who has it worse" game. Being the even-keeled person that I am, I am OK with saying we both have it hard. . . . An example:

THE DAY HE LEFT

Him: riding out on his floating steel chariot, heart thumping, adrenaline rushing, the adventure starting.

Me: holding his hand as he prepares to leave, keeping my patience when his superiors come to chat with him, cutting into our last few seconds together. Waving good-bye as he rides away. Driving home to the big empty house, seeing his dirty laundry, the empty Monster can he'd finished off the night before, not quite bringing myself to throw it away, not just yet.

I'd rather be him.

CHRISTMAS DAY

Him: probably stuck in the middle of the desert, maybe out on a mission, receiving stale, crushed gingerbread cookies in the mail, waiting for a Christmas gift that hasn't made it yet, singing "Jingle Bells" in his head to drone out the chanting blasted from every loudspeaker on every mosque in town.

Me: sitting at home with my family, opening up gifts by the fire, making butterball cookies with my mom, waking up to Santa Claus–stuffed stockings, clinging to my cell phone, hoping for a phone call from my husband.

I'd rather be me.

Yes, we've both had it tough—we've been separated from each other before our new marriage has even had a chance to solidify, for holidays, birthdays, and anniversaries; if we speak, it's in the middle of the night in 15-minute increments, forcing us to trust that the other is thinking about us, loving us, even if they can't let us know.

But let me also tell you why we have it good. We have a little more perspective. We squander our minutes together a little less, knowing that they are limited. We have an opportunity to write each other love letters. We learn to be proud of one another and proud of ourselves. And when we say, "I love you," the small crack in the voice shows that we really mean it . . . and, for me at least, the silver lining that I don't have to watch a single football game this whole season.

While I don't always love this life, while I wish that I knew right now where my husband is and what he is doing, while I sometimes feel alone, sacrificing so much for something that most people find an inconvenience to their pocketbook or a nagging annoyance on the evening news, while we both have it hard, and it's easy to slip into the "who has it worse" game, I find it helps to focus on what I have learned, how this has helped us, and how lucky I am to really know it.

HAMID

NAME: **CAPT DOUG TRAVERSA**
STATIONED IN: **KABUL, AFGHANISTAN**
HOMETOWN: **TULLAHOMA, TENNESSEE**
MILBLOG URL: **TRAVERSA.TYPEPAD.COM**

Today was the usual half-day of a Thursday. Our interpreter, Hamid, and I spent a lot of time waiting for meetings, and we worked getting the ANA troops paid for their convoy duty. I was the approving officer for four convoys, so they had to write up the approval letters, Hamid had to translate, and then I signed them all so they could get paid. The personnel officer was very happy that I was taking an interest in helping. Franz Kafka could not have written a more twisted and convoluted system than the ANA pay system, even if he had a hangover, a toothache, and just had his leg gnawed off by a rabid hamster. Nothing is easy here. Falling off a chair requires three different forms, signed in blood, and approved by the Ministry of Defense.

Hamid and I had lots of time to talk, which he really enjoyed. I learned just how awful his life is. He is an earnest, serious man, 27 years old, and never gives the impression of being irresponsible or not taking his religion and culture seriously. He lives with his mother and two brothers on a hillside overlooking the capital, and he says his house is very nice. It is conveniently located in relation to everything except work. He would love to have us over for a meal to meet his family, and I would love to go, but I doubt we would be able to. No one knows he works for us except his immediate family. They don't want to get attacked by insurgents or angry neighbors.

Further questioning revealed that his house has only two rooms. It used to have four, but the house was divided, and his uncle owns half of it now. He has electricity for only two or three hours in the evening, and so their house gets pretty warm. In the winters they have a wood-burning stove, but the house gets very cold. He loves eating at our chow hall because there is such variety. At home they eat a rice and meat dish that rarely changes from day to day. He does not like it very much, but the rest of the family does. I've seen Hamid wear exactly three different shirts in the five weeks I've known him. It's probably all he owns. He gets paid good wages by Afghan standards, but I know he supports his mother with some of that.

We discussed funerals, as COL R and many of the ANA troops were heading to one. Death is common over here, and the life expectancy is in the upper 40s. Muslims are not supposed to cry at the burial, as it can send the dead person to hell (as best I understood Hamid on this point). Despite this, there is much weeping and screaming of anguish at funerals here.

He also told me that the police had just arrested a man who had been posing as a woman and hijacking cars and kidnapping women. Men would pick him up, thinking he was a prostitute, and he would chloroform them and steal their cars. This whole thing was pretty amazing to him. So I told him all about America, sex-change operations, breast implants, transvestites, etc. I explained that when you live in a free country, there is a lot of weird stuff that can happen, too.

At lunch, we discussed his hopes in life. He would like to get married, but his mother must arrange it. First his older brother must get married, and that is in the works. The brother's wife will move in with them in the tiny house. He also explained that wives and mothers-in-law fight a lot because sons must pay equal attention to their wives and their mothers. After his brother is married, Hamid may ask his mother to arrange meetings with a girl. However, Hamid must first go through all his cousins and tell Mom that he doesn't want to marry them. Then he can look to marry outside of his cousins. At this point, he asked if we married cousins in America. I said in many places you could, but generally we did not. I tried to explain about in-breeding and recessive genes, but who knows how much he understood. I did make it clear that for health reasons it was usually better not to marry a cousin.

Hamid does indeed have a girl he is "impressed by." That is Afghan for "she's so hot!" He rarely gets to see her, but once his brother gets married, he can start hinting to Mom that she might be a nice girl to set him up with. Despite this, Hamid is very sad. He wants to get married, but it is at least two years off, and at 29 a good chunk of his life is over. Most of his friends are married and have kids. I told him lots of Americans wait until they are over 30 before they get married.

"Yes, but you can have sex any time you want. We must be married," he replied.

Well, I can hardly blame the poor guy for being frustrated. He's going to wait for marriage, and it's killing him. I told him that plenty of Americans wait until they are married to have sex, and we aren't all having nightly orgies. Plenty of guys never have sex. (I suspect there is a significant number of guys so afraid to even talk to a girl that they never get to first base.) Hamid gave me a look of skepticism, but I told him there are plenty of religious people in America, just as there are in Afghanistan, and they wait for marriage. I think he finally believed me.

I will close with a story he told me, which is poignant and heartbreaking. I will write it as closely as I can to the way he told it, which was very moving. This was about his life in Pakistan, shortly before coming back to Afghanistan.

"Pakistan was so green, so beautiful. When it rained in the spring, it was warm and lovely. I remember once it was raining, and I put on my raincoat, and my friends and I walked three miles in the rain to a café. It was dark, and there were lights everywhere, and they shone off the water, the rain, the streets. We sat and drank tea and watched the beautiful girls go by. But here in Afghanistan there is nothing. We must be inside by 8 P.M. There is no electricity. There is nothing to do. I wish I could leave."

"Why don't you go back to Pakistan?" I asked.

"My family was with me there. Now they are here, and I must take care of them."

When Pakistan is your Garden of Eden, you know you are at the very bottom of what life has to offer.

Our day was over. He needed to go to the front gate to catch a taxi, and I walked him out. "Today was a very good day," he said. "I am glad we had so much time to talk. Normally we are in too much of a hurry. But I enjoyed it very much."

As did I, my friend.

THE COOLEST PLACE TO BE

NAME: **SGT ROY BATTY**
STATIONED IN: **BAGHDAD, IRAQ**
HOMETOWN: **YELLOW SPRINGS, OHIO**

Most of the time, the coolest place to be on post is the coffee shop that I call my other home. It's nestled in between two Hadji Internet cafes, and since the Internet places have wireless LANs, one can sit in the coffee shop, enjoy the Arabic television, surf the Internet on your laptop, and best of all, smoke!

The place is full of the gray twisting tendrils of various exotic tobaccos and their respective memories: hookah shei-shei smoke—that can only be Baghdad and missing Barbara like I would miss a critical part of my body; or Djarums—full of the cloying scent of cloves and Vikki and the misplaced nostalgia of high school; or Gauloise, that always smells like burning horse shit and reminds me of Nicole and Paris and the restaurant on the Champs-Élysées with the world's largest bowl of chocolate mousse.

The coffee shop is the place where the dustbowl anarchy of Iraq fades away, and my mind becomes engaged with something other than the drill instructor routines of deployed military life. This is the place where reality fades and is replaced with memories and thoughts and imagined realities; all coursing through the light-dazzled tube-ways of the Internet to arrive on my laptop, spat out onto my screen in little binary squiggles of black and white electrons.

When the cybercafés close amid the commo blackout, the hip place to be is the battalion Hadji store. I am half convinced that the commo blackouts are engineered by the secret army of Iraqi interpreters that live on the FOB, and who own and operate the various Hadji stores dotted around the base. They don't have Internet connections, but they do have tables and backgammon and German MTV on a big-screen TV, and their hookahs are much bigger and more impressive. The drinks are all the same as the coffee shop's, but it doesn't matter, since none of them are alcoholic, being banned by some distant Grinch of a general. So when the blackouts descend, everyone packs into the place and clusters around whatever female is holding court tonight, and tries to be as witty and solicitous as possible. This is pretty hard, not having alcohol to lubricate the process, so everyone puffs away on the flavored shei-shei smoke and consumes as much Jordanian soda pop as possible, as if attempting to get high on the sugar content and lack of oxygen. I like it better during the day, when the TV is tuned to CNN and the place is not quite packed to full capacity.

In the back is a large store that offers the usual pirated DVDs/Xbox/PlayStation games, as well as leather shoulder holsters and various computer accessories. This is where I bought the Iraqi SIM card for my cell phone and the silver metal CIA briefcase that I carry my ThinkPad around in. The place appears to be owned by an Iraqi with the code name A.J.—a short, muscular fireplug of a guy who speaks perfect English, with an American accent to boot, although he has never left Baghdad. All of the interpreters use code names, to avoid getting "three in the back of the frickin' head" if they ever decide to venture off post in anything other than an armed convoy.

A.J. is really cool, very energetic, and he teaches me a new phrase in Arabic every time I see him. Today it is *"al-'amthall noor al-khalaam."* Or, "Proverbs are the light of speech," which shows, if nothing else, how much Arabs like to use proverbs.

I DREAM OF DJINNI

NAME: **CAPT MATT SMENOS**
STATIONED IN: **AFGHANISTAN**
HOMETOWN: **SANTA MARIA, CALIFORNIA**

I tried to explain that she was a genie—or a *djinn*, as it's pronounced in Arabic. For me, Barbara Eden strutting around in a pink halter top and pantaloons had always fit vaguely into my understanding of the mythology of the Middle East. To my friend and interpreter, Aresh, it made no sense at all. I tried to explain who she was and what she was doing as he and I ate lunch in the television room at our little base, but I soon realized that this was an American idea and kind of a dumb one. Define surreal: "A white guy from the suburbs, eating grilled cheese sandwiches in a wooden hut in Afghanistan, explaining *I Dream of Jeannie* reruns to an Iranian-born Afghan employed as a Dari/Arabic interpreter by the U.S. government."

Aresh wanted to know why she was (relatively) naked and why her "husband" (The Major) allowed her to come and go (so abruptly) while dressed like that. I explained that The Major never chose her, that they were not married, and that, in fact, it often seemed he wanted to be rid of her. Yet, she had chosen him as a master, and there was no getting rid of her. This explanation did nothing to clarify the concept for my poor interpreter. But Aresh is a good kid, and as frustrating as the conversation was for him, he satisfied himself by telling me he was glad no women he knew could make things happen like the woman in the show. Next week I'm starting him on *Bewitched*.

AMBUSH

NAME: **1LT ADAM TIFFEN**
STATIONED IN: **IRAQ**
MILBLOG URL: **THEREPLACEMENTS.BLOGSPOT.COM**

I cannot believe what I am hearing. The screaming over the radio is horrifying. Something, somewhere, is seriously wrong. At the first sound, all movement in our command post stops. My eyes are riveted on the green radios sitting on the top of the old wooden desk. A quick glance around the room tells me that every other soldier is frozen in place.

The radio static is heavy, the voice making the transmission frantic. I can barely make out a few words: "This is Titan 5 . . . an RPG . . . ambush . . . casualties . . . grid coordinate . . . UX 2468 7531. . . ." It is enough. Jumping to my feet I run over to the map against the wall. I quickly pinpoint the coordinates that I have just heard through the static and the gunshots. The location is a straight shot west, about six kilometers. Not far.

Turning around, I see that the other soldiers are all still frozen, waiting for the next transmission. I exchange glances with the other platoon leader and announce to no one in particular: "I'm going out there." I turn and grab my gear. Shrugging on my body armor, I run into the hallway shouting: "Let's go! Get to the vehicles! There is a unit in contact that needs help! Move!"

The soldiers in my patrol tumble out of their cots, where they have been lying, exhausted. Grabbing their gear, they take up the shout:

"Come on!"

"Let's move!"

As I run out of the building, still pulling my body armor on, the heat hits me like a blast furnace. Behind me, soldiers are flying down the steps and running to the vehicles. Climbing into my seat and fastening my helmet chinstrap, I can hear the guttural roar of the engines. We are loaded up and out of the gate within four minutes.

The HMMWVs speed out past the concrete and concertina wire obstacles. My driver takes the turn around the barrier so sharply that for an instant I am certain that we are going to hit it. The front bumper clears by an inch, and we are through.

As we begin to speed down the broad paved main street, I pick up the handset for the platoon net and gather my thoughts. "All right, this is what is going on. A unit was hit about six klicks west of here on ASR Robins. It sounds like they have been hit with RPGs and small arms fire and have several casualties." There is silence in my vehicle as my crew listens in on the conversation. "One more thing—we may be targeted as we respond. Be on the lookout for an ambush, especially a VBIED."

Insurgents have been known to hit units that move to assist a unit in contact. Overhead, I hear the metallic clacking of my gunner charging the M2 .50-caliber machine gun. He has racked a five-inch round into the chamber of the long-barreled, lethal weapon system. It is a reassuring sound. The M2 has a rate of fire of more than 10 rounds per second, and the rounds can easily punch through concrete walls.

Turning west we begin to pick up speed. "Thunderbolt X-Ray, this is Warrior 2/6, we are headed west on route 'Robins,' moving to Titan 5's position. We should be there in about five Mikes. Do you have an update on Titan 5?"

In front of us, civilian traffic hastily pulls out of the way as the patrol runs screaming down the road. I can tell that my driver has his foot clamped all the way down on the accelerator. The clear, paved road stretches west into the distance, empty and desolate except for scrub brush and trash lining the sand berms on both sides of the road. It is a stretch of empty desert between two towns, and out here traffic is thin.

Over the battalion net, I can hear Titan 5 calling for a medevac to pick up his casualties. Someone has been seriously wounded. Above me, I hear my gunner swear an oath under his breath. Looking up, I can see a plume of thick black smoke in the sky. It can only mean one thing. Something is burning.

Adrenaline floods my system, and my heart starts pounding rapidly as we round a bend in the road. A HMMWV is completely engulfed in fire. Flames billow from the windows, and black, choking plumes of smoke rise high into the air. The smoke is thick and acrid from the burning tires. A chill runs down my back, and I realize that there are no soldiers anywhere to be seen. Nothing moves. It is terrifying, like something out of a nightmare. Where are all of the soldiers?

A hundred meters past the burning armored vehicle, I can see the charred, torn, and twisted remains of a pickup truck. What used to be a gray Mazda is now scattered all over the road. I key the battalion handset.

"Thunderbolt X-Ray, this is Warrior 2/6! We have arrived on site. There is a burning HMMWV and what looks like the remains of a VBIED. There are no soldiers anywhere! What is the current location of the Titan element? Where are the wounded soldiers?" My only thought is to get to the troops that need help and secure their position. The only problem is I can't find them.

"All right, stop here! Secure this location! White 1, move out about 300 meters and block off the west end. White 3, set up a blocking position 300 meters away on the east side. Tell your gunners to watch for follow-on VBIEDs and do a good dismounted sweep for IEDs!"

My vehicle comes to a screeching halt, 75 meters from the burning armored vehicle. Dismounting, I hear a loud staccato popping sound. The ammunition stored in the vehicle is cooking off, the bullets exploding in the heat of the fire.

I key the handset again: "Thunderbolt X-Ray, this is Warrior 2/6, I need the location of the Titan element! Where are they?"

There is a moment of silence, and then Thunderbolt X-Ray replies: "Wait one."

Surveying the scene, I see that the ground is littered with spent brass and links. There has been a major firefight here, and it looks like hundreds, if not thousands, of rounds have been fired. The berm to the north is separated from the road by a 20-meter stretch of empty ground, and rises 15 feet in the air. It is the most likely place to set up an ambush.

I notice a half-filled 30-round magazine lying in the road amid the scattered brass and shell casings. Reaching down, I pick up the battered magazine and place it in my cargo pocket. With a flash of light reflected off a canopy, the Apaches fly out of the sun. They are so quiet I do not even hear them until they are circling in a tight formation above my location. The circle is so tight that the lead Apache looks like it is standing on its side. I can see the pilot looking down over his right shoulder at the carnage below.

"Apache flight, this is Warrior 2/6. What is your call sign?"

"Warrior 2/6, this is Blue Max 2."

"Blue Max 2, this is Warrior 2/6. I need you to sweep the area to the north and west! Look for insurgents and also check for American troops. I know that Titan is here somewhere and is set up for a medevac, but I can't find him."

The pilot immediately banks north, and I get his crisp and clean "Roger" over the net.

Looking east and west down the road, I can see that the other vehicles in my patrol have moved into position. To the east, another three-vehicle patrol has arrived, responding to the urgent calls over the radio.

With a tremendous blast, the burning armored HMMWV explodes from the inside out and shreds itself into pieces of shattered and twisted steel. The armored glass bursts outward, and large chunks of armor go catapulting through the air, landing 20 or 30 meters away. The sound is almost deafening, and it takes me a second to realize that something inside the vehicle—likely a Claymore or several grenades—has exploded due to the heat of the fire.

My driver comes running up to me, his rifle held at the ready. "Sir, I don't know how to say this. I think I saw a body in the back passenger seat, before the vehicle exploded."

My heart stops. Looking up, I can see that the HMMWV is just a mass of charred steel, flames, and smoke. I force myself to speak. "Are you sure? Are you sure that is what you saw?"

My driver falters. "Sir, I . . . I don't know. It could have been the headrest or something else. I just thought I saw a body slumped over."

I clear my throat and key the hand mike. "Thunderbolt X-Ray, this is Warrior 2/6, the HMMWV has just been destroyed by secondaries. Do we have a location for Titan 5 yet?"

This time Thunderbolt X-Ray responds quickly. "Warrior 2/6, this is Thunderbolt X-Ray, roger. Titan 5 has headed south along route 'Maples' and has linked up with an element from Avalanche. They are secure and are conducting air-evac of wounded personnel right now. Continue to secure the site; more units are en route."

"Roger, Thunderbolt X-Ray. Are all Titan 5 personnel accounted for?"

"Warrior 2/6, this is Thunderbolt X-Ray, that's affirmative. All Titan 5 personnel are accounted for."

Closing my eyes, I breathe a sigh of relief. My driver must have seen something else. The hollow knot in my chest eases, and a weight lifts off my shoulders. Titan 5 is secure.

I hear my gunner calling out to me from the other side of the vehicle. "Sir, sir! There is an IED over here. I think that there are two of them!" He has done a sweep around my vehicle to check for IEDs and seems to have found some.

"Roger, show me." Walking around the vehicle, I can see a burned and blackened 155-mm artillery round lying out on the dirt, amid the wreckage of the charred Mazda pickup truck. From this distance, I can easily see a long white cord running from the nose of the round, which has been packed with some type of plastic explosive. Lying as it is on the dirt, it seems less an IED than a kick-out from a VBIED.

When the vehicle bomb exploded and tore itself into shreds, some of the artillery rounds from the bomb were kicked out by the explosion and failed to explode. This does not, however, make them any less lethal. I can see at least four, possibly five, of these kick-out rounds lying scattered on the pavement and on the dirt. Four or five battered and primed artillery rounds less than 100 meters from my position.

Great.

"All right, stay back. Conduct another sweep up to the northern berm, and I will call EOD."

"Thunderbolt X-Ray, this is Warrior 2/6, we need EOD at this location. We have either secondary IEDs or kick-out rounds from a VBIED scattered all over the place."

"Warrior 2/6, Thunderbolt X-Ray, that's a good copy. EOD will be en route."

In the distance, to the southwest, I can see the Apaches circling something. To the east, I see a plume of dust rise as two M1 Abrams main battle tanks arrive on scene. "Warrior 2/6, this is Reaper 3, where do you want us?"

"Reaper 3, this is Warrior 2/6, it is good to see you. I want one of your tanks to take up a blocking position on the eastern side and one to circle south around the HMMWV and take up a blocking position on the western side of the road. Watch out for follow-on VBIED attacks."

"Roger."

One of the 60-ton monsters drives past my position, slung low and squat with surprisingly sleek lines. The turbine engines grumble and the steel-padded treads squeal, sending up a hot cloud of dust and dirt high into the sky. Now I feel that the site is finally secured.

An hour later, EOD has detonated five 155-mm shells in a controlled explosion, and so many units have arrived that the place is swarming with troops. The senior man on the ground far outranks me, and some of the soldiers have found bloodstained fighting positions dug into the berm in the north. With the amount of blood found in the positions, it is likely that at least some of the insurgents never made it out alive.

Another HMMWV pulls up, and three soldiers dismount. I can see that their uniforms are stained with blood. One, a sergeant, has his hand and arm swathed in white bandages. They are from the Titan 5 patrol, escorted back to brief the battalion command on what had happened during the ambush. They look around, as if reliving a dream. I can't help but notice that they seem to be in good spirits, as if relieved at being back at the scene of the ambush and still in one piece. One is standing quietly to the side, watching the flames continue to consume what is left of the HMMWV. I walk up to him. "How are you doing, Sergeant?"

He turns and smiles. "Hey, sir, we're OK. My lieutenant is hurt pretty bad. He took some shrapnel in the leg, and we had to apply a tourniquet to stop the bleeding. A couple of the other guys were hit. My arm got scraped up pretty good, but all in all, everyone is still alive."

I turn my eyes back to the still smoldering HMMWV. "What happened?"

"Well, we were traveling east along Robins when our vehicles were hit by RPGs. This pickup truck was rigged as a VBIED, but for some reason it did not explode, so the insurgents hit it with an RPG to try to set it off. After it exploded, we took some pretty heavy small arms fire. They must have had at least one RPK there up on the berm." He points. "We returned fire over here, and then some of our guys were hit by shrapnel. Basically, we fought until the ammunition ran out, and then we withdrew to evacuate the wounded. My SAW gunner opened up on a couple of them on the bridge, and I saw at least two bodies fall into the water. They took a pretty good beating. I think we killed five or six of them."

In my head I can picture the entire sequence of events as he describes it. I glance at my watch. It all occurred about two hours ago. "When did you leave? We got here about 15 minutes after your call went out, and we couldn't find you guys. I didn't know if you had all taken off, or if you were all lying somewhere in a ditch."

He shakes his head. "It was my LT that made that call before he was hit. We disengaged once our ammunition starting running low and headed out to evacuate the wounded. We probably left no more than a few minutes before you guys showed up." Turning away from me, he stares again at the burning vehicle, then glances at the berm to the north, now crawling with soldiers.

Reaching into my cargo pocket, I pull out the battered, half-full, 30-round magazine and hand it to him. "Here, you guys dropped this."

He reaches out and takes the magazine, weighing it in his palm. Then he smiles as he looks back up at me. "Shit, sir, if we had known you were coming so quickly, we would have just stayed here."

A TASTE

NAME: **1LT WILL MANGHAM**
RETURNED FROM: **AFGHANISTAN**
HOMETOWN: **MOBILE, ALABAMA**

'm at the bookstore, and the woman at the table to my left has just finished rambling on to some poor guy about trying to find a 2006 Infiniti something or other because, "It's the only one with a navigation system that works in Hawaii." And she wants the rear-facing camera when she backs up because she hates the beeping, and you can only get the rear-facing camera if you have the navigation system. But the only one with a navigation system that works is a 2006, and she can't find a 2006. And my mind jumps back to a day in March of this year. I went out with a friend's platoon, and we hiked about two hours from our company patrol base uphill to a small village.

This is the kind of village that's so remote that there's no possible way for the kids to get to school and no way to get outside help for injuries. There's just no access. A central government has little influence on a place like this.

As we were approaching the village, an old man with crazy eyes and a white beard ran down the mountain to greet us. This was a welcome sign because it signified that he was taking us in, that we were under his care. After you are greeted in this way and guided into the village, there is basically no chance that you'll get attacked because the Pashtun notion of hospitality is very powerful.

As soon as we entered the village, the whole place was mobilized for our visit. A group of us were led onto a porch that had an incredible view of the valley. We talked for a while and let some of the old men and kids play around with some of our equipment, while our corpsman looked at and tended to some ailing villagers. Then tea was brought out to us, along with fresh bread.

The elders insisted we have lunch with them, and we agreed. The crazy-eyed man then made a stabbing motion with his right hand, and I realized that he was going to slaughter a goat for us. After almost three months in this country, it was the first time this had happened. One of the Marines loaned the old man his bayonet, with which the man was much impressed. Then two younger men held down the goat while the old man cut its throat to bleed it. If you want meat in Afghanistan, chances are you're going to have to kill something. There are no grocery stores in the mountains.

After the goat was bled came the skinning and the gutting. The old man casually disposed of the unwanted entrails, and suddenly a dark red piece of organ was thrust into my face: the liver. You want me to eat that? But I could not refuse. I had never refused any food that was offered to me, including a hunk of very bad cheese. The old man cut off a rectangle of goat liver and threw it back like it was candy. He cut off four more chunks. One went to the platoon commander, one went to a squad leader, one to our interpreter, and one to me. I held the liver up, considered it, and put it in my mouth. It had the same texture as raw fish—somewhere between that and a gummy bear. The flavor was actually appetizing. The only thing that threw me off was the warmth. The goat had been alive 15 minutes ago, and here we were eating its insides with a 70-year-old Afghan. I thought about that for a few seconds while I was chewing; then swallowed it down.

I noticed that even our interpreter wouldn't eat his liver raw. He was from the city, and these were country people. We must have all had the same strange look on our faces because the old man laughed at us and went back to tending the fire. I can only guess at the reason behind his laughter, but I think he knew that we live a very different life in America from the one he lives in the middle of the mountains. The sun rises in the morning, he starts his fire, he makes tea for the people he loves. I have no idea what he must be thinking at such a moment, but we had been given a taste of an entire reality, of a whole different consciousness.

ANOTHER TASK FORCE MISSION

NAME: **1SG DON CONNOLLY**

STATIONED IN: **IRAQ**

This one starts at 0200. I was going to be better this time. Prepared my gear, did everything I needed to, and in bed asleep by 2130, with the alarm set for 0130. I would be, if not well rested, at least in good shape to go through the mission. Eyes popped open at 2250, and nothing I did would get me back to sleep. Figures.

At 0155, I put on my gear and head out to a now-familiar sight—my soldiers moving around in the darkness doing the final preparations for the mission. Over the radio, platoon sergeants conduct an unending series of checks and verifications:

"Did you get the _____ team picked up at the CP?"

"Have all vehicles done radio checks?"

"Where the heck is _____, and why isn't he here now?"

"Get over to vehicle _____ and check _____!"

My vehicle this time is an M1114 armored HMMWV borrowed from another company. Looking at it yesterday, it was clear that they didn't loan us their best. This morning, a new gremlin shows up in one of the radios that wasn't there when we did radio checks yesterday. We can't fix it but figure out a work-around that will get us through the mission.

Final checks for my crew:

"Hearing protection?" Check.

"Eye protection?" Check.

"Ammunition for the turret gun?" Check.

"Water?" In the cooler with the ice.

And the list goes on.

Not a problem with my crew, as my driver and gunner are both experienced and have done it countless times. I check anyway. They check me.

0230: We move from our staging area toward the departure gate. On the way, we link up with what to me is a very ironic sight. Most of my military career has been spent studying Soviet/Russian-designed weapons and equipment and how to defeat it. The unit we are linking up with is equipped with that very same equipment. We are working alongside an Iraqi Army company that is equipped with BMP armored personnel carriers and Kalashnikov rifles.

We stage alongside the IA vehicles and wait. They look nervous, sitting atop their BMPs chain-smoking. After a few minutes, my driver and I get out and stretch. They look on curiously while we discuss a couple of details. Then I turn and say good morning in Arabic. A couple of them try out their English, which amounts to, "What's your name?" and "My name Hasim."

The word is passed: "Mount up!"

0300: Out the gate. Driving under blackout conditions with night-vision devices. We receive instructions to keep the speed down, far below normal. The BMPs can't keep up with our normal speed.

By the time daybreak comes, we have made it to our objective and are ready to start. We will seal off a series of small villages and search the buildings and surrounding areas. This will be a "cordon and knock" operation, much more polite than a "cordon and search." We will do what we need to do, search what we need to, take down census information, but we will do it courteously unless given reason to do otherwise.

The first few houses and farms are searched, and I stay with my vehicle, monitoring the radio nets. By the time we move to the next area, I get out and move with the search teams. We slowly move into the hamlet, carefully looking at everything because there have been numerous attacks nearby. SGT V's team enters the first house. It apparently has not been used for some time.

On to the next. This one is lived in, with cows, goats, and chickens in the yard. Everything goes by the unwritten script—the women and children go into a quiet huddle somewhere in the yard and try to pretend we can't see them. The men stand anxiously, some with a defiant look, others with trepidation. Many are simply resigned to it. Today, most seem helpful.

At the third house, there is an older couple who seem overly helpful. Sometimes this means they are hiding something. Not this time. The man shows us right where he keeps his AK-47 for quick access against the "Ali Babas" who raid at night. The woman scurries about, laughing as she warns us about the low door lintels so we won't bang our heads. They rush ahead of us to open cupboards, doors, the trunk of their car. The rooms are mostly bare with concrete floors. They roll their sleeping mats out at night, but for many, that is the extent of their furniture.

As we leave that house, the man manages with hand signals to convey that he is the patriarch of the small hamlet we are in—all the houses, all the residents, everything is his.

The team moves to the next house and, rounding a corner, find we have met another part of the platoon. There is a large group of women and children huddled around something in the yard, but they present no evident threat. I check with the search team in the house; they have found nothing amiss.

Moving back into the yard, I see what has drawn the crowd—the medic, PFC N, is open for business. He dispenses aspirin, antacid, antibiotic ointment, whatever he has to relieve suffering. N is a good medic. I have worked with him before. He is young, quiet, competent, and caring.

The people are joyful to have that kind of attention. They carry an old woman over to where N works. She is the matriarch of the clan, perhaps the mother of the man at the last house. Whatever the relationship, all show respect for her and concern for her condition. There is something wrong with her feet and legs; I never find out exactly what. N and the interpreter go to work, while the platoon sergeant does his own kind of work.

These people are very family-oriented—it is all they have. They are virtually all completely illiterate. There are no books, no papers, nothing. They are born, grow up, farm, marry, have children, grow old, and die.

They are proud to show off their children, and the platoon sergeant responds by taking out a picture of his baby daughter. The women are excited and pass the picture around, chattering away. On the other side of the crowd, I also take out a picture of my three-year-old daughter and join in. Now N has plenty of room to work. The platoon sergeant and I have drawn most of the people away.

We are each working the crowd, admiring the children, while the mothers (and a few fathers) admire the pictures. Many of the women actually kiss the pictures and then hold them up to heaven with a short prayer phrase. In this culture, it is considered bad luck and invokes the "evil eye" if you admire someone's family member or possessions without giving praise or credit to Allah.

The platoon leader and I have our cameras out and, with the exception of a few younger women, the people are eager to have their pictures taken. The women are interested as the platoon sergeant and I describe, mostly using signs, how many and how old our children are. At this point, I do something I have not yet done since coming to Iraq. A word to the platoon leader and the word goes out over his radio net: "Send Private C down to where the large group of people is ASAP." A couple of minutes later, Private C appears, walking quickly but carefully, ever alert and scanning for danger. He has his M4 carbine slung over his back and carries a shotgun. He has grown even more in the few months we have been here and now towers several inches over me as we stand together.

He quickly figures out what is going on, but I tell him to bear

with me on this. We turn and face the people, and I point to my
name tape and then to his. There is a look of disbelief on everyone's
face. I have the interpreter tell the people that this is my son, and
that we together made the decision to come all this way to Iraq to
help the people as much as we can. After a moment of astonish-
ment, they cry out in a flood of excitement. They have never seen
anything like it. We are escorted into the presence of the matriarch,
still seated on the ground where the medic was working on her. The
relationship between Private C and me is explained, and she lifts her
face to heaven. She looks back at us, and I see a tear coursing down
her cheek.

LIST OF GEAR FOR SANDBOX DEPLOYMENT

NAME: **1SG TROY STEWARD (Bouhammer)**
STATIONED IN: **SHARANA, AFGHANISTAN**
HOMETOWN: **AMHERST, NEW YORK**
MILBLOG URL: **BOUHAMMER.COM**

Many people reading this blog are getting ready to come over here in the near future or have loved ones already over here. I have put together a list of good-to-have equipment, based on my experience here in Afghanistan and that of friends in Iraq. Some of these items won't be needed until you get in-country, so you may want to set those off to the side and have them sent once you get settled.

1. Any extra Class VIII you can bring from HS is good to have.
2. Wolf Hook Single Point Slings.
3. Desert Tan spray paint.
4. Space blanket(s).
5. 100 mph tape, 550 cord, TP, other expendables you think would come in handy.
6. Drop Leg Holster (BlackHawk or SERPA) and Uncle Mike's Holster for wearing around every day (Drop Leg will wear a hole in ACUs over time). I also have one for my IBA so I can have my 9 mm handy when in the gun hatch going through towns.
7. Weapons lube that *doesn't attract sand* (Miltech or Remington Dry Lube).
8. Two copies of addresses, phone numbers, account numbers, etc.
9. Two pairs of *good* boot insoles.
10. A good tactical flashlight (SureFire, even though you will get issued one with M4).
11. Red/white light headlamp.
12. Spare pair of running shoes.

13. MP3 player with extra pair of headphones.
14. Enough batteries to last you 30 days.
15. ChapStick.
16. Lotion.
17. 30 SPF or higher sunblock.
18. Bar soap—for some reason it's almost always in short supply.
19. Small, compact rolls of TP. A lot of places make travel size. Half the time you get to a Porta-Potti and the jackA$s before you yanked the TP.
20. Baby wipes—30 days' worth. Expect that the power and water will either go out, or the water will be contaminated, at least once a month.
21. Gold Bond Foot and Body Powder.
22. Small clip-on LED light. Clip it to your IBA. It will come in handy—quite often.
23. Drink mix for 16- and 20-ounce bottles of water.
24. Weightlifting supplies.
25. Small photo album with pics from home.
26. Hand sanitizer (small bottles to put in ankle pockets).
27. More books/magazines than you think you will need.
28. DVDs, for you and to loan out for swapping purposes.
29. Tactical gloves—military gloves are sort of clumsy. (I love the $9.95 Whitewater brand gloves from the clothing sales.) Also standard flight Nomex are good.
30. Lens anti-fog agent. Shaving cream works in a pinch, but you have to apply it every other day or so.
31. Good pair of shower shoes/sandals. I recommend the black Adidas—lasted me all year.
32. Small pillow (air inflatable).
33. Cheap digital camera (at least 2.1 mp).
34. Boot knife.
35. Gerber multitool.
36. Febreze—sometimes the laundry opportunities are few and far between.
37. Armor Fresh.
38. Extra boot laces.

39. Stainless steel coffee cup with screw-on lid.

40. Soccer shorts/normal T-shirt to sleep in, hang out in your room in.

41. Sweatshirts for wintertime hanging around.

42. A couple of poncho liners for privacy, cover for nasty mattress, etc.

43. A set of twin sheets with pillow case.

44. Good regular-size pillow.

45. One or two good civilian bath towels.

46. Buy a good set (more than $200) of winter desert boots. All they will give you is a regular summer set and a set of Gore-Tex-lined for waterproof needs. Desert is a cold place at these altitudes in the wintertime.

47. Bring a laptop. Also may want a PSP or some other handheld gaming device.

48. Get an external USB hard drive (greater than 60 GB). You will need this to back up data to and to store movies and MP3s that you will fall in on from previous teams.

49. Get a Skype account and download the software from skype.com. This is how I talk to home 95 percent of the time. If you call computer-to-computer, it is totally free. You can also Skype out from your computer to a regular phone for 2.1 cents a minute. There is nothing cheaper than that.

50. Decent headset with mic for computer (Skype).

51. Webcam for video calls back home.

52. Bring a minimum of 18 each M4 magazines per person. Nine that are loaded and nine that rest. Plan to do M4 mag changeover once per month.

53. Bring eight each 9-mm mags, for same reason above. Change these over every two weeks.

54. Order a LULA Magazine Loader & Unloader. It will be the best $14 piece of plastic you ever bought. I have 12 mags loaded at all times, and when I do change over, it will do it in a fraction of the time and save your hands and save the ammo.

55. Try to get your state to get, or purchase yourself, one 12V DC to 110V AC inverter per man for your trucks. They are crucial

on mission for charging personal items, cell phone, ICOMs, and especially ANA radios (they only have rechargeable batteries).

56. Dump the IBA tactical vest you get issued. Get a Tactical Tailor MAV chest rig. (Does not matter if you get one-piece or two-piece, as you want to keep the front open for lying in the prone. You don't want mags pushing into your chest making it hard to breathe.) I wish I had bought mine at the start. It makes a *huge* difference on the back and shoulders when carrying a loaded rig.

57. Get a comfortable pair of desert boots. I wear only the Converse eight-inch assault boots (non-zipper ones). Oakley, Bates, and several others are similar in style and comfort.

58. Bring some good snivel gear for the wintertime. Extra polypro winter hat, gloves, neck gators, etc.

59. Lock deicer for the wintertime.

60. Disposable hand and feet warmers.

61. Canned air, lots of it for electronics, weapons, etc.

62. Lens wipes for optics.

63. Screen wipes for computers.

There are probably many other things that could go on this list, but a lot of that is personal preference. The purpose of this list is to provide some insight into things that could make anyone's tour easier.

MAHN

NAME: **CAPT MATT SMENOS**
STATIONED IN: **AFGHANISTAN**
HOMETOWN: **SANTA MARIA, CALIFORNIA**

Sun-dried brick ramparts and soaring, silver parapets signaled a neck-craning, awe-striking terminus to our dusty, rattling convoy as we rumbled through the gated arches of Kayer Khot castle. A relic of the 19th-century British occupation, this megalithic fortification is actually very simple in design: a few mighty walls and towers lined with gangways and stairs, weather-beaten fighting positions and airy lookout posts, facing defiantly over the seemingly infinite leagues of barren hills and plains. As we passed into a large courtyard, a few gray-clad envoys from the local garrison jogged up to meet us. My breath caught in my throat as I noticed the burnished amber-golds and rich autumn reds of the leaves on trees, the likes of which I'd been sorely missing for months on end. The vegetation and fall colors reminded me so much of home that I soon found myself sitting alone in a cold, parked Humvee, stunned, mouth agape.

I was hardly unhappy to find myself alone, as my companion on the two-hour ride from our base had been one particularly gregarious guardsman. He had been, according to his story, to every special-forces school, every kind of combat training, and fought in so many battles that it would take far longer than a two-hour Humvee ride to relate. But he did his best, to the accompaniment of a bored-silly Air Force captain banging his helmet against the window in misery.

Left alone with my trees in the blowhard-less silence, I stepped out of the cramped gun truck and walked toward a low-hanging tree branch. Eyes fixed on the spectacular sight of sunlight diffused through a natural palette of color, I reverently approached the stand of trees, tripped . . . and fell on my face. As I tossed around in the soft dirt to find the culprit of my calamity, I locked stares with the small, round face of a boy in the dirt beside me. Skinny, with dark hair and eyes, this little guy tried to gather his simple brown shift and straighten his cap while he beamed at me with a huge smile, too rich for such a poor nation. I think I smiled back at him, some stupid grin like a half-drawn squiggle on a dirty piece of paper.

As I dragged myself back up, checking my various pouches and clips, his eyes darted around at the scraps of paper and trash he'd no doubt dropped when the huge, tan man had stepped on him. I tried to kneel down and help, but he was too quick. In a flash, he was on his feet again. With a trained eye and a sure foot, he bolted around, retrieving the bits caught by the breeze, scooping and jamming the mess back into a torn plastic bag. As he completed his rapid retrieval, he stopped dead, looked up at me—there was that smile again—and snapped me a heroic little salute. I was about to return it when we were interrupted.

"Hey! Wee-Mahn . . . get back to work!" I was startled by the close proximity of the sudden shout. The boy jumped, and his smile faded from his face. "Welcome to KK, Cap. I see you 'found' the help." I turned to see an old comrade walking quickly toward us. I looked back to where the boy had stood, but he'd vanished. This young sergeant had worked with me for a few months at another base before being relocated to Kayer Khot as an instructor. He is a good man, in my opinion, and had impressed me. We had spoken frequently, and he really seemed to care about the mission and our responsibility to help the Afghans help themselves. He had a gruff manner and shared a certain rustic, "old-school" attitude about foreign cultures. Unlike others, who might let that attitude affect their behavior, he had a kindhearted and surprisingly patient keel when dealing with our counterparts.

We shook hands and exchanged pleasantries, and he led me toward the local garrison's operations center, a worn but well-appointed white structure. It was simple, square, reminiscent of an old-fashioned, one-room schoolhouse. He told me how much happier he was at KK, and that he really felt good about the progress he'd seen in his troops. Ever bored with shoptalk, I asked about the boy.

"He's a good kid," he said, holding the door for me as we entered the ops center.

"Is he Pashtun? From a local tribe?" I asked as I gulped a bottle of water.

"Who knows? I don't even try to tell them apart. He and his brother came with their father, who helps us with carpentry and odd jobs."

"What's the boy's name? Or do you just call him 'Wee-Mahn' all the time, like the movie," I joked, recognizing the *Austin Powers* reference.

"Kind of, his name actually is Mahn." The door squeaked on its hinges, and the room was suddenly filled with voices as the survey party filed in. Civilian engineers and self-important senior officer types faked gutsy laughter and patted each other's backs and began dragging chairs around tables. They were discussing grid locations, elevation, local water supply, access routes, and personnel housing facilities. Apparently some high-toned and fancy to-do would be on its way to this poor, innocent castle in the coming months. I liked it the way it was. I took a seat by the window and waited for an opportunity to sneak out. The young sergeant was called away to answer some "critical planning question" about colonels' parking spaces and whether there was room for a water fridge and a soda fridge. Could we improve upon the volleyball court? It all sounded way above my pay grade. And my tolerance. After about an hour, I mumbled something about a toilet and slipped out of the door.

It was somewhat warmer this far south of my usual base. I caught a glimpse of Mahn, tirelessly hauling plastic bags of trash around the camp. I could still make out the big grin on his grimy face. I wondered if he'd been working like this the entire time since we'd arrived.

The presence of trees combined with the absence of colonels made the day even more inviting. I took a walk along the inside of one of the huge castle walls. I knew I was wrong to judge my companions so harshly. They had the best intentions and really did strive to accomplish what they considered great undertakings to improve this nation. I just never agreed with the priorities. Unfortunately, middle-management doesn't come with consular veto authority or anything like that, so I frequently wandered off, rather than lose another debate. They just seemed so singularly focused on improving the surface phenomena, like worrying about the paint job on a car that doesn't run. I always felt we should start smaller, focus on fundamentals.

My dramatic reflection was interrupted by an echo of laughter. Behind me, Mahn and another boy, whom I took to be his brother, were following me. Hands shoved in imaginary pockets, heads leaning forward—a perfect mimic of my "melancholy musings" pose. They were so amused with themselves that they couldn't help laughing at one another. The laughter turned to playful pushing, and eventually they were rolling on the ground in one of the most entertaining battles this ancient fortress had likely ever seen. Their faux mockery was very funny. It was as if they were telling me not to worry about them. They knew what needed to be done, and although they were just "the help," their voice would count for something someday. I waved to them, and they saluted me again before scooping up their trash bags and running off.

Another hour found me back in the Humvee (thankfully, with a new driving companion). My driver and I tested our radios with each other and with our gunner before giving the thumbs-up to the lead vehicle. As we rolled out through the giant walls one last time, all of our gazes lingered on the colorful trees in the courtyard. I looked around for Mahn or his brother, but they were nowhere to be seen. As we turned back onto the main road, my driver commented that it was nice to see that the seasons still change in this country. I kept thinking that I couldn't agree more.

ROBBIE

NAME: **SGT ROY BATTY**
STATIONED IN: **BAGHDAD, IRAQ**
HOMETOWN: **YELLOW SPRINGS, OHIO**

I am sitting on my camp chair in the corner of my room, the laptop on my bunk, iPod inserted deep within my ears. Hedley Moose is asleep next to me, exhausted after another night of avoiding the restless bulk of a snoring ex-Marine. The bed is cluttered with a 1:50,000-scale tactical map of Baghdad, my black Cordura wallet, ever-present Camels, a bright yellow *Arabic for Dummies* book, and Chuck Klosterman's awesome book, *Killing Yourself to Live*. After finally putting down Neil Stephenson's bulging *Quicksilver* for the hundredth time as being brilliant but absolutely unreadable, I picked up Chuck's tome and have been reading it every chance I've had for the past 24 hours. Which means that I am about halfway through it. He writes almost exactly the same way as I hope to, except for the fact that he is actually funny.

Peter Gabriel surfaces on the tiny, scratched screen of the Nano, singing quietly about Mercy Street. I close my eyes and the white-tiled ceiling disappears as I slowly rise through it and drift away to somewhere vaguely Celtic, full of dark rain clouds over coal tailings, thick with the wet smell of distant sheep. Amber, scotch-colored water pours over my hands as I dip them in a cold northern loch somewhere in the memories of my childhood in England.

I don't have anything to write about. We'll have to see what happens tonight on patrol. Baghdad has a way of throwing inspiration into the path of your HMMWV, either with the wet plop of over-ripened fruit or with something considerably denser and unfortunately louder in volume.

Actually, it just did. Resigning myself to writer's block, I put down the iPod and went outside to smoke a cigarette. Schrader and Smith were out there, so I went over to say hi. We were just starting to talk when we were interrupted by a weird whirring noise, sort of like a radio-controlled car in low gear.

We turned to see what it was, and a short black robot trundled around the side of the building on little round all-terrain tires. The intruder was just under a foot high and about three feet long. A tiny, two-inch silver camera was mounted on the top of the front bumper, and two spring-loaded antennas bounced along merrily at its rear. This was one of our newest toys; something I had heard about but had not actually seen yet. It's an EOD robot, but a cheaper version just for MPs. Designed to investigate possible roadside bombs but small enough to be carried in the back of an HMMWV.

Robbie the Robot trundled obliviously past us, turned right, and drove underneath a parked semi, its antennas bouncing and scraping the undercarriage of the truck. He then cruised off in the general direction of the battalion TOC.

The three of us looked at each other, wondering if we had actually seen this mechanical apparition. We had, so we peered around the building, expecting to see whoever was controlling the cute little thing, but no one was visible. I don't know the range on the radio controller, but it must be pretty far. No telling where they were hiding.

Robbie was disappearing in a small cloud of gravel dust, and, on a whim, I ran after him, following the bright, little blue LED mounted on his rear. I caught up with him, got in front, just to the side, and got down on all fours on the gravel. As he rolled by, I leaned over, mouth wide open, right in front of the TV camera. I would have loved to see the view on the distant TV screen. Understandably, he stopped instantly.

I laughed to myself and stood up, looking at him from the side. The robot paused for a minute and then lurched forward and then slowly started circling around me. I was amazed to see the little silver camera start traversing back and forth. Obviously he was trying to find out what halitosis-ridden monster had just tried to bite his head off. Robbie did a slow 360-degree turn around me, and I stepped in front of him, blocking his escape. The camera shook for a second and then rose up on an articulated arm that had been hidden inside his body. I leaned over and pointed a finger at him, like a boy admonishing a wayward puppy.

"Go home! Go home now!" I mouthed at him. I don't know if there is a microphone on the camera, but I couldn't see one. The camera rose up another inch or two, and then, amazingly, slowly shook its head left and right. No.

I burst out laughing, absolutely delighted. Apparently whoever was on the other end of the video feed had a decent sense of humor, too.

Robbie lowered his head, backed up, slowly rolled around me, and resumed his exploratory journey. The last I saw of him, he was headed off in the dust, antennas bouncing joyfully, silver head checking out the scene, trundling off in the general direction of the showers. The female showers.

Ah, to be a bored soldier in Iraq, with million-dollar toys. These are your tax dollars at work. At least he made my day, so it was worth it, I hope.

IN THE CHECKOUT LINE

NAME: **KELLIE COY**
HUSBAND STATIONED IN: **CAMP TAJI, IRAQ**
HOMETOWN: **MARION, OHIO**

I'm standing in the checkout line with my 11-year-old daughter, thankful that the twin ten-year-olds are not with me. I'll have enough questions to answer due to the women in front of us. "I can't believe we're still over there," the bleached blonde says to her friend. "It's not doing any good! We should just get out!"

My daughter, smarter for her age than I wish she was at this moment, knows these two are talking about troops in Iraq. How do I explain that her father's work is not a waste of time? That all the pain we've felt from his absence, all the tears we and others have cried are not in vain? How can I convince her of this when people like these two women are all too often what she and her siblings hear?

Oh, yes, there are those that say, "You tell your Daddy that I said 'Thanks.'" And even a few that recognize the sacrifice the children make and go as far as to tell them, "Thank you. I know it must be hard." But those are hard for kids to remember when the negative people speak so loudly. I look down at my daughter and see she's watching for my reaction. This is a crucial moment. A time to teach her a life lesson. So I bite my lip, literally. And I hold back the urge to speak in anger.

After we're settled in the car, she looks at me and asks, "Mom, I know you wanted to say something to them. Why didn't you?" I look her in the eyes, smile, and tell her, "Daddy's working in Iraq so that one day the Iraqi people will be able to speak their opinions, like those two ladies, without fear." Then, like most mothers do, I start to go into more of an explanation than is needed, when she interrupts me with "I know, Mom." And gives me a look of understanding.

Later that night, after the kids are tucked into bed, I'm sitting on the couch thinking—thinking about the day's events and what tomorrow will bring. I send up a prayer of thanks that my husband is safer than most, along with a prayer for those who aren't as safe as he.

And I don't forget to thank God for my children, who so completely believe in their father and what he's doing that I don't need to worry so much about what other people say. Because what's in their hearts is a blind love and belief that only a child can have.

A life lesson was taught that day, but I believe I was the student.

COMBAT

NAME: **ARMY GIRL**
STATIONED IN: **AFGHANISTAN**
MILBLOG URL: **DESERTPHOENIX.BLOGSPOT.COM**

How did I feel when I was in combat? It was scary. I was afraid. I wouldn't be telling the truth if I didn't put that out there first. After you go outside the wire so many times, you start to feel comfortable or complacent. That will get you killed, and it almost got us killed. So, no more complacency. Every time I'm out, my mind runs through the hundreds of possible ways we could be hit; from that building over there, from that rooftop on that side, from the mountains/hills on both sides, from that car driving up to us or that person lurking around our group. I look for kids. I look for things in the road. I watch for motorcycles with people wearing things that look too baggy, because the only fat Afghan is a wealthy one, and he's not going to be blowing himself up. Your senses become heightened, and you're ready at any given moment for something to happen. You expect it. You think of countless ways the enemy could ambush, attack, or approach you.

After we got hit, I was furious. Rage and anger were the only things that I could feel. It was as real and solid as the blood in my veins, and it was unlike anything I'd ever felt before and ever hope to feel again. It got me through and helped me do what I needed to do. I pulled security and administered first aid to my buddy. I got inside the gate, jumped out of my truck, and cleared my weapon. Training is what got me going. I have no idea what made me jump out of the truck, instead of riding it into the aid station, but all I could think about was following procedure and clearing my locked and loaded weapon. It was on burst and the safety was off, so it was the safest thing to do. I walked to the aid station and was stopped on my way there by a soldier who was far smarter than I. He treated me for shock and forced me to calm down and lay down. I got to the aid station, was checked out and treated for minor injuries, and spent the rest of the day and many hours into the night working. I had so much adrenaline pumping through me that I felt little pain till the following day, when I felt like I'd been run over by a five-ton truck.

WHAT IT'S ALL ABOUT

NAME: **FC1 (SW) ANTHONY McCLOSKEY (Tadpole)**
STATIONED IN: **AFGHANISTAN**
MILBLOG URL: **ARMYSAILOR.COM**

A t the end of the movie *The Green Berets*, John Wayne tells a little Vietnamese boy, "You're what this is all about. . . ." He was absolutely right. I cannot speak to the motivation for much of what we do at the political level, but I can say that for those of us out here, boots on ground, every day, the women and children of this country are what it's all about. Each day that I see families

living in the conditions that they are forced to endure over here, I am thankful that my own family is safe and secure back at home. Afghanistan has given me one great gift: It has made me very thankful for all that I have. When I rotate back to the world, life will have a far richer flavor.

Although I do sometimes feel resentful at my being over here because of my separation from those I love, I have to admit that the resentment fades away when I look at these children. I feel for them. By what luck was I fortunate enough to be born in the U.S., or any First World country, for that matter? That alone is reason to give thanks.

A DIFFERENT PERSPECTIVE

Name: **AMERICAN SOLDIER**
Returned from: **IRAQ**
Milblog URL: **SOLDIERLIFE.COM**

This last month stateside has given me a lot of time to view things from a different perspective and evaluate some things that I might have overlooked otherwise. I made a trip to Idaho and visited my good friend Chad. I opened up a few times to Chad and told him some of the experiences I had over there. The whole trip was worth it.

The day I left, something occurred that really topped it off. While in line to get my tickets, I saw another soldier. We really stick out like sore thumbs. Anyway, I get to the kiosk, and he was right next to me. He asked me if I was coming or going. I told him I had been back for a few months now, and I came back early due to being wounded. I asked him his job, and he said he was a crew chief on a C-5. He said he had just gotten back the night prior. In a stroller, he was pushing his eight-month-old baby, whom he had never seen until the day before. It put a smile on my face.

Well, I kept bumping into this guy along my travels, and I swore I knew him from somewhere. I just couldn't place it. The Army can seem very small, but I didn't remember him from any prior bases I was at. While on layover, I saw him and his family. I approached him and asked him about the aircraft he flew in over there. At that point, I figured he might have been on the same plane I was on when I was evacuated. I described the flag in the hull and a few other things. Sure as shit that was the same plane he was the crew chief of. He tended to me while I was laid up on a stretcher. I was in and out for the duration of the flight, but I remembered his face. What are the chances of that?

We parted ways, and I was just happy that I had met him. I really didn't know how to respond. So I went to the terminal of my next flight. He was passing by, and he came up to me pushing his baby. The words that came out of his mouth really stuck with me. "In the 16 years of my career, I've always wondered about the guys that we flew out. You have made my career come full circle by meeting you." The man had tears in his eyes. He explained that he always wondered about the ones who were hurt. He knew the disposition of the ones in boxes, but the ones on stretchers like me, where did they go, and how did they make out?

We had some more words between two soldiers who were strangely reunited, one on a trip fresh from the war and another enduring the mental war. It was good to have that experience; it closed a few things that might have hampered me a bit longer.

ON OUR OWN

NAME: **CAPT ERIC COULSON (Badger 6)**
STATIONED IN: **RAMADI, IRAQ**
HOMETOWN: **ST. LOUIS, MISSOURI**
MILBLOG URL: **BADGERSFORWARD.BLOGSPOT.COM**

I usually write contemporaneously, but this is something that happened several months ago:

Ar Ramadi, Iraq. 0300.

We left the FOB at 2130 and have been winding our way through the city ever since. We are nearing the end of our route.

It is one of our first patrols on the ground in Iraq on our own. No trainers, no unit we are replacing. Just us. Many of the soldiers in our unit have spent years training to do something like this. Wondering what it would be like. Wondering if we would measure up.

It has been a quiet night in Ramadi. Earlier, we looked at many possible targets but found none. Then the radio call comes.

"Badger 3/6, Kilo 1/1."

"Go ahead, Kilo 1/1."

"We have a suspected cache of explosives and weapons here. We were wondering if you and your EOD could come take a look at it."

"Roger, Badger 3/6 on the way. We are about five blocks from that location."

We pull up to the target area. The Coalition Forces that called us have at least two platoons on the ground.

I get out of the truck, look around, and think, "Wow, here I am on the ground in a combat zone, in Iraq. And hey, no one has taken a shot at me. This is OK."

Surreal does not even begin to describe the situation. I could have been on a training exercise at NTC or an urban warfare training ground, but no, it really is Ramadi, Iraq. All the preparation has been for this moment. Not just the deployment prep, but all of my

Army training going back to basic training at Fort Benning, Georgia, over 15 years ago.

The street reminds me of a postapocalyptic Southern California. The homes are in a distinct Mediterranean style with stucco walls and red tile roofs. This street is atypically wide, at least for Ramadi— 30 feet. But the homes are close together, with eight-foot-high fences separating them.

The maneuver forces that called us here are standing in a vacant lot that looks like a mini-landfill between two homes.

"Hey, Badger, over here."

My platoon leader and I walk over.

"Check this out."

The soldier who called us points to several pieces of large military munitions that until this time I have only read about in books: Soviet, Chinese, South African.

"And look at these."

More bomb-making material. The stark realism that we are no longer training hits me like cold water in the face; both startling and refreshing. Working with our EOD element, we scan the entire 15 x 15-meter lot, moving very carefully in case there are booby traps.

I remember thinking at some point that I should be cautious. Any bullets shot at me would not be the fake laser of the MILES gear, but real 7.62 x 39 mm from an AK.

After scanning the area, we begin sorting the items into different piles: nonexplosive, bomb-making materials here; possible intelligence items there; a bag of black ski masks; and all types of explosives ranging from artillery shells to rocket-propelled grenades. And finally, sitting in the middle of everything, small arms ammunition.

We are confident the area is now clear. Everything is inventoried, and all the nonexplosive material is placed in a vehicle for transport back to the FOB for potential intelligence exploitation. Then we search for an appropriate place to detonate the explosive material.

We enter the two-story house associated with the property, a place I imagine a middle-class Iraqi family once lived. It was clearly abandoned long ago by the owners, the conflict here too much for them. It looks as if insurgents might have made use of the home recently as a base of operations. We search it thoroughly for any sign of life. When it becomes clear that the house is not currently in use, or in any condition to be used ever again, we decide to do a controlled detonation inside. So as to better contain the explosion, we move all of the explosives into the lowest and most central part of the house, under the central staircase. After 15 minutes, we finally get it all in there. Everyone is then moved out except the EOD techs, who will perform the actual detonation. We move all the vehicles to a safe distance.

"This is EOD, two minutes."

The fuse is lit.

"One minute."

"Thirty seconds."

"Fifteen seconds."

"Ten seconds."

"Fire in the hole."

"Fire in the hole."

Boom. The night sky is lit up for less than a second, as the would-be insurgent bombs disappear in a cloud of dust and smoke. An already dilapidated house leveled.

Less than 60 seconds after the dust begins to settle, another call comes across the radio. They have another cache that needs to be cleared.

"Badger 3/6, Kilo 1/1. We have another one."

"Roger, we are coming."

We move to another vacant lot just down the block. There is even more bomb-making material here, a veritable insurgent armory, but it is all centrally located. Mostly explosives, but we also find a large number of small arms, AKs, and sniper rifles.

This cache has been buried in a large hole that was once part of a building foundation, a building long since torn down. At the bottom of the hole where we find most of the explosives is a box of sweating dynamite. Now that concerns us. Conventional munitions are stable. This might not be. We decide to move the mortar shells and RPG rockets, the bulk of our find, to take inventory, then pile the military munitions back on top of the dynamite.

Then the same procedure as before: Move away, count down, *boom*.

As we slowly drive back to the relative safety of the FOB, the horizon turns a golden pink, and the dark night sky melts into pale blue clouds. Our truck jostles over the bumps in the road, and I lean my tired head against the door frame. Our first real foray into combat is now complete. We walked on the battlefield ground of Iraq. We executed and coordinated a mission. And we took away valuable enemy resources. As we pass through the security gates of the FOB, a feeling of confidence comes over me. We can do this.

REST IN PEACE

NAME: **1LT STEFAN C. RALPH (GruntMP)**
STATIONED IN: **SOUTHERN AFGHANISTAN**
HOME STATE: **WESTERN MASSACHUSETTS**

Saturday night I got a phone call from my team chief. He was calling to see if we were OK. They were in a blackout down there (no calls out, no Internet) because someone had been KIA (killed in action) and they didn't know who it was. Yesterday morning we heard that it was a USSF (Special Forces) that was KIA up near Tarin Kowt, one of the forward operating bases up north in Oruzgan. I didn't think much of it because I hadn't worked with any of the teams from Tarin Kowt, so I didn't feel directly connected. Well, last night I found out that it wasn't an SF soldier that was killed, it was an ETT (embedded training team). That changed the whole picture for me, because I know at least one ETT at each of the FOBs up in Oruzgan. I couldn't find out who it was through the channels that were open to me last night, but I was able to confirm that it was an ETT. A little uneasy, with a desire for morning to come so I could make some calls and shoot off some e-mails to get some info, I went to bed.

I got up and started making phone calls. I didn't get ahold of anyone until a little after 8 A.M. The person I talked to couldn't remember the soldier's name, but he thought he was a 2LT, he was from Utah, and he was a big ol' boy. This last statement was the first jab in a series that in a very short time would end with a KO punch I already knew was coming. I kept making calls. Dex came into the Internet café and sat down next to me, and I told him what I had heard. He said he had gotten a call last night and been told it was a 2LT from Utah and he was 35. Two hard shots, a cross and a hook. Now I knew, goddammit I knew, but I didn't want to know.

My phone rang and I saw who it was. He was calling me back to let me know what I already knew. Before the bearer of the news said anything, I asked, "Hey, sir, was it 2LT Lundell, Scott Lundell?"

"Yeah."

"Thanks, sir. I went to officer candidate school with him and I was with him up at DR. Thanks."

"I'm sorry."

"Thanks, sir. Bye."

I closed out the windows on the computer and walked out of the café, trying to get up off the canvas. So what do you do when you find out you're now in another club, a club you knew one day you would become part of, but not a club you look forward to becoming a part of—the one of combat veterans who lose a personal friend in a firefight? At first I kind of walked in a shocked, saddened state. Then I called some people that I love and are close to me, because I just needed to tell someone and talk, but once I got them on the phone I realized that what I needed was to just be alone and cry. I pulled up some pics off my external hard drive with Scott in them and watched the last video I made up, where Tycz and I go into Scott's room while he's on the computer and we have a witty little exchange. Then I stop the video and just cry and want to kick a hole in the sky and drag Scott's soul out of heaven or wherever he may be and put him back here on earth so he can go home to his wife and children. But I can't, I know I can't.

I remember the last conversation he and I had. It was the morning I left DR. We sat in his room and talked about how we both felt that the approaches being taken to Afghanistan and Iraq were wrong, lacked military might and resolve, and were overly concerned with public/international image. We left that conversation open-ended, with the intent of picking it up again sometime in the future. It will remain open for eternity. Scott was one of the few people who was on the level with me when it came to my view of our nation's inability to properly conduct *military* actions, and the undue danger it puts the lives of U.S. soldiers in.

I've been trying through a couple different channels to find out, for my own peace of mind, what exactly happened. I have yet to get any details. What I do know is that he was wounded by small arms fire, it took some time to recover him and medevac him, and he ended up succumbing to his wounds while at Tarin Kowt, where they were working on him. What I also know is that he's gone and I will miss him.

I'm up off the canvas. I've had a pretty good day, considering. Scott's been on my mind a lot, as would be expected. He had a lot of heart. He was built pretty similar to me, but on a six-foot, four-inch frame, so I am pretty sure that whatever wounds he suffered they knocked him out of the fight and he probably wasn't conscious from the time he got hit until the time he passed. I decided to connect with whomever I could from my OCS class, so I sent out an e-mail to the addresses I had to confirm the intended recipients were correct. I'm still getting confirmation from that e-mail. Once I get a few more I'm going to let them know what happened to Scott. As far as I know he is the first soldier from my OCS class to be KIA. I am still raw on some level. Writing this e-mail has brought tears to my eyes, but the reality is I still have six months and some change left here, so my head is back in the game and I'm ready to roll out whenever we go next.

Interestingly, even this series of unfortunate events has not led me to hate my enemies. I might have more of a desire to hunt, kill, and destroy them than I did before, but I won't let myself begin to hate them. I fear that if I allow myself to hate them I wouldn't be far from beginning to hate all Afghans, and I am too intelligent and honorable to fall into that trap. But I will say that when the chance does arise to kill some of the fighters that are affiliates of the fighters that killed Scott, I'm going to engage and destroy as many as I can. Will it bring Scott back? No. But it will serve two purposes. The more of them I kill, the fewer of them there are shooting at me. And in my head, heart, and soul, every one of them I drop is a message that for every one you take from me I will take ten or twenty or as many more of you as I can. It's about settling up. They took a brother from me. That doesn't and won't go unanswered.

One thing is for sure, though; I won't allow myself to get so wrapped up in settling up that I make tactically unsound decisions that will put me at any unnecessary risk. Given the chance, I will pick my fights wisely and at the time of my choosing, so I can maximize the damage I inflict upon my enemy while minimizing the risk to my soldiers and myself. Well, I'm sorry that this has devolved into an angry rant, but that's part of it, I guess.

"Whom shall I send? And who will go for us?"
And I said, "Here I am. Send me!"
Isaiah 6:8

Rest in peace, Scott Lundell.

KIA 25 NOV 06, Tarin Kowt District, Oruzgan Province, Afghanistan.

A brother in arms who is loved and missed.

The debt will not go unpaid.

I love you. I hope it was painless.

OUR WOUNDED WARRIORS

NAME: **RN CLARA HART**
STATIONED IN: **A MILITARY HOSPITAL**
HOME STATE: **ILLINOIS**

Many times when people learn I am a civilian nurse working in a military hospital they ask if I take care of any wounded soldiers. When I reply, "I do," they always ask how they can come and visit the wounded. I always tell them, "You can't." People are shocked by that blunt response and frequently tell me, "I just want to say thank you."

I realize most people are very well intentioned and really do want these guys and gals to know how appreciative they are. However, we are very protective of our wounded warriors, and here are the reasons why. Think back to a time in your life when you were your absolute sickest. Or a time you were in horrific physical pain. Or a time when you were so devastatingly depressed you could hardly climb from your bed. Or a time you were grieving the death of a dear friend or family member. Or a time when you realized the life you thought you had or looked forward to having was no longer possible. Or a time when a husband, wife, boyfriend, girlfriend says, "I can't do this anymore," and leaves you alone.

Many of these wounded experience some or even all of these things at the same time. The IED that shredded their leg so badly it had to be amputated also killed their buddy or buddies. The family they thought they could depend on isn't there. They are trying to come to terms with just how drastically their lives have changed. They are trying to manage emotional and physical pain, issues with infection, and the need for multiple surgeries to clean their injuries. These soldiers and Marines, depending on the severity of their injuries, will easily go back to surgery 10, 20, 30, even upward of 40 times. If you really stop and think about it and put yourself in their place, would you really want a stranger walking into your hospital room?

Frequently the celebrities come by to visit. I remember visiting with a soldier when someone knocked on the door and an MP stuck his head in and asked the soldier if he wanted to see Mr. X. The soldier did not. The MP said OK and closed the door. We talked a bit more; then I left him to get some sleep. As I was leaving and closing the door to his room, Mr. X's PR person comes running over and says to me, "He really doesn't want to see Mr X?" I told her no. She then said, "Well, we're only here this once—maybe he should reconsider. He saw you, didn't he?" I told her the soldier did not want a visitor and walked away. These soldiers know me. I've seen them in horrible pain, I've held their hands while the tears roll down their faces, and I've listened while they tell the kind of stories nightmares are made of.

I know people want to show their appreciation for the difficult job these soldiers and Marines are doing. Please be sensitive to their needs and not your own.

JINGLE TRUCKS

NAME: **CAPT DOUG TRAVERSA**
STATIONED IN: **KABUL, AFGHANISTAN**
HOMETOWN: **TULLAHOMA, TENNESSEE**
MILBLOG URL: **TRAVERSA.TYPEPAD.COM**

O ne of the first things that struck me about Afghanistan, besides the stunning levels of poverty I saw everywhere, were the gloriously colorful trucks. The style of the art reminded me of India, and they had many chains with pendants hanging from the bumpers. I would soon learn that these were called "jingle trucks." I did not immediately learn why, but I spent many days trying to get good photos of them. We are never allowed out of our vehicles unless we are on a base, and jingle trucks never seem to come on base, so photos must be taken from inside our moving vehicle. Despite these difficulties, I managed to get some clear pictures.

The most striking thing about the artwork is that it depicts

beautiful landscapes, usually with woods, grass, lakes, rivers, and many exotic animals. There are often beautiful cottages or new, modern buildings. All of this is done in bright colors; no pastels here. The poignancy is that the artwork depicts everything these people will probably never experience. The area of Afghanistan I've seen is uniformly brown, and trees are rare, and grass almost non-existent. The only animals I ever see are endless flocks of sheep and mangy dogs. Jingle trucks are the only bright color in an otherwise drab landscape, expressing the hopes of all for a land of beauty they can only dream of.

I finally had a chance to learn the secret of why they are called "jingle trucks" when one came onto the Afghan Army base where I work. It was parked, but there was a good breeze blowing, and I heard wind chimes. It was the chains and pendants hanging from the front bumper. This had to be the answer; surely the jingle referred to the music from  the pendants! But I had to nail it down, so I took my interpreter, Hamid, with me to find the driver and asked him why they hung all the pendants from the bumper. Was it for the music or for decoration? He shrugged and said, "Who knows? Both, probably." So much for an authoritative answer. Of course, it's not really important. I just appreciate seeing them. I never tire of looking at them as we head to work or back home. They are my favorite works of art, living testaments to the hopes of a people beaten down for over 25 years. And to think, they pay me to be here!

WRITING LETTERS

NAME: **CAPT LEE KELLEY**
STATIONED IN: **IRAQ**
MILBLOG URL: **WORDSMITHATWAR.BLOG-CITY.COM**

Yesterday was a good day. I had a lot of work to do, the minutes sped past me unnoticed, and I was able to do something to strengthen both mind and body, which means I did some writing and hit the gym when I went off shift. No one in my unit was hurt or killed yesterday, no mortars or rockets hit the FOB, and I fell asleep with a satisfying sense of fatigue and a firm optimism about the days to come. Before bed, I sat at my desk—an ugly thing made of plywood and two-by-fours—in the light of a small lamp and composed some letters. My eyes welled up because it's difficult to write letters that you only want to be read if you die.

I started with one to my dad, sounding formal, even though we never talk like that:

Dear Dad,
I know you raised me well, and I appreciate that. As a parent, I know it's not always easy. . . .

To my dear wife,
If I don't make it from sunrise to sunset today, please know how much I always loved you. . . .

To my beautiful daughter,
Chloe, you have been such a light in my life, and I hope that you continue to shine as you grow into an adult. Know that I will be by your side always, and . . .

My son,

Why this day was my last we'll never know. Why I decided to write this letter is yet another enigma. But I believe there is a reason for it all, and I wanted you to know that I love you so much, buddy. . . .

I have been wondering why I haven't written this type of letter before. We all know mortality can strike us at any time. We can be the unwitting target of a drunk driver, our hearts can simply stop beating, or we can be diagnosed with cancer. I could have written them back home, in the long hours of the morning, when the sun vaults from the horizon, and suburban America rouses itself with percolating coffeemakers, and the dew-covered newspapers cover the lawns like dead animals. Each minute can be our last, no matter who or where we are—it's the human condition.

In the Sunni Triangle, even though statistically fewer people get killed in combat here than die daily on America's highways, you feel like death is closer, breathing down your neck, taunting you. And you laugh at him. You live and laugh right in his dark foreboding shadow because what else are you going to do—cry about it? You just focus on the mission and contribute the best you can. I don't think about death all the time, but I do find myself getting philosophical about it more often than ever before.

All these years I could have been composing a letter each day, once a week, or every month to my loved ones. But I didn't write those letters. I never have, until last night. I am well into this deployment, and I feel confident that I will return home and chase my dreams as I never have before. I know in my heart that I will wrap my arms around my two wonderful children. Still, these letters will be sealed, and on the envelopes I will write:

To: _____

From: _____

OPEN ONLY IN THE EVENT OF MY DEATH

I'm thinking those who read this will find it saddening. But it's not. It's a very good thing. I have been thinking about mortality a lot lately, and I am the kind of person that wants to leave words to certain people, not only memories. This is important to me. Leaving my writings, my blog, and my journals and notebooks is simply not enough. I want them to know I composed a letter directly to them, in my own handwriting. I like thinking that if something catastrophic should happen to me out here, and I never make it home, the people I care about the most will know exactly how I felt about them before I died.

They can sit down and look at the envelope in their hands, run the letter opener along the edge, listen to the soft rip of the paper. One likes to think that our actions in life demonstrate our appreciation for those we hold dear, but this is unfortunately not always the case. My loved ones will have no doubts as to how much they mean to me and how proud I am of them. I will make it very clear. Will I write more letters, now that I've opened myself to this line of thinking? I don't know. But after these were done, I felt better. I let it all out. Got it off my chest.

When I return from this war, I'll take care of these letters. I won't even read them again. I'll have a nice glass of red wine, or a dark beer with lemon in a frosty mug, and then I'll burn them in my own little postdeployment ritual. I'll smile at the flames as they eat away the now-muted possibility of my death in a combat zone.

For I will be home.

When you were born, you cried and the world rejoiced.
Live your life in a manner so that when you die the world cries
and you rejoice.
—NATIVE AMERICAN PROVERB

BOREDOM

NAME: **SGT BRANDON WHITE**
STATIONED IN: **AFGHANISTAN**
HOMETOWN: **DIAMOND, OHIO**
MILBLOG URL: **GWOT.US**

The boredom is irreversibly maddening in this place, where keeping your mind occupied is the name of the game. And I am losing, miserably. It's like getting to level three in Super Mario and never quite making the leap over that gigantic pit of nothingness. I can see King Koopa off in the distance there, irking me on with his fiery nostrils, but alas I am unable to attack him. That is a mission for the ANA. I can only mentor.

I wish I could say we were in our seventh-inning stretch, but I can't; not yet. It is only month six. I sit out on the patio of our building watching a bird pick at the lone Christmas decoration we have emplaced, a piece of red garland perhaps three feet in length, which bedecks our small camp's tree. Not a Christmas tree, mind you, just a tree. How the hell does it live with the lack of water in this place? Man, I wish a mortar would land and take it out. Perhaps that would cure the damn boredom.

I wonder how my wife is doing. Are the bills being paid? I hate paying bills. I'm glad I don't have to pay bills right now. I know writing will keep my mind sharp. But what to write about? I saw a local contractor washing his feet with the runoff from a running washing machine yesterday. He was using the hose that sprouted from the rear of the machine, hosing off his sandals as well. Now there's a story. How do these people wear sandals year-round? Wow, it's cold out here.

I once again step to the edge of that pit; I lean out ever so slightly and try to make sense of the black nothingness below. All at once the old familiar images begin flashing in rapid succession in my mind, like a warm hand on my shoulder encouraging me on into insanity. I see a fly-covered corpse lying in a sewage-infested culvert in An Najaf, black from the number of flies. I see an orange and white taxi with holes the size of tennis balls lacing its exterior. Inside, blood and bits of skin are splattered everywhere.

No, I can't. I won't go there again. I look across the pit. The princess is standing there. She waves a white hanky at me. I must get to her. I must leap over this pit, save the princess, and collect my coins.

MORTAR MORNINGS

NAME: **SPC MICHAEL O'MAHONEY**
STATIONED IN: **IRAQ**
HOMETOWN: **WASHINGTON, D.C.**

You're frozen. For a split second every muscle in your body tenses, and your mind draws a blank. Was that incoming? Wait for the alarm. If it was an incoming round, the siren blares off with a recorded voice and electronic bell: "Incoming! Incoming! Incoming! Bing bing bing. Incoming! Incoming! Incoming!" Stay calm, get to cover, listen for the splash, look at your buddies and smile. . . . Wait.

Everybody has their own "So there I was getting mortared" story. I was once pulling gate guard on my little FOB with a young infantry private I had never met before. We sat in a 113 (armored personnel carrier) that acted as the gate. If someone needed to get on or off the FOB, you just started the vehicle and threw it in reverse, let them drive by, then pulled back into your place. So there we sat one morning. I was in the driver's hatch and PFC L was behind me in the crew compartment with his SAW. We heard the first round strike about 100 meters away, inside the FOB. We looked around for someone to tell: "There's incoming!!"

Another round strikes, this one closer, only 50 meters away. We heard it whistle before it hit. I looked over. "Dude, get your fuckin' hatch closed!" So there we were, an infantryman and a scout, neither of us having been on a 113 before, pulling, punching, slamming, and smashing these hatches that refuse to come down over us to help aid in our protection. The familiar whistle is coming. "Get down!"

Just as we got our heads below the armor, the round struck not 10 meters from us. The dirt and shrapnel sprayed the vehicle, and a cloud of dust descended on us. As I and this guy I've never met before huddled in our convertible armored vehicle, we laughed with each other as he gave me the requisite "I love you, man." I dusted some earth off his helmet as we heard the next round whistle over. It landed farther away. That was it. We poked our heads out of our shelter to survey what was left of the earth, and our backup—about 20 meters behind us—came running up: "Medic! Are you guys OK in there? Oh, holy shit, we thought you guys were done for sure!" Our gate took a nice peppering, but that was it. We all sat around and had a good laugh about how the 113 had instantly vanished from their eyes in a cloud of dust and black smoke. I've had some close calls, but in all the times I've been mortared, that was the closest one.

Well, that's my opener for stories. If anyone back home reads this: If you're too far right to make any sense, leave me alone, and if you're too far left to make any sense, leave me alone. It's easy to say, "*We* have to go to war," if you're not *we*, and it's easy to say, "Bring home the troops," if they are not your brothers getting left behind on the return trip.

MY FORK

NAME: **CH (CAPT) BRAD P. LEWIS**
STATIONED IN: **IRAQ**
HOMETOWN: **SACRAMENTO, CALIFORNIA**
MILBLOG URL: **CHAPLAIN.BLOGSPOT.COM**

I can't imagine that there is anyone over here that does not want to go home. It's very fulfilling to be a part of something so big and to play a role in the freeing of an entire nation. But it's like Dorothy said, "There's no place like home." They treat us pretty well here, but there are some things that just can't be replaced. As I sit down for meals and talk with soldiers about life, service, home, girls, boys, families, etc., everyone misses something. For one it's coffee out of his favorite mug. For another it's the morning newspaper. One guy will miss the smell of his children or the taste of Mom's lasagna. Everyone misses something. Everyone looks forward to getting back to that something. Everyone dreams of normalcy. That's where the sacrifice of these great people is most clearly seen—in the little things they willingly give up, to live and work in a rat hole. And they don't complain or blame or whine. They just keep fighting and working and dreaming of going home. These are truly great people.

Like the next guy, I, too, want to go home and hold my wife and my kids, to sip coffee from my own mug, to work in my yard. But having been deployed to several locations in a very short period, I miss one thing more than any other. For me, plastic is the problem. It's those silly plastic forks with the hollow tines, where everything you eat gets jammed in there, and it just feels funny in your mouth. I miss real silverware. Ah, the feel of smooth aluminum or steel or tin or whatever they make silverware out of (maybe it's silver). I'm no utensilogist, but I know a good fork when I see one. Knives and spoons are not an issue. Forks are what I miss. Like I said, I'm no different. Just like the next guy . . . kinda.

You see, unlike the next guy, I have the perfect spouse. She knows me and loves me anyway. She's perfect. So, recently I was home just long enough to drive my kids to school a couple of times and kiss my bride. And just before taking off again for parts unknown, she bought me a fork! It's not a very fancy one. Neither is it a girly fork. It's perfect. It has a nice big handle that's a manly black and silver; it's easy to hold on to, with perfectly straight and smooth tines. I love my fork. So now when I go to eat breakfast or lunch or dinner or just an afternoon snack, I reach into my pocket and pull out my little friend . . . and we enjoy a meal together. There's no place like home, even when it's the size of a fork.

BE AFRAID

NAME: **CAPT DOUG TRAVERSA**
STATIONED IN: **KABUL, AFGHANISTAN**
HOMETOWN: **TULLAHOMA, TENNESSEE**
MILBLOG URL: **TRAVERSA.TYPEPAD.COM**

J ust when I think nothing will surprise me, Afghanistan throws me a curveball. Let me set the stage. MAJ Apple, Wali and Hamid (our interpreters), and I were sitting in our office having a Deep Discussion about life, liberty, and the pursuit of happiness. Somehow the topic of gays serving in the military came up, and MAJ Apple and I both think they will be able to openly serve in the military very soon. (I mention this to set the stage, not to start a debate. Personally, it wouldn't bother me. If they want to come over and fight for their country, it's fine with me. Welcome.)

Once this topic came up, Wali asked why people were allowed to be openly gay in our country. We explained that in a free society, people are allowed to do pretty much what they please, as long as they are not hurting others, etc.

"But it is so revolting. A man would shame himself to do this."

"Wali," I asked, "what would happen to a man in Afghanistan if he openly declared he was gay?"

"That would never happen," replied Wali, acting as though that was as likely as the Pope converting to Islam.

"I know. But let's just pretend. For instance, let's say a famous TV personality decided he wanted to try to change things here, so he announced on TV that he was gay."

Wali interrupted. "But that would never happen."

"Maybe it would. Just tell me what you think would happen."

"His family would kill him immediately," he said, without batting an eye. Remember, Wali represents moderate, Westernized Islam in Afghanistan.

"Why would you kill someone just for being gay?" I pressed.

"Because my religion says so." Again, as matter-of-fact as though he was explaining why a rock falls to the ground if you pick it up and then let go.

"Let's suppose he escaped from his family. What would the government do? Would they arrest him?"

"Yes."

"And would they then kill him?"

"Yes. This is an Islamic republic. Our religion says to."

"And if someone wanted to leave Islam and join another religion, they would be executed for that too, right?"

"Yes."

The sad thing is we could have been talking about football scores or the weather. He was not remotely embarrassed or hesitant in any of this. Hamid, however, was very quiet the whole time. I wonder what was going through his head.

"Well, if you believe all this, why would you want to move to America? We allow people to switch religions if they wish or believe in nothing at all."

"Do you have people from different religions marry each other?" he asked.

"Yes, all the time," replied MAJ Apple.

"What do they teach the children?"

"Usually they teach them both religions and let them decide for themselves," said MAJ Apple.

Wali seemed a bit surprised by this. Steam was starting to come out of his ears.

"America is not like Afghanistan," I continued. "Our government does not tell us what to believe. We are free to believe whatever we wish. That is our greatness. We can say whatever we wish, as long as we aren't threatening to kill someone or violently overthrow the government. We can get on TV and say we think the government is awful, and no one will arrest us."

MAJ Apple gave a brief explanation of how our country was founded by people who wished to worship in their own way.

Once this was done, I asked again, "Do you think you could be happy in America? Muslims can leave the faith there, and no one will kill them."

"That's OK. As long as I can worship my way, I don't mind what others do."

So there you have it, the incongruity of a man who thinks it is perfectly normal to execute gays and apostates in this country but doesn't think it's a big deal if he's living in the U.S. No matter what your views on homosexuality, I doubt any readers of *The Sandbox* want to execute gays (well, maybe some Taliban reading this trying to gather intel). Same thing with people who leave your particular faith. Would you kill them? (Hopefully that's a rhetorical question.) Yet I live with seemingly normal, pleasant, hardworking people who would think nothing of doing this. This is not an isolated incident either. Other Americans have heard the same thing from their interpreters.

Now take this mind-set, set temperature to high, and nuke for ten minutes, and you have some idea of the hatred and violence in the hearts of the men we are fighting against. Do you think diplomacy is going to work?

Do you think you can reason with them?

Be afraid. Be very afraid.

NAME: **CAPT DAVID DIXON**
RETURNED FROM: **IRAQ**
HOME STATE: **TEXAS**

A few days ago, Vice President Cheney came to Fort Hood and addressed members of the community and the post on the eve of the 1st Cavalry Division's return to Iraq. The vice president was surrounded by Purple Heart winners and those who had earned Bronze Stars with valor or higher medals. That was, at least, the initial qualification given to be able to stand behind the vice president. The cameras were all there, and I have no doubt that the public will see the vice president and the soldiers. However, I was not there to hear the vice president's speech, whatever it was. Instead, a fellow captain buddy of mine and I were across post, at the rear detachment headquarters of a 4th ID brigade. I helped him in his duties as the summary court-martial officer as he inventoried and loaded up a 23-year-old soldier's personal effects for shipment to her family. As we stood there, looking at three cardboard boxes and a metal futon that comprised the totality of what she owned, many things struck us.

It was a sad experience for us. While we both lost soldiers during our first tour in Iraq, we did not know this soldier but felt as if we did. It seemed somehow wrong to be packing up a stranger's goods, not because of anything extraordinary we found, but because of how extremely ordinary everything was. She had a cheap television, a small microwave, some DVDs bought from the PX, a paperback book or two, a few pairs of shoes, a clock radio, and a plastic-drawer dresser full of clothes. We wondered, as we watched the movers photocopy my buddy's inventory of her meager possessions before taping shut the boxes that the soldier's father and mother would have to open in a few days, whether it would scare or reassure Americans to see this.

We wondered if it would make people a little less easy about glibly "supporting our troops" if they knew that this 23-year-old woman didn't leave behind copies of the Constitution, books on warfare, or even an American flag. She didn't have any pictures of her standing in front of Old Glory or even any inspirational posters extolling patriotism, valor, and the like. She left behind shoes and a television. She was a normal American, or could have been, had she not been killed in Iraq. She didn't drape herself in the flag in life; we have draped her in death. She could have been anything; she was a soldier, but she never got the chance to be a wife or a mother, never got the chance to pursue whatever interests she may have wanted to when she returned from the Middle East. She loved and laughed just like the rest of us, but she is gone from us now. It is too easy to say, "She was a soldier and gave her life doing what soldiers do," but it is a hard thing to say when you stand there and watch what little she left being packed up for a grieving family.

I fear too many Americans think of soldiers without truly thinking of them as people. They may be soldiers, but they are so much more. They are soldiers now, but may not always be—they will become musicians, and teachers, and businessmen, and journalists, and car salesmen. The difference is they are willing to die to protect those other Americans who are musicians, teachers, businessmen, journalists, and car salesmen before they go and join their ranks.

As my buddy and I thought and talked about all of this, we wondered if the press would come away from the politics of it all and perhaps come to the quiet rear detachment where senior NCOs and soldiers soberly watched yet another young American's effects be quietly packed and shipped to yet another grieving family. We wondered if the vice president would step away from the podium and see soldiers doing their duty, trying to help one of their own who died doing her duty as best they knew how.

Most of all, though, we wondered about our society at large. We wondered if they could grasp that this 23-year-old soldier who had given her life for them left behind only shoes and a television. It got us thinking about what separates a soldier and society. Finally, we figured it out. What is a soldier? A soldier is someone who leaves behind in death the very things most of us spend our entire lives trying to acquire.

97

ROAD WORK

NAME: **CAPT ERIC COULSON (Badger 6)**
STATIONED IN: **RAMADI, IRAQ**
HOMETOWN: **ST. LOUIS, MISSOURI**
MILBLOG URL: **BADGERSFORWARD.BLOGSPOT.COM**

Highway 10 heads west out of Baghdad, through the suburb of Abu Ghraib, turning north briefly where it winds its way between the city of Al Fallujah and the military Camp Fallujah before it resumes it western traverse to Ar Ramadi. After Ar Ramadi, the road swings southwest, rolling through open desert to Al Rutbah and then finally the Jordanian border. Today, though, I am heading east, out of Ramadi toward Baghdad.

Highway 10 is a six-lane divided highway that would look familiar to any American or Western European. It has seen better days, true, but I have seen highways in the U.S. with almost as many problems. Green signs in Arabic and English point the way to various cities, towns, and routes. It is all so familiar, yet alien.

One of my platoons is going to Fallujah to support another element. I am going with them to check on their progress and see if I can make their lives a little more comfortable. We move out of Camp Ramadi midmorning. The route clearance patrol, like all Coalition Force patrols, brings traffic to a halt. After three years of war, it is instinctive to the Iraqi driver: Do not approach a Coalition convoy unless you want to meet the business end of a crew-served weapon.

I imagine being an Iraqi driver: As I approach the entrance and exit to a Coalition military camp I hope that I am able to pass by without a convoy coming out; if I see a convoy coming out, I let out an epithet. My trip is going to be much slower now. The truck blocking my way indicates I did not make it past the camp in time. It is going to take much longer now to reach my destination. I curse the Coalition for my inconvenience and then shrug. Inshallah.

As we pull out onto Highway 10, I see a few cars start to halt. If they are going to Ramadi, they will only have to spend a few kilometers behind us; however, if they are going much farther, their choices are either slow down or become imaginative in their use of the roads.

It is clear and cold. Hardly a cloud in the sky. We are thankful for the warmth of our vehicles. The mood is almost giddy. After several days of maintenance, this platoon is glad to be back on the road. The chatter in the vehicle revolves around what we see, gossip from the battalion, and anticipated leaves. My presence gives the soldiers plenty of opportunity to let me know what is going on with them.

"You know what I miss about home, sir?"

"No—what?"

"Being able to go to Blockbuster and pick up a movie."

"Or just being able to get up and go to the refrigerator," adds another.

"Just being able to walk around in my underwear."

"Or naked."

We all chuckle and look back out at the landscape, searching for possible threats.

"Is that new?"

"What?"

"That gas station."

Sure enough, a new gas station is in operation along Highway 10. It takes up the space a small truck stop would back in the States and is apparently serving mostly the orange and white taxis one sees everywhere. I recall seeing the early construction stages of this facility but had thought it a long way from completion, if not an abandoned project. But here it is now, with a small hand-lettered sign in English, servicing at least 30 taxis and the odd private car. Signs of life in the local economy.

My attention is pulled back to the task at hand.

"We have a white rice bag with something in it, right side," crackles through the radio.

"Roger," says the platoon leader in reply. "Push up past the two vehicles in front of us," he says to the driver of our truck. "Twenty-six moving."

We find a white rice bag, which clearly has something in it. I am reminded of the last time I went with these soldiers on patrol and found an IED just like this.

The arm operator deftly moves the arm out to interrogate the package. Nothing happens as he pokes and prods. Finally, he decides to pick it up with the arm.

"It's light," he says.

He swings it out to the side so we can all get a better look and evaluate it from the relative safety of our seats in the armored truck. If it was high explosives, it should have fallen out of the rice bag by now. But that's what we thought last time.

"I'm going to shake it."

The bag bounces up and down until it finally falls off and rolls down the embankment and away from the road, harmlessly into the desert. Nothing.

"Clear."

"Twenty-two, it's clear, nothing. Go ahead and push."

As we begin to move out, I look behind me and see the traffic beginning to pile up behind us. We are like a moving road crew. Except we have provided no way for the traffic to get around us. I don't feel bad, though. Proceed around us at your own risk.

And some Iraqis choose to go around us. They drive off the road to our left or right and make a wide sweep, using a combination of side roads and cross-country driving to get past. We watch the vehicles closely, but they pose no threat to us. They are simply people trying to go about their lives.

We are moving again. The conversation dies down, and we continue to scan for threats and contemplate the landscape. I see sheep herders with their flocks. I am reminded of the Navajo who tend their flocks on an equally hardscrabble landscape. I think of my mom and the landscape of northern Arizona. People talk about how different we are from the Iraqi people. But mostly what I see is how similar we are.

We continue to roll, kilometer after kilometer, taking our time to scan our sectors, looking for that thing that is out of place. Conversation is limited, but we take time to grab something to eat from our various bags. Items from home are offered up and shared equally. My in-laws have sent a smoked and dried steak, an early Christmas gift I am sure I was supposed to wait to open. I offer some up to the soldiers with me; not sharing would be the ultimate insult. The driver opens some nuts, and we pass them around. A family of four out for a Friday afternoon drive.

Oncoming traffic offers a change of pace. Bus after bus after bus. They are flying flags, the flags of Iraq and various Islamic banners. Shia green and white for purity. I wonder if I will see the black flag for martyrdom. These buses with their banners proclaiming their love of Allah are heading south to Saudi Arabia for the Hajj. A point of entry on the far southern Iraq border has been opened specifically for the Hajj, so the Iraqi faithful can fulfill their obligation to at least once in their lifetime go to Mecca. The buses remind me of Americans on their way to see a football game. And why not? We have raised football to the level of religion in America. More the same than different.

We are approaching Fallujah now—the next sign says, "Fallujah next two exits," or something to that effect. We pass over the cloverleaf and see the entry control point into the city. Big green road signs direct you to the exit, or to Baghdad, Samarra, or Basra.

We continue to scan vehicles as they approach us or go around us. We look at old blast holes and other debris by the side of the road. We check here and look there. We find nothing.

Having passed the now-empty prison at Abu Ghraib, we are approaching our unmarked turnaround point. Once we reach that point, we block off traffic coming the other direction and move over, the long line of traffic behind us relieved to be able to resume normal speed. I wave to some of the people we have held up as they pass. Some stare coldly, others wave back, I hope recognizing that we have provided them a service, even if we have slowed them down.

The mission is almost finished now, just a few more kilometers. We continue to check junk on the side of the road. We would take an IED attack behind us very personally.

Nothing. Finally we enter Camp Fallujah. Highway 10 is clear. At least it was when we got off the road, but the insurgency will be back at it again. For now, though, mission complete, and all Badgers safely in their den.

DON'T TOUCH THAT

NAME: **ROB**
STATIONED IN: **IRAQ**
MILBLOG URL: **SNIPEREYE.BLOGSPOT.COM**

Most missions I didn't look forward to, because more than likely my teammate and I would be bored to death, watching the never-ending nothing. Boredom—the worst punishment and a passive form of torture, as far as I was concerned. But this mission I loved the moment I heard of it. The infantry company responsible for the city was having trouble keeping their "wanted posters" up for longer than a few minutes. Every single poster portraying the high-value targets who were possibly in the area was expediently ripped off the wall and thrown away. That's where we came in: Anyone who ripped down the posters was to get a well-placed shot, close enough to unquestionably deliver the biggest scare of their life. The team leaders fought over who would go. We all wanted this one. It was like putting a kid in a candy shop.

Rick and I got it and headed over to the palace that C Company lived in, to meet with the company commander and the platoon leader.

"Matrix 1! Matrix 8! You guys ready for some fun?" the commander enthusiastically yelled as we walked into the TOC.

"Hell yes, sir!" I replied, taking off my Kevlar and pulling my pen and notepad out my pocket. Fun in the Army is a rare thing to come by, so you have to enjoy it when it comes around.

"All right, we want to place posters of high-value targets we're looking for," said the commander, "and we want them to stay up longer than 20 minutes. So, where do you think we should put them?" We were looking over a large satellite-imagery map of the city, laminated to a table in the center of the TOC.

"How about here . . . and here," I said, pointing out locations on the map. "There will be tons of traffic, so the posters will get seen, and there are some apartments across the street we can use for positions. And Rick and I will be close enough to talk to each other."

"Sounds good. Now . . . can you guys stay out there for a day or so, or what's your boss got you doing?"

Rick and I knew this was coming. They always want to milk us for every minute possible. But this was months into the deployment, and we knew the city well enough to know that staying out in this area after the fun was over would just be a waste of our time. There would be a whole lot of nothing to watch, and curious bystanders would likely venture out when it got dark and try and find our positions. It was pointless to remain out there.

"Sir, I think the boss has got other missions for us with one of the other companies when we get back from this one," I told the commander with a deadpan stare.

"All right. Well, Red 6 is downstairs," he replied in a disappointed yet suspicious tone. Rick and I walked out like two schoolboys who had just evaded detention. Downstairs, we linked up with the platoon leader and went over the mission details, then went back to our palace to prep and get a few hours of sleep before we infiled.

Infil time came, and two eager sniper teams were waiting on the back of the stripped Humvees while the platoon got their weapons mounted and troops situated on the other Humvees. The sun wasn't out yet, and the air was cold. I enjoyed these moments before a mission. From where we were on the FOB, I could see the horizon, the city, and a village on the Tigris River. It was peaceful in a way—everyone around me scurrying about and getting ready to leave the FOB, and all I had to do was wait on the back of this Humvee and enjoy the view while I thought about my mission.

The sounds of weapons locking and loading, radios transmitting, and soldiers complaining or telling filthy stories was what usually happened while we made our way to the gate of the FOB. This morning was no different. Once you're in the city, the smell of garbage and sewage fills the air. Trash, graffiti, rundown buildings, and cars on their last mile all cram together as if there is nowhere else on the world they could fit.

"This will work, sir! Let me off here," I yelled to the platoon leader in the front of the Humvee. As the vehicle slowed down, I slid off the back and broke into a dead sprint. Walter and Brian had already been dropped off and were stacked at the apartment building entrance waiting for me. I sprinted through the street as the convoy drove off to infil Rick's team.

I took point, and we entered the dark and quiet building. We pulled down our night vision and crept up the stairway to the top floor. I reached the apartment door and slowly turned the handle. It was locked. I didn't have time to pick it, since the QRF would be back soon to put up the posters, and we needed to see exactly where they put them. So I took a few short steps back, ran to the door, and struck with my right boot just above the door handle. I loved this part of the job. The door flew open, and we stormed in.

The apartment was clear. We set up in the secondary bedroom, cracked the windows, closed the blinds partially, and pulled in some chairs from the other rooms. The windows were already dirty on the outside. Perfect. The setup was now complete.

Moments later the QRF arrived and began to plaster up the posters on the walls directly in front of our position. I stood in the open window watching exactly where our posters/targets would be. A soldier on the ground noticed me standing in the window and abruptly stopped. Without hesitation, I gave a few IR flashes with my night vision and radioed in, "Red 6, Red 6, we are in position and signaling you with IR flashes, over."

This soldier didn't catch the transmission and raised his rifle up to my window. I found the IR beam from his PQ2 bouncing around my chest. Furiously, I closed the window and hollered into the radio, "Red 6, tell your fuckin' men we're up and quit lasing us like we're a goddamn Haji!" The snipers we replaced had warned us of this. Friendly fire is a bitch. They advised carrying chem lights and yelling out something familiar that Haji wouldn't think of saying. Their choice phrase was "Fuckin' retard!" I liked it and was one step away from using it. Fortunately, I didn't have to. It would have compromised our position.

Once the circus was gone, we waited for the sun to rise and the city to come to life. I wasn't the least bit tired. It was like trying to sleep on Christmas Eve.

Moments after the sun came up, a man curiously walked over to one of the posters and launched into a fit of rage. "I got one," Brian quietly mumbled, as he watched through the scope of his rifle and switched his selector lever from safe to semi.

"Wait until he grabs it," I replied, watching the man yell and flail his arms around as if he'd just caught his wife cheating. From my vantage point, his reaction was amusing. He reached up to grab the top of the poster. BAM! A round from Brian's rifle impacted a large glass döner kebab sign just above his head. He jumped back in a frightened panic and searched the windows and rooftops for the shooter, while small pieces of glass signage fell on top of his head. Brian and I chuckled and gave each other a sly grin.

"Target," Brain whispered.

"Roger," I replied.

Needless to say, that guy didn't mess with any other posters for the rest of the day. Hours later, a group of four young men strolled through the neighborhood like they owned the place. I knew they'd be trouble, and I was right. The leader of the pack went into the same fit of rage as the earlier guy. I raised my cheek to the butt stock of my rifle and took aim. I was completely focused on my enraged target as things began to move in slow motion.

He forcefully ripped one down. BAM! I placed a shot into the tin roof of the building, several feet above his head. I was feeling nice and wanted to see exactly where my point of impact was from this elevation and angle. Range, elevation, and angle determine a bullet's trajectory and final point of impact. Whenever those factors change from what you zeroed your scope at, your point of impact changes. I had to be sure where my rounds were going. And now I was. But since all the doors and windows in our room were closed, my ears had been flooded with a piercing ring that traveled through my head and sliced away at my sanity. I couldn't hear anything else. It was so intense I almost broke concentration but pushed through it.

The first shot had been so far above his head he didn't even seem to notice he was being shot at! So he continued down the side-walk to the next poster.

"Don't do it buddy...." He grabbed the top of it.

"Fine then!" BAM! My round impacted exactly where I wanted it to, shattering a glass sign inches above the tall man's head. He tore off his jacket and held it above his head to protect himself from the storm of glass. In a panic, he threw his arms in the air and ran back over to his group of friends, who were in a frozen state of fear.

I slowly closed the cracked window and watched. Unsurprisingly, the group dispatched the youngest to search for me. With utter fear and curiosity, the young boy was sent out to retrace his friend's path. He walked slowly, as if he was navigating through a minefield, scanning the windows and rooftops across the street with panic in his eyes.

"Some friends this guy has!" I said to Brian and Walter as we watched the boy unsuccessfully search for us.

"What a bunch of idiots," Brian replied with a chuckle.

ODD DREAMS

NAME: **FC1 (SW) ANTHONY McCLOSKEY (Tadpole)**
STATIONED IN: **AFGHANISTAN**
MILBLOG URL: **ARMYSAILOR.COM**

I have been having quite a bit of trouble sleeping lately. This has worked wonders for my ability to get a lot of reading and writing done, but it has not helped my physical condition. I have been exhausted due to a lack of sleep. I am seriously considering going to see a doc, but I don't want to be a whiner. I'll go if it gets too rough.

When I do sleep, I have been having really weird dreams. Usually about being shot at or things blowing up around me, and recently I had a dream that I was walking up an extremely narrow pass, on an extremely high rock wall, and I fell off. As in most falling dreams, before I hit the bottom, I woke up.

Last night, though, I had an unusual dream that got me to thinking. I dreamt that I stepped on an old Soviet mine, and it blew me to kingdom come. When the mine exploded, I woke up with my heart racing, and I was a little disoriented. Here's what got me thinking: I grew up in the '80s, and I always wanted to join the military. As a child, I assumed that I would grow up and fight Soviets and kill Russians. Of course, by the time I joined the military, the Soviet empire had collapsed, and the Russians were our friends. C'est la vie. How ironic would it be if a Soviet mine did me in? Wouldn't that somehow seem strangely appropriate?

What is even stranger is that today a stray dog wandered into a minefield and didn't get too far before he found a mine. For a couple of moments, it was raining dog meat. An interesting phenomenon, to say the least. A buddy of mine was so startled by the blast that he spun around and locked and loaded. No doubt that if there had been an enemy there, it would have quickly become a dead enemy.

I'll tell you this: I have never been much of a religious man. And

I am not overly superstitious (maybe a little). But there is one thing, and one thing only, that I will accept completely on blind faith. And that is a sign that says "Mines." You tell me that an area is a minefield, and I will believe you, no questions. Mines are scary things, and it only makes them scarier that they still work after all these years.

I'm just glad I wasn't the dog.

WHEN MATT GETS HOME

Name: **CAPT MATT SMENOS**
Stationed in: **AFGHANISTAN**
Hometown: **SANTA MARIA, CALIFORNIA**

When Matt gets home . . . things are gonna happen.

When Matt gets home . . . it's gonna be great.

When Matt gets home . . . we'll all be happy.

When Matt gets home, Matt's kids are going to shout and imagine and play. They'll hug their mom and tell her secrets. They'll never let anyone tell them they're not good enough.

When Matt gets home, Matt's wife will forget the past, live in the now, and see what a bright future lies in wait for her. When Matt gets home, he'll go anywhere she goes.

When Matt gets home, Matt's mom will sit down, take a breather, have a cocktail (or five), have a laugh, and enjoy herself and her success. Matt's mom will stop and look at the palm-tree majesty and white-sand dreamland she has earned. She'll realize everything is gonna be OK.

When Matt gets home, Matt's dad will unfurl his sails, put on his sunglasses, and ride the waves with his son. Matt's dad will lean on his mast and crack a beer. He'll sip it and survey the clear, blue majesty of his world, once only a dream expressed in trinkets and tacky wallpaper. Matt's dad will be content to be a pirate a few hundred years too late. Matt's dad will watch the sun set on the ocean.

When Matt gets home, Matt's brother will keep doing what he's doing. Matt's brother will keep kicking ass, living his dreams, and being Matt's hero.

When Matt gets home, Matt's friends will party like rock stars. From the wine tour to Megan's floor, they'll be in celebration. They'll smile and invite each other to lunch and fight over the check. They'll sneak out the turnstile at 8:47 for coffee. They'll decide, together, that this place has too many damned stairs and all take the elevator. They'll be cool. They'll realize that sometimes, just sometimes, every now and then, things truly happen for a reason, and a bunch of people in drab buildings become more than just individuals. They become full-color, moving pieces in a divine plan that helps a man get up in the morning. They'll realize that some days just don't start until he hears their voices. They'll realize how unbelievable they are, and that no matter what happens, he'll never forget them.

When Matt gets home, Matt's coworkers will realize that the rockets will launch anyway, eventually. When Matt gets home, maybe they'll clock out just a little bit early once in a while.

When Matt gets home . . . it'll all finally happen.

Want Matt's advice?

Don't wait for Matt. . . .

VBIEDS ALONG
THE TIGRIS

NAME: **SGT ROY BATTY**

STATIONED IN: **BAGHDAD, IRAQ**

HOMETOWN: **YELLOW SPRINGS, OHIO**

The boring and dangerous checkpoint missions are behind us, and once again the infantry company returns to its original mission. We are happy to be free again, with the open Iraqi countryside waiting to be explored. Except today we are not going out into the scrub-grass desert, but instead are headed to Samarra, a central Baghdad neighborhood. We are supposed to do the usual IP station assessment, followed by a joint patrol. It's a new area for us, and we're looking forward to some fresh scenery—if fresh is the right word, given the odoriferous nature of downtown Baghdad.

My li'l droogies, as I call them a la *Clockwork Orange*, are rambunctious and full of spunk this morning, and we joke back and forth on the new intercom headsets, busting on each other as we drive. The day is crisp and blue, scrubbed clean by the rains that have started to become more frequent here as we move slowly into the Arabian winter. The temperature is in the low 80s, which feels like heaven after the rotisserie hell of the summer months.

We emerge from the blasted lands, driving through a small slum pockmarked with houses completely made out of scrap metal. Kids and dogs come running out of the shanties, the children dashing with their arms outstretched, thin voices shrill above the whine of the diesel engines, wailing for infidel candy. Sure enough, the gunner in the lead truck tosses handfuls of Jolly Ranchers to them as we speed by, and the kids dive into the dust to snatch up the treats. The dogs chase us, tails wagging ferociously, barking their heads off, bravely driving away the cumbersome metal monsters. Nix veers at one pooch that is a little too courageous, and it narrowly escapes becoming the next bloated carcass swelling in the sun on Airfield Road.

We careen onto Route Wild and head north, into the city, and the civilian traffic swerves and ducks around us, diving for the safety of the curb as they turn on their flashers. Nobody wants to get shot on this beautiful fall day. The city is its usual chaotic self—crazy traffic, faded signs scrawled with Arabic script, shoppers choking the markets. I love working with this infantry company, since we get to go to all sorts of interesting places, not just the same useless checkpoints on Route Pluto. Today seems especially alive, and even the locals seem pretty content; not too many suspicious stares are thrown our way as we maneuver into the heart of the city.

The traffic gets a little thicker, and we slow down as we approach a wide traffic circle surrounded by multistory buildings. A green park, dotted with palm trees, graces the center of the traffic circle, with a central podium that probably once held a statue of Saddam Hussein, but which is now empty in sort of an anticlimatic way.

I notice a cluster of activity to our right, just around the corner of a building, and then I see blue-shirted Iraqi cops converging on the hubbub. First, there are just a couple, and then more, and now they are running, a sure sign of something wrong, as IPs never move quickly. Our convoy inches forward, and I advise Cooper, my gunner, to keep an eye on the building. I crane my neck forward, watching the area through the dusty windshield of the HMMWV.

Something dark and twisted comes into view, lying in the middle of the street, which is dirtier and more cluttered than usual. It takes a second to figure it out, and I slowly realize that it is the engine block to a small car. Beyond it are a few twisted pieces of metal, apparently the frame of the vehicle. A small ambulance is just behind the wreckage, and local people are loading burnt, mangled bodies into it. As I take in the fact that I am looking at dead people, a metallic voice in my ear announces that we have wandered into the scene of a car bomb attack. Apparently it happened just minutes ago, even though none of us heard the explosion. Sometimes I hear them back at the barracks, usually in the early morning; a sudden, deep rumble as someone's apartment block goes up in flames.

I'm immediately concerned about the possibility of secondary VBIEDs (Vehicle-Borne Improvised Explosive Devices) and ask the team leader of the point vehicle to move forward into the middle of the perimeter. I get back a sharp answer: "We are in the middle of the fucking perimeter." I look outside my window and see that my door is a foot away from a big, '70s-style Cutlass sedan—a white and orange taxi cab. Some local guy is anxiously peering underneath it, and as I look at him, he turns his head, and our eyes meet for a second. We are both thinking the same thing. I tell SGT Egan that while he might be in the middle of the fucking perimeter, I am sitting next to a big fucking car, and it is very uncool. He moves forward grudgingly.

The squad leader announces over the radio that our translator, Joey, is getting out to talk to the IPs to find out what happened. I get out, too, ostensibly to pull security on him, but really because something inside, unspoken, urges me to get a closer look.

The ground is densely peppered with black metal fragments, burnt pieces of clothing, and as I squint at the asphalt I can see the occasional body part—blackened, burnt, torn, but identifiably human, if you look at it long enough.

There is a strange feeling to this—not of horror or terror or sadness, but quite the opposite. It feels normal. There are tiny pockets of grief or shock around the scene, but they seem incongruous, out of place, almost . . . inappropriate. Because boring, old, regular life continues in the middle of it.

A young girl, maybe 13 or 14, leans over a second-floor railing and screams at the crowd below, gesturing frantically at something. She holds a dirty baby, and as I glance at her I see more children clustered around her smudged skirt, peeking out through the bars. Yet more kids appear out of the gloom of the apartment, and they line up, much like the village kids do when we make security stops in the desert. The children have blank looks on their faces, their mouths little round O's. Is that her parents being loaded roughly into the ambulance? I don't know. No one seems to pay any attention to her.

A policeman picks up a ragged bundle from the blackened street, and as I turn to look at something else, it registers in my head what the package really is: a severed arm. A woman walks between two of our HMMWVs, pushing a baby stroller—one of those European types, all blue fabric and big double wheels. I look to make sure it really holds a baby (it does), and I note the look on her face—the same level of interest you would have when you see that dish soap is on sale for a buck twenty-five. She pops the stroller backward for a second, clears the front wheels over the curb of the traffic circle, and continues on her way.

A young police officer across the circle slaps his hand across his face and wails, one arm outstretched toward the wreckage, and a comrade grabs him, holds him back for a second, and then they collapse together in the middle of the street. I can't hear his sobs, because of the wailing sirens. More ambulances are coming in.

An old man walks by, a foot away from the mangled engine block, carrying a bag of groceries. He barely glances at the scene, perhaps just once, just for a second. His face is normal, relaxed. How many of these has he seen?

The place is full of cops now, all waving their AK-47s, rushing around with great energy but no direction. A small fire truck arrives, and a black-clad fireman sprays the wreckage with an anemic stream of water. There are an uncomfortable number of men in civilian clothes clutching pistols, which makes me nervous until Joey stops a police lieutenant and we learn that they are detectives.

The lieutenant is pissed and is also clutching a small black Glock. He yells angry words, curt orders, at some other officers nearby, but I can't see anyone react to them. Joey talks to him in Arabic, and he replies, loudly, venomously. I'm not really paying attention to them. I'm watching the rooftops and balconies for snipers.

I ask Joey if the neighborhood is Shia or Sunni. He asks the lieutenant, who stops and glares at me with intense eyes. He replies sharply: The neighborhood is mixed, neither one nor the other. He softens a bit as he talks and then adds that this traffic circle is always crowded. Apparently whoever did this just wanted to kill as many people as they could. They didn't care who, or what sect they were, or where they came from. They just wanted the maximum amount of carnage.

Joey and the lieutenant go back to their conversation, and I go back to watching the chaos, splitting my attention between watching for snipers and just looking. A policeman walks by me, his long, blue shirtsleeves coated red up to the elbows with blood. I don't think he has realized this yet, and he marches by without glancing at me. Something tinkles as I brush against it with my foot, and I look down to see a scorched and scarred piece of metal. Some innards blown out of the car, and I look at it curiously for a minute, turning it back and forth with my boot. I can't tell what it is.

There is a flurry of activity off behind me, and I turn to look. Joey relays to me from the lieutenant that they think there are other VBIEDs in the area, and that someone has found a suspicious vehicle down one of the five streets that feed into the traffic circle. I point my rifle down the road and glass it with my sniper scope, but nothing looks out of place. A number of IPs get on their vehicle PA systems and start shouting orders at the people down the road, telling them to back up.

If you want to shout frantic orders at people, Arabic is a pretty good choice. The guttural syllables sound really compelling, particularly when amped to deafening levels. The only better choice might be German. I have no idea what they are yelling, but it makes me want to move. People start going quickly, and the perimeter is pushed out farther.

More Coalition convoys arrive from other side streets, and they start strengthening the perimeter. Joey and the LT go back to their conversation. Apparently they know each other or are related or something because they start laughing, and they kiss each other on the cheek. They light up cigarettes and chatter away. The LT gives me a light. Three Arab women in traditional black robes walk past, the last one with her head tilted back, up to the sky. Her face is transfixed, eyes closed, mouth frozen open as she cries. The cigarette tastes good, reassuring. I drag on it heavily, exhaling smoke as she walks away.

Our squad leader decides it's time to go. There isn't much for us to do here. The other units have the perimeter. The bodies are loaded up and shipped out to wherever dead bodies go in Baghdad. Maybe we can go find the other VBIEDs, or maybe we get out of here before they show up. Anyway, we have a police station to get to.

Ten minutes later, we are sitting in the sun outside the Samarra IP station. We are eating fresh Iraqi bread and goat cheese, fetched for us by a bright-eyed Christian kid who speaks perfect English, taught to him for the past four years by the soldiers. Younger children cluster around the HMMWVs, begging for more Jolly Ranchers. The sun is warm on our faces; the bread is hot, straight out of the oven, flat, eye-shaped, traditional. I eat it hungrily and think again of the policeman and his red-stained shirtsleeves.

Just another day in Baghdad, one which ends beautifully as we drive home through the Green Zone and out across a bridge over the Tigris. The sun is setting over the water, and I hand my camera up to Cooper to take a snapshot. The water is flat and golden, and the bridge is high enough that I can't smell the sharp nasal punch of the raw sewage below.

I think for a second of the people who didn't live to see this sunset; people out playing with their kids on a balcony or stepping out of the door to grab something from the store down the street. One second they were here, and the next they weren't. I think of fresh bread and an arm lying in the street, and I am glad for the company of my soldiers, next to me in the tight metal womb of our truck. We ride back to the FOB, smoking and joking, and it is good to still be alive.

A SURREAL DAY

NAME: **SPC GORDON ALANKO (Teflon Don)**
STATIONED IN: **RAMADI, IRAQ**
MILBLOG URL: **ACUTEPOLITICS.BLOGSPOT.COM**

It's been something of a surreal day. The air outside is thick with the smoke from the garbage dump, where it seems there is nothing to burn besides some sort of plastic. The acrid stench gives way to the crisper smoke from the assortment of burn barrels, which are once again busy devouring remnants of unkept letters and packages from homes far away. The night sky seems impossibly bright overhead—just a few days ago, it was nearly impossible to walk around at night without bumping, tripping, and stumbling along. Now it's easy to move. It's especially noticeable in town, where we gain next to no benefit from dousing our vehicle lights. The dim twilight is still more than enough to see by, and our trucks are large enough to stand out, even in the more urban areas. But I'm getting off track. Back to this last 24 hours.

Let me preface this story I'm about to tell with a little background: Chuck Norris is a gigantic cult phenomenon. Everyone knows a joke or two about the man: "Chuck Norris has two speeds: sleep and kill." "There is no natural selection. There are creatures that die and creatures Chuck allows to live." "Chuck Norris doesn't have a beard because he doesn't shave; Chuck has a beard because razors are scared of him." References to the man are everywhere, and nearly all of them are as odd or inane as those. Whether they make sense or not, these little sayings are written inside bunkers, latrines, vehicles—anywhere someone might think to write something.

While I was out on mission last night, one of the Bradley Fighting Vehicles that compose our security escort called up the escort commander on the radio during a lull in movement:

Red 1: Sir, did you hear they're taking one of my Bradleys
   tomorrow?
Red 6: Negative. Why?
R1: I guess Chuck Norris
   needs it for something.
R6: Say again?
R1: Chuck Norris is com-
   ing here tomorrow, and
   he's taking one of my
   Bradleys.
R6: Is this one of those jokes
   you guys tell all the time?

We were sitting in the truck
saying to ourselves, "What does
Chuck Norris need a Bradley for?
Can't he just roundhouse kick
the IEDs away?" and, "Y'know, if
he'd come here three years ago, we
wouldn't still be here now!"

It turned out to be true.
Every soldier's hero, Chuck Norris, came to the ghetto of Iraq today.
I wonder how many kids had their illusions shattered.

Tonight we went out on another mission, a short one, to clear
part of one of the main routes between here and all the other military bases in Iraq. Coming back, we had a bomb explode near us.
However, it was no ordinary bomb. This one was a shell, strapped
to what appeared to be a roller skate, which was pulled across the
road in front of us. Apparently the bad guys have been watching too
many old cartoons and called Acme to order their bomb. My truck
has now earned the nickname "Road Runner," for having survived an
attack by Wile E. Coyote.

Chuck Norris and bombs on skates. That's about all I can handle for one day.

MAN FOOD

NAME: **C. MALONEY**
HUSBAND STATIONED IN: **IRAQ**
HOMETOWN: **SEATTLE, WASHINGTON**
MILBLOG URL: **CORPSDJOUR.BLOGSPOT.COM**

"**I**f you can't eat it, or you can't wear it, we probably don't need it." That's the directive from the CO. So, what does my husband get this year at Christmas for being a good boy? Well, let's look at the environmental requirements (not an easy task, may I add, considering I have talked to him once, for 10 minutes, in the last month):

It's the desert, and it's cold. You know, when you think about it, a nice lump of coal might not be such a bad idea! It could help keep him warm, at least. I fret, however, that such efforts might be misconstrued and seen as not in the spirit of Christmas, so I guess I'll pass.

Hmm . . . something he can wear. Well, it must be green. And not Army green, but Marine green, because believe it or not, even their T-shirts have their own distinct shade of drab. I'd send Under Armour or some kind of long underwear, but it can't be made from polyester or other synthetic fabrics that melt when exposed to flames. I don't want anything melting on his skin—he's too young to need any sort of skin peel just yet. Maybe once he's a real "leatherneck." What options does that leave me? A nice pair of socks. Good thing I live on base and have access to the right kind, in the right shade. Look out, cutie—you got a sweet pair of socks coming your way!

Now, something he can eat. Wherever he is, I know he's eating MREs at least once a day. My husband doesn't have a big sweet tooth (disappointing, I know!), but he does like Sour Patch Kids—so those are in. My mom sent him some canned oysters out of the pantry last time he was in Iraq, and he raved about that. I am firmly against sending him booze; I hear weapons and alcohol don't mix, so that's out. My man likes *man* food, but pork is a no-go in the country, which means Slim Jims are out. So what's he getting? Oily, stinky canned fish, all-beef summer sausages, and a can of Cheez Whiz. Sounds terrible to me but it might just beat having to eat another unsavory MRE.

And that's about it. My baby has socks and man food coming his way. A few pictures of our house with the lights I put up, a note to say "I love you," and a promise to celebrate whenever he gets home. Don't worry, sweetheart, Santa will find you, and we'll make sure that this Christmas is as merry as it can be.

Saalam. Peace.

MUDDY CHRISTMAS!

NAME: **SPC IAN WOLFE**
STATIONED IN: **IRAQ**
HOMETOWN: **MINNEAPOLIS, MINNESOTA**

Since the rainy season started, I have discovered that there are several different kinds of mud. At first I thought, "How bad could it be?" Now I know. The worst mud is the thick mud; it can add up to three inches to your height. This is good for most, but I am already too tall for anywhere but America. This mud is especially thick when rocks and gravel mix into it. When I arrived here at the end of the last rainy season, I wondered what all the ravines were for. They can barely carry all the water that comes down. They would make nice swimming holes if the water didn't look like it's chock full of all sorts of nasty bacteria. I am in the Medical Corps, which may explain my bacteria fear. The one upside of this thick mud is that sometimes a mission gets canceled because it is too muddy to get to our destination village. Although I do enjoy the missions, it is nice to have a relaxing day.

The second kind of mud has been dubbed by some "chocolate mousse." It is a filmy, and yes, chocolate-looking mud. It sits on top of the dirt and is not quite as irritating as the thick kind. The main problem is that there are very few places to walk here that aren't either muddy or flooded with water. When you walk, it splashes up on your pants. It also splashes all over as vehicles drive by. I end up stripping in my doorway before I go inside.

The third type is the frozen mud. I enjoy its crispness in the early morning. It is nice to walk on hard ground that doesn't collect on your shoes. The only downside is that it can be surprisingly slick. But I think it is the closest thing to snow we will get this Christmas.

Despite being away from home and doing a job that we all wish was not a necessary one, Christmas will not be too bad. Most of us realize that we made the decision to do something when no one else would and have made this sacrifice for the good of others. The people back home have recognized this and been great. I have never seen so much mail in my life. I think almost everyone in my group has a tree in their living place. American companies and families have been sending us tons of stuff to make our holiday season as good as it can be. We almost have too much. It gets passed around and shared with the entire base and with the Romanian and Australian soldiers who are here with us.

Despite all the mud, danger, and being away from home, it will be a memorable holiday season. I am fortunate to be with the people I am serving with and also to have so many people supporting us back home. Thanks to all the people who have sent their wishes, prayers, support, and packages. Maybe the mud will turn to snow.

NAME: **CAPT DOUG TRAVERSA**
STATIONED IN: **KABUL, AFGHANISTAN**
HOMETOWN: **TULLAHOMA, TENNESSEE**
MILBLOG URL: **TRAVERSA.TYPEPAD.COM**

On Christmas Eve, my hut mate Mike asked all of us in our side of the hut to sing some Christmas carols for his wife and daughter. He was going to record them on his camera and send the file to her by e-mail. Of course we agreed and tried to figure out a song the four of us all knew. We got it down to "Rudolph the Red-Nosed Reindeer" or "Jingle Bells, Batman Smells." Standing at the end of our hall (right next to MAJ Apple's room, so only a single sheet of plywood would protect him from the audio onslaught), the Barbershop Quartet from Hell sang "Rudolph," then watched ourselves on Mike's laptop. I'm glad to say that I'm not the only awful singer in our group. I had pretty stiff competition.

At this point, we thought it would be pretty cool if we could sing "You're a Mean One, Mr. Grinch." So we hunted the lyrics down on the Internet, and we were all set. Yes, we did sing it, and yes, it was pretty bad. And that's being generous. In fact, MAJ Apple yelled through the wall, "For the love of God, please stop!" The files were way too large to send, however, so Mike got online with his wife and daughter with a video feed, and we all crowded into Mike's room and sang both songs again. They seemed to enjoy it, which proves that love is not only blind but also deaf.

Yesterday we had our Christmas lunch at Central Movement Agency, the Afghan Army base where I work. It all started a couple of weeks ago, when MAJ Apple was touring the new HQ building with the CMA commander, COL Fatiullah, and his staff. In the course of their conversation, COL Fatiullah asked  when our Christmas holiday was coming up. He didn't know much about it but knew it was important to us, and they wanted to help us celebrate. We agreed to have a lunch together, all the ANA troops—officer and enlisted—and all of us, in their chow hall. SMSgt White headed up a team to collect candy and decorations. The morning of the lunch, COL Fatiullah came into our office and asked what we would like to eat. MAJ Apple explained that we wanted to eat with the troops and eat exactly what they ate. COL Fatiullah was nonplussed. He wanted the lunch to be special, since it was an important holiday for us. We told him that in the military we all ate together on Christmas (and most other times, too), and it would be special just to be together. So he agreed and said all his officers would eat with the soldiers, too.

The meal was a smashing success. Everyone seemed to have a good time. The soldiers grabbed up the candy happily, and lots

of people wanted their photographs taken. It was one of the best Christmas meals I've ever had. We really did feel like we were with family. Here is a picture of one of our centerpieces—a card from five-year-old Lauren, which says simply, "Please stay safe. Love Lauren."

We'll try really hard, Lauren. Merry Christmas.

PICTURE US SMILING

NAME: **CAPT LEE KELLEY**
STATIONED IN: **IRAQ**
HOMETOWN: **SALT LAKE CITY, UTAH**
MILBLOG URL: **WORDSMITHATWAR.BLOG-CITY.COM**

L ife doesn't seem to give you time-outs. Put your hands up in the shape of a "T," and the stress is not softened, the edges not blurred; you can't sit down on the bench of life's sideline and just catch your breath. The clock doesn't stop so that you can better deal with whatever hardships or difficulties you are experiencing. Likewise, war doesn't screech to a halt during the holiday season. The enemy does not celebrate Christmas, nor do they try to respect it, the way we show deference during Ramadan and other religious observances. They don't circle December 25 on their calendars and scribble "Kill no Americans today" in Arabic. When you're in a combat zone, it's a little harder to get into the spirit.

But you know what? We have Christmas trees in almost every office. Some of us have little trees or stockings in our rooms, surrounded by presents in festive wrapping. Some offices are decorated more than others and have wreaths with little Army figures rappelling from them. There are cookies and treats in almost every area, morsels of charity and love from the home front. Everybody is receiving care packages. Children from local schools in our hometowns have sent us beautiful cards. They adorn walls that are otherwise covered, for the most part, with matters of warfare, kill tactics and such. We are all eating way too much holiday candy. The stuff is everywhere.

When you enter the chow hall, there is a six-foot Christmas tree surrounded by big boxes that are wrapped as if they were gifts. The festive decor is way overdone, but that's what makes it so nice. Right now there is no such thing as too much America in Ramadi. Bring it on, we say. The metal support beams that line the chow hall are covered from top to bottom in wrapping paper. When you come out of the serving line and enter the area with the salad bars, there is Christmas music playing and cakes that reconstruct the nativity scene and cakes in the shape of snowmen.

We are still fighting a war in a very deadly region. We are still focused. We work our shifts and immerse ourselves in the mission and make the most of each moment. But we are completely aware of the spirit of the holidays that is lighting up our hometowns. We hum Christmas tunes under our Kevlar helmets. We want to be there, but we accept that we cannot. Many of us will use an instant messenger service and webcam, or a satellite phone, to see and hear our loved ones on Christmas Day. Technology does shorten the miles, and for that we are definitely thankful. I know folks who are going caroling around the FOB. And I am willing to bet my next paycheck that someone will dress up as Santa Claus.

So picture us smiling, not bleeding. Imagine us laughing instead of staring at the desert sunsets wistfully. Know that while we are painfully aware of the drama of our present state of affairs, this hard reality, we think of you often. In everything we do there is the simmer of Christmas cheer bubbling below the surface. It is a good thing in a place where good people are living and fighting. We've spent most of our lives in America. And while it is difficult to fully remember the joy of Christmas out here, it is much, much harder to forget.

In the end, it has to become just another day. But it is another day down, scratched out on the calendar. An emblem of progress and a reminder to count your blessings, not your difficulties. We are 24 hours closer to finishing this chapter of life and returning to those things that we know and love.

One Christmas tree is pretty big. It has blinking lights, ornaments, tinsel, and candy canes hanging from it, and, in a nice dark touch that exemplifies the mood of war, a belt of .50-caliber ammunition placed carefully around the bottom. The multicolored lights reflect off its brass casings. It's actually quite beautiful.

Thank you for all the support this holiday season. It means more than you know. Merry Christmas from Al Anbar Province.

THE HOLIDAYS IN IRAQ

NAME: **SPC JAMI GIBBS**
STATIONED IN: **IRAQ**
MILBLOG URL: **AMERICANBABBLE.COM**

It's kind of a relief that the holidays are over. Someone put it well here when he said, "Now all we have to get through is Easter and Independence Day. And those holidays won't be nearly as hard as this was." So very true.

I worked both Christmas and New Year's Eve. The usual 12-hour shift. On Christmas, I walked into work at 0700 and, like clockwork, a round came into Anaconda. A little Christmas present for everyone. I, of course, took the liberty of blasting Bing Crosby Christmas music for everyone as they stumbled into the clinic to check in at my desk after the "all clear" was given. All sleepy-eyed and groggy, most were able to mumble a "Merry Christmas," while the rest were wise enough not to even open their mouths.

In the evening, I felt little Christmas cheer as I spent hours and hours trying to call back home. Imagine thousands of troops trying to call the U.S. at the same exact moment. I opened all the wonderful presents everyone sent to me and had a cup of "Christmas cheer" with my roommate to celebrate the holiday.

Backing up a day to Christmas Eve: I had to make a run to our battalion early in the morning. Even though it isn't too far from the clinic, I always try and take advantage of the van, to save myself from the half-mile walk.

Yes, we have a van. It's kinda funny looking. The type you would see zooming around the streets of Europe somewhere. It's more long than wide, white, with a stick shift, which makes it even more hilarious when you're driving it off curbs and flying by armored vehicles with gunners on the top. It's ironic the way they strictly enforce the 20 mph speed limit but let you take sharp right turns

off paved roads over curbs and park wherever there's enough room to fit your vehicle.

So I'm scootin' down the road in my little Euro-van, and it's a very chilly day. Upper 30s is my guess, from the way my breath is sticking to the windshield. Armed Forces Radio is on, and they're playing Christmas music. The sky is a perfect blue and, for once, not a soul is on the road. There are no gun trucks or trash collectors. I find myself in a bubble of Christmas cheer. I could be driving anywhere right now on this calm Christmas Eve morning. I am reminded of Nebraska. The complete stillness in the crisp air and the solitude is something you can only find in vast midwestern winters. I wanted that half mile never to end because it took me back to better times. Here we grasp at any little moment that helps us feel normal.

We rang in the New Year with sparkling cider. Being a bit more organized than Christmas, New Year's Eve was quite pleasant. Even though I was working 1900–0700, I could feel the positive energy in everyone. They had music blasting and were grilling hamburgers and hotdogs. I have always felt that Christmas is meant for family, and New Year's is meant for friends. Well, this year it was for both. It's a fantastic feeling looking at these people and knowing they are both friends and family. Even though I was stuck working, people still made the effort to come give me a hug and wish me a Happy New Year.

It was odd knowing that at midnight it was really only 3 P.M. back home. I got a bit depressed thinking that I'll be spending a majority of the next year here. As if I shouldn't even bother with goals and resolutions like everyone else. But I decided that maybe I should take this time and really live it. Smell it. Be it. Explore who I am, where I've been, and what has made me this person today.

The first bright morning of the New Year was spent in a bunker with the rest of my sleepy company. Again, the insurgents decided to throw a round at us—a wake-up call, if you will. At this point, we just laugh and say, "Happy New Year!"

THE ENEMY

NAME: **1LT ADAM TIFFEN**
RETURNED FROM: **IRAQ**
MILBLOG URL: **THEREPLACEMENTS.BLOGSPOT.COM**

The front gate of the Alamo opens up into the sprawling town. A mass of triple-strand concertina wire and Jersey barriers block out traffic and channel incoming vehicles through a chicane of concrete blocks. The front entrance is reinforced by an up-armored HMMWV, a gunner sitting in the cupola manning a long-barreled .50-caliber machine gun. The gunner scans oncoming traffic looking for signs of trouble, while the driver sits patiently and monitors the radio. The vehicle must be moved for any traffic to enter or exit and is a last-ditch effort to prevent a car packed with explosives from slamming into the Alamo and reducing the building to fire and ash.

Nearing the front gate and stepping around the wire, I wrinkle my nose as I catch a fresh draft of hot wind from the city. The sewer stench of the city permeating the air is something I will never get used to.

At the front gate, a man stands patiently, waiting to talk. He is wearing a dark blue robe and worn brown sandals. His rolled-up sleeves reveal faded swirling tattoos and Arabic markings on his skin. His unshaven face is rough, made up of sharp angular planes that are hardened by hooded, expressionless eyes. Looking into those dark brown eyes, I can tell that he wants me dead.

Without taking my eyes off his, I motion for the interpreter. Steve walks over and stops suddenly, as if sensing the tension between the stranger and myself.

"What does he want?" I ask.

Steve begins hesitantly, stumbling over the first few words of his normally flawless Arabic. The man replies so softly that Steve has to lean forward to catch his last few words.

"He says he has come for his brothers."

"Who are his brothers?"

"He says that one of his brothers was killed by Americans yesterday, and that the other brother was taken and arrested."

Unconsciously, I nod my head. I know who he is talking about. The day before, an IED had hit an American patrol. Immediately after the blast, the soldiers had spotted a blue Bongo truck fleeing from the scene. The patrol reacted quickly and gave chase. The truck fled until its tires were shot out. As it ground to a halt, two armed men had jumped out and started running. My patrol had arrived on scene just after one had been shot dead and the other had surrendered.

The two brothers had been insurgents. This one likely is as well.

Standing before me is the enemy.

The bastard is trying to stare me down.

Resting my right hand on my pistol, I feel an involuntary rush of adrenaline.

"Tell him that he can have his brother's body. I will show him where it is."

At the mention of his brother's body, his gaze cracks. For an instant, the corners of his eyes tighten with grief, and then his features return to the intense, hate-filled stare. Motioning with my right hand, I turn and walk over to the Iraqi Police station. Behind me, the man follows, shadowed by two of my soldiers pulling security. They have picked up on the lethal atmosphere and are moving with extra care, their eyes scanning for trouble.

I can feel his gaze on the back of my neck.

Walking into the comparative cool of the police station, I step through the shadowed concrete corridors and into a back room. There, on a wooden pallet, is a body bag with his brother's remains. An Iraqi policeman walks in, and Steve quietly explains what the man is there for. There is a slight stench in the air that no words could properly describe.

The man steps around me and walks up to the bag. I can see him grip his blue robe with his right hand, holding the material so hard that his knuckles have turned white. After a long moment, he turns to face me.

"And my other brother, the Americans arrested him. Where is he? How can I get him?"

I look at him for a moment, not saying anything.

"Your brother was arrested after he attacked an American patrol. He has been confined, and they are doing an investigation. If he is guilty of terrorist activity, he will be charged and sentenced by an Iraqi court of law. If he is not guilty of terrorist activity, you have nothing to be afraid of. If he is innocent, he will be released, and you will see him again. If, however, he is guilty, he is going to be going to prison for a very long time."

The man looks at me, his jaw working in anger. For a brief second, I get the impression that he is going to attack, and then suddenly, as if the energy has gone out of him, his shoulders slump slightly, and he looks down at his brother's body.

"Can you help me move him to my vehicle?"

I can tell that it was painful for him to ask me for assistance. Looking steadily at the man standing before me, his face half cloaked in the shadows, I consider his request. Part of me goes out to the man in sympathy. For the loss of a brother.

And then I remember all of the bodies of innocent civilians that my men have found rotting in the sun, their hands bound behind their backs and their eyes blindfolded before they were shot in the head by insurgents that had suspected them of helping us. This man is an insurgent. His brother had tried to kill Americans.

My resolve hardens, and I shake my head to clear my thoughts. I will get him what he needs. "Tell him that the Iraqi police will help him carry the body." The policeman in the corner nods and leaves the room to get a colleague to help. For my men will do no such thing.

MOUNTAIN FURY

NAME: **1SG TROY STEWARD (Bouhammer)**
STATIONED IN: **SHARANA, AFGHANISTAN**
HOMETOWN: **AMHERST, NEW YORK**
MILBLOG URL: **BOUHAMMER.COM**

D ay six of Operation Mountain Fury started with a good breakfast shared with my ANA brothers. The half of Recon Company we have here is doing a really good job, and the 10th Mountain boys really like them and say they are the best ANA they have ever worked with. Face and I drank coffee, while the ANA drank chai tea. I ate some oatmeal along with some Afghan sweet bread—we'd picked up some sweet bread the other day while at the bazaar, and it is good stuff in the morning with coffee. The ANA had made a small fire to get warm, so we sat around that and chatted while we ate the bread and drank our coffee/tea. I also showed the ANA how to do a toast, and we all toasted while I called out "Salute."

Today was going to be a slow day, so we tended to personal, vehicle, and equipment maintenance. Since we had the generator going, the cell phones and iPods got charged. We also performed maintenance on the vehicles, weapons, and radios. By noon we were pretty much done with everything, and since we react to what happens on the battlefield, there was nothing to do. We were letting things settle down after some busy days and wanted the enemy to get complacent.

Around noon, Face and I decided to take the ANA out without 10th Mountain and do another presence patrol of the one village he had been in two days prior. We planned to depart around 2 P.M., after the ANA were done with lunch.

Things started to change around 12:45, when our terp came running over saying there had been an accident, and one of the

ANA soldiers, the cook, had been severely burned. Apparently he was cooking lunch for the ANA soldiers on a pressure cooker, and it was not sealed properly. It had blown up, and he was burned pretty bad; he had second-degree burns to his face, neck, upper chest, and left forearm. He was screaming in pain, and the U.S. medics came running. There is not much you can do for burns, so the medic put burn gel on, gave him a hit of morphine, and Face gave the guy an IV to help replace fluids.

I noticed that he was already starting to blister, and some of the blisters were already popped. I knew we had to get him out of there, as there was too much dirt and filth in the field for him to be that exposed. He could not ground-evac because of the dust, so I sent up what we call a 9-line medevac request and called in an air medevac.

After a very long 45 minutes, he was numbed up from the morphine pretty good and not screaming and moaning anymore. The bird finally came in on final, and I went out to set up yet another landing zone (LZ) with a VS-17 orange panel and purple smoke. I called the bird and told them the markings again, and they spotted us. By this time the injured soldier was able to walk, so a couple of ANA soldiers and I helped him onto the bird. I handed the air medic a paper with the treatment and drugs he had been given and the guy's vital signs.

After the bird left and finished blasting us with sand and rocks, Face and I linked up and decided to continue on with our presence patrol mission. It was already 30 minutes past when we'd wanted to depart, but that was OK. We needed to get the ANA out of there and their minds off of their injured buddy. So we called the ANA leadership over and told them to be ready to go in 15 minutes. Right before the bird flew in, the 1st Platoon of the 10th Mountain company we were attached to had pulled into the patrol base from a short mission they had earlier. This insignificant action played a bigger part later in the day.

We told the ANA Recon XO to go whatever direction he felt comfortable with to get to our objective. There were several ways to get there, and we wanted it to be his decision. We departed, and everything was quiet and normal, as we would like. As we went from one village to another, we started to get close to the hardball road that would take us to our objective. There were several very tight bridge crossings that were barely wide enough to get the Humvee across. Since I had a better vantage point from up in the gunner's hatch, I would tell Face "a little left" or "a little right." The last thing you want to do is flip a six-ton truck into a ditch, and these ditches were very deep.

We got past the third crossing point when a guy approached from our left side on a motorcycle. He almost did not stop, so I started to swing my gun toward him. He just stared me down and did not wave or smile. I turned around and watched him as we went past and told Face that I did not trust the guy. Just as we went past him, another guy on a bicycle was going the opposite direction and passed us. He also did not wave, smile, or even look up at me. I turned to watch him, as you never know what they might try behind your back. I was just telling Face that this was not a friendly village when "time stood still," again.

As I was turning my head back to the front and talking to Face, the ANA truck in front of us blew up. It had only been about 10 days since I had one blow up right behind me and kill two ANA soldiers, and now I watched every detail as the one 60 feet ahead of me exploded. I remember seeing parts and pieces fly everywhere. I also remember seeing the flash of the fireball very clearly. Several natural instincts kicked in within milliseconds. First, I buckled my knees and dropped down to shield myself from any secondary explosions, direct attack fire, or flying debris. At the same time, I was yelling to Face, "I am fine! I am fine!" I then popped up and clicked the safety off the MG and started scanning for targets.

137

Face stopped the truck and was also looking at the scene in front of us for targets. The ANA had opened fire from the other trucks at people nearby. The normal practice after an IED hit is for a trigger man to jump up and take off. However, people also run from things blowing up. As I saw which way the ANA was shooting, I was looking through my MG scope and trying to get a PID (positive identification) of a threat target. All I could see was men, women, and children running for cover as bullets kicked up dirt and dust around them. From the moment of the blast, only about four seconds had elapsed—time slows to a crawl as your mind works in overdrive. I was processing everything I was seeing and trying to see a threat before it saw me. Unable to find a runner or a threat, I started yelling for the ANA to cease fire. I was afraid they would shoot an innocent, and thankfully they didn't. I am not sure how, but they didn't.

Now Face and I turned our attention to the smoking heap of a truck in front of us. Face and I had already confirmed what each of our jobs would be in case this happened (something we do before every vehicle movement), so he ran to assess the situation and render first aid while I provided security and worked the radios. I called to the company we were attached to first and let them know what had happened.

They had heard the explosion and shooting, so they were already moving to get guys mounted up. I gave them our grid loca-

tion and called in the initial report. I knew there was at least one wounded, and I thought we might have one KIA already. I watched the ANA carry this lifeless-looking body from the truck with its arms and leg dangling. After Face got a good idea what was going on and knew that there were wounded that needed treating, he sent Jawed, the terp, back for the CLS bag. Jawed ran it up to him, and Face was busy again providing first aid to burns and giving IVs.

He and I were the only Americans there (as is usual with the ETT mission), so he handled the ground work while I kept an eye out and called not only the 10th Mountain, but also my higher ETT HQ, sending up another 9-line medevac request. I could tell the truck was destroyed, so I was already working a request to get a wrecker out there to evac it. As I was finishing up with talking to my HQ, the commander of the company we were with (call sign: Devil 6) had gathered enough info from my initial report to call a medevac through his channels. I think he had seen how long the earlier one took and did not want to have to wait that long again. Devil 6 called me and told me he had a bird en route and told me he needed the last few lines of the request. I gave them to him and told him I would cancel my other medevac request. Devil 6 also told me he was working a wrecker, so I did not need to get that either. It sure is nice to have that level of support in situations like this.

A few minutes later, his QRF platoon arrived and asked me where I wanted the LZ. I told them where I was going to put the bird and told them where I wanted their security. They sent their medic up to help out Face also. By then he was ready for help. The injured soldier had thrashed around and yanked out three IVs before Face finally got a fourth one secured enough to stay. The guy had terrible head and face wounds, along with a pretty mangled lower right leg. From the time of the blast until when the bird set down was just under 11 minutes. In fact, the helo got there so fast we were not even looking for it yet, and it just popped up on top of us. Later I found out it was the same bird that evaced our earlier soldier and was on its way back to its base when our request came in.

After both soldiers (the Recon 1SG and one of his NCOs) were evaced, Face returned to the truck. He started telling me about the guy's condition and how much medical supply stuff he had gone through, when he looked down and said, "Damn, I got his blood all over my uniform." I then informed him that he should look at his hands, which were probably 60 percent covered in blood. He wasn't happy about that either but forgot about the uniform.

I got down from the gun (10th Mountain was there providing security now) and inspected the truck and blast site. All appearances suggested a land mine, but we were unsure if it was victim-initiated or remote-controlled. We coordinated with the ANA and 10th Mountain on the action plan. Some ANA went with the 10th, and they started searching through coochie tents about 200 meters away. The ANA was also stopping and questioning locals.

We garnered quite a bit of information from one and ascertained that the guys on the bike and motorcycle were working together. They saw the 1st Platoon coming in earlier and had planted a land mine to blow them up, but it was a dud. So they went back, dug it up, put down a new one, and barely finished before we showed up. The guy on the bike had the dud land mine on the back of his bike wrapped up in a cloth. I remember seeing that object.

We also found out that ACM stayed in a nearby mosque the night before, so several gun trucks of 10th Mountain and some ANA went over there, along with Face. I stayed at the truck, waiting on the wrecker and helping with the forensics. They found quite a bit at the mosque, at least enough to warrant Americans entering it and searching. They found medicine bottles, an AK-47 magazine chest rig, ammo for AK-47s, and an entrance to a huge tunnel complex. All of the stuff was confiscated, and we marked the spot on our maps.

Face and the rest of them returned right about the time that the wrecker was leaving with the truck. At this point we packed everything, and everyone up and headed back to our patrol base. It was already dark and time to get back. Luckily nobody had been killed, but about four guys were hurt, including one that is still in the hospital and getting reconstruction surgery.

That morning we sat around and drank our drinks of choice and enjoyed each other's company. That evening we were down three guys, Face had a lot more experience giving IVs and medical attention in stressful situations, and I was very proficient on doing 9-line medevac requests.

And we thought it was going to be a slow and boring day.

SUNSET

NAME: **CAPT LEE KELLEY**
RETURNED FROM: **IRAQ**
HOMETOWN: **SALT LAKE CITY, UTAH**
MILBLOG URL: **WORDSMITHATWAR.BLOG-CITY.COM**

ome soldiers take pictures of everything. Some just take pictures of what they consider unique—things they don't think they'll ever see back home, like palaces, or Iraqi children, or themselves behind a .50-caliber machine gun looking like a battle-hardened, steely-eyed killer. But it's interesting when there's a beautiful sunset. I see a lot of my fellow soldiers pulling out their digital cameras to capture it, though pictures rarely do a sunset justice. Don't get me wrong. A sunset is a wonderful thing to behold, and even more so when it happens to take on colors and formations that really rest upon the retina with a splendor that's impossible to deny. But we've all seen thousands. And we'll presumably see thousands more.

It reminds me of the movie *Smoke*, in which a guy takes a picture of a busy street corner in front of his smoke shop every single day at the exact same time for decades. When he shows a friend, the friend says, "They're all the same." But upon further consideration, he realizes how poignant the photo album really is, and how each day is in fact unique, and he even sees some people he recognizes who have died in the years since the photos were taken.

Sunset out here can be like that. Most days, you don't even notice the conversion from light to dark. The light is irrelevant, its strength superfluous to what you're working on. But sometimes it catches your eye, especially one like tonight when the orange looks like melted copper spreading across the horizon in a river of floating lava, playing hide and seek with the moon across the smooth curvature of the earth.

Years from now, you'll look at the picture, and it will just seem like one of a million beautiful sunsets. But it won't be. It's a sunset from when you were deployed in Iraq, and it takes on a special meaning, carries more weight somehow. For the rest of your life, you'll probably never be in this place again, looking at the sunset from this perspective, either geographically or mentally. Others might look at it and say, "Oh, that's pretty." But you'll know it was more than that. You will remember taking the picture on a particular day, and you may very well use the quality of life you had back then as a barometer by which to judge just how bad something really is.

The pictures will help you remember your combat experience, which I think is important, because once you've gone to war, what else in life can really match the endless tests of patience, courage, physical fatigue, sleep deprivation, stress, and camaraderie? I think we'll be able to handle more than we ever thought possible, conquer obstacles once insurmountable. Yes, the work is satisfying. But the experience of being here will be all the sweeter once it is an artifact of the past—a conversation at a party, a dream sequence in the documentary of your life.

I took a lot of pictures today, in part just because I happened to have my digital camera with me. But part of it is the ever-growing anticipation that I will be departing this eyesore of a base sometime in the next few months. I want pictures to help me remember, so that I can counterpose living on this FOB with life hereafter, making it seem eternally richer. Oh, it's not so bad. You make the best of it. You have food, shelter, clothing, "recreational facilities," the Internet, movies, video games, books.

But let's be honest, shall we? The "suck factor" outweighs satisfaction. The cons kill the pros. Of course, you'd rather complete the mission and be in your own home with nothing but a box of crackers and a beanbag pillow than live here with every amenity under the sun. Having a bad day, soldier? Think the world is being too hard on you? Just pull out your photo album from the year you spent living on a forward operating base in the Sunni Triangle.

THE DOG

Name: **SGT ROY BATTY**
Stationed in: **BAGHDAD, IRAQ**
Hometown: **YELLOW SPRINGS, OHIO**

So it is a new year, and once again I am disappointed that we are not all zipping around the skies in shiny silver jet packs. I thought we would be there by the impossible Year of Our Lord 2007. But no, here we are in freakin' Baghdad, watching Mesopotamian hillbillies waste each other with assembly-line machine guns designed in 1947 and trying to relearn hard-won lessons from a bitter little war 40 years behind us. It's all a bit depressing.

I could deal with all that, though, if it weren't for the mud. We enjoyed a week's respite while the clouds held back their torrents, and a weak and impotent sun slowly transmogrified the mud back into its usual tan-gray talcum-powder form. Now it's returned with a vengeance, like some monster Jell-O from a cheap 1950s sci-fi horror flick. *Revenge of the Chocolate Mousse. Bride of the Mocha Blancmange.* Or my personal favorite: *It Came from the Porta-Potti.*

Rumor has it that last week 1st Platoon lost a soldier to it. One moment he was walking to the latrines; the next second he was gone. All they found was his boonie hat lying on top of an innocent-looking mud hole, a few air bubbles plopping around it. No one's seen him since.

Mud victims or no, life goes on pretty much as normal, if such a word can be used on whatever twisted planet Baghdad rests upon. Midway through our deployment, and we have all gotten used to the routine. Admittedly, said routine is pretty easy here at FOB Shield. Too easy, if you ask me. We go out for a few hours every couple of days and spend the rest of the time either playing Xbox or languishing in the Motorpool of Lost Souls, trying to make torque wrenches out of commo wire and the remnants of ammo crates, since the mechanics

(a) flatly refuse to actually work, and (b) won't give us any of their tools. The other day I managed to take apart a steering gear box and change the MWO with my Leatherman and a P-38 can opener.

Today we have a new mission, an interesting one. We are going to an IP station on the fringes of Sadr City. Up until now, it's been left out of the whole training and assessment thing we have been pretending to do with the other stations in town, since we were pretty darn certain that the entire staff was Mehdi Army. Someone higher up has decided that we will single-handedly convince them to turn their backs on their sectarian buddies and embrace the cause of democracy through the combined tactics of giving them the occasional case of drinking water and maybe a bullet or two. Giddy with the success of winning previous counterinsurgency wars by handing out free shit, we are going to have a go with these guys.

But first we have to do PT. So I wake up at 0730, trudge to the latrine for the morning tinkle, only losing one shoe to the morass outside the front door, then present myself to the MWR gym. The gym is tacked onto the back of the strange structure we live in. I say strange because it was clearly something else back in the days when Saddam Hussein first raised it out of the desert sand. Its commonly accepted name is the "D-cell," MP lingo for detention dell. Civilian translation: jail. The back half is a vast, dark, echoing cavern where the infantry stay during their occasional sleepovers at Shield. We call it the Thunderdome.

The gym is hidden away inside its bowels. Most of the rooms have tile walls, vaguely stained, which suggest that it was either once a series of showers, or one of Hussein's secret gas chambers. The floor is made up of those funny foam segments that you see in kindergarten classrooms, linked together like a huge puzzle. The pieces are uniformly black-gray, though I suspect at one time they were cutely pastel. The rooms are filled with a variety of aging cardio machines, pieces of weightlifting equipment, and a surprisingly imaginative series of entertainment rooms, including a video game room, billiard room, and two phone/Internet chambers. With some hard work and ingenuity, someone has made the most of a bad area.

I spend half an hour on a creaking, mutinous cross-trainer machine, followed by 20 minutes on a treadmill, and am surprised that I feel good. Really good. Like a million bucks, that kind of Tony the Tiger enthusiasm that seems to get more and more rare the closer you get to 40. Even the bracing thrill of the ice cold shower afterward does little to daunt my good mood—in fact the screams of my comrades around me freezing their balls off just increases the grin on my face.

An hour later we are rolling out of the mud-strewn gates in our trucks. I am appropriately fortified with nicotine and caffeine and looking forward to the tawdry sensations that only Baghdad can offer. Our convoy is particularly full today, with three International Police Liaison Officers (IPLOs), their translators, and some pudgy Military Intelligence dudes and their interpreters. The MI guys have become a bit notorious with us lately, since they seem unusually incompetent, at least when it comes to preparing for missions.

The other day we were late for our SP (start point) because they had not done maintenance on their truck, which promptly went dead just as we started to move out. Once they got that fixed, it turned out that they had not changed the fill on their SINCGARS radios. Once they got both of those problems taken care of and we were finally on the road, they realized they had not written down our frequencies during the OPORD brief. "Lost in the sauce," as we say. Today we cut through that problem by stuffing them into our own trucks, despite their objections.

We didn't have to wait long for Baghdad to offer up something unusual. As soon as we had driven out of the gate, I noticed a column of dark smoke a block away. It looked a bit like the smoke from a VBIED, or car bomb, but no one had heard anything. It could have been just another trash fire in a city that seems to breed trash fires, but it was not in a usual spot for one and seemed just a bit too big and a bit too black. It looked like it was along the route that we would be traveling; maybe we'd get a look.

Sure enough, a few minutes later we emerge from a *mahallah* side street and there it is; some sort of vehicle in the middle of a major road, fully engulfed in flames. A HMMWV is parked in front of it, blocking one of the lanes. We wheel around to check it out.

Turns out the HMMWV belongs to the Iraqi Army, and a number of IP trucks pull up at the same time we do. A ragtag crowd of people has already formed around the burning vehicle, pointing and gibbering and moving back and forth with sudden flares of movement, the way crowds do. People lean over the balcony railings of nearby buildings. Kids stand around with open mouths, their attention moving from the popping and blazing wreck to us, then back again. Traffic clogs up around us, drivers cautious not to get too close to all of these men and their guns.

I get out of my truck and direct Nix to park it sideways across the street, providing more cover to the guys in front of me. I usually have the last truck in our convoys, so we are responsible for the rear security. I direct my gunner, Cooper, to watch the traffic behind us and to scan the rooftops for snipers. I join him, standing at the back of the truck, using its bulk as cover, and scan the balconies and windows in the buildings behind us, peering through the telescopic sight on top of my M4. The chubby MI guy gets out of his rear passenger seat and takes up a stalwart position at the front of the truck, chewing his bubble gum and watching the car burn in the middle of the road.

We have new, high-speed radio headsets, so the team leaders can talk to each other and the squad leader when dismounted, and

through it I pick up what has happened, in bursts of static and bits of conversation. SSG Huhn is up at the front of the column, conferring through his interpreter, Sam, with the Iraqi Army and police on the scene. Seems that the Iraqi HMMWV came across a kidnapping in progress. The IA guys shot at the kidnappers, who took off, leaving their car behind, and the locals torched it in retaliation. These kidnappings are the newest fad in Baghdad, and there's been an explosion of them in the recent months. Anyone and everyone can be a target, as long as they have money. Ransoms can be hundreds of thousands of dollars, sometimes millions, and hostages are often killed or simply never seen again. It seems that this time, for once, the bad guys lost.

"Meester, meester!" I turn around, and there are a cute little boy and his sister standing in the middle of the road, wrapped up in thick bubble jackets against the winter cold. He wants some candy but has chosen a bad place to make his pitch. I try, not unkindly, to shoo him away, doing a fair exploding-car charades bit with my hands.

"Boom! Go 'way, kid, it's not safe here."

He really wants some chocolate and ain't budging—but his sister picks up on the message right away. I return to my search for snipers and RPG gunners, but I can hear her behind me, tugging at him.

"Imshee, imshee." Let's go, let's go.

As is normal for Baghdad, everyday life goes on around the spectacle, as if nothing were happening. Men walk down the street carrying groceries and seem surprised when I suggest to them, via the pointy end of my rifle, that perhaps they should not walk near my truck. A hefty woman draped in traditional black robes walks right past me, coming from behind, lugging a massive plastic gas can. After she passes, I suggest to the MI guy that as long as he is going to watch the front of the truck, I would appreciate it if he did not let anyone get near it, particularly if they are carrying large amounts of flammable liquid. He pops his gum and nods.

There is not much more for us to do. The police and Army are here, but oddly no fire department. The truck continues to crackle and burn merrily, to the satisfaction of the crowd. As usual, a couple of knuckleheads try to inch around the backed-up traffic and roll up on our blockade. There's always someone who thinks they are special. We have another job to do, so SSG Huhn radios to the team leaders, and we mount up and head on down the road.

Away from the burning car, traffic is fairly light. I ride in the TC seat, toes tapping as we go, with the hand mic for our internal freq jammed up underneath my Peltor headphones. Between the SINCGARs and the headset radios, the airwaves are full of convoy chatter. Nowadays, we always go out with at least six vehicles, for security, and everyone is going on about something. Cracking jokes on their mates, sending out tactical info on the movement of traffic, pointing out potentially suspicious bits of junk on the road, or relaying info from the various maneuver elements that are trolling around the city. I send up a steady stream of comments, letting the squad leader know the status of the convoy as we clear various obstructions—intersections, turns, checkpoints. We want to make sure we all stay together.

The weather is at odds with my good mood—dark gray, raining off and on, and bitterly cold. For most of the year, Baghdad is solidly tan, but in the winter it is a depressing combination of slate gray and shit brown, glazed over with subfreezing temperatures at night, sulkily rising to the high forties or low fifties in the middle of the day. The palm trees look completely out of place in this weather, as if they have been trucked in as props on a movie set. In fact, if you want to know what Baghdad looks like in January, watch Stanley Kubrick's *Full Metal Jacket*. All of the scenes in the last half, set in Hue City during the Tet Offensive, were filmed in the docklands of London. The combination of half-destroyed buildings, black plumes of gasoline fires, and the unremitting gloom of Great Britain in soggy wintertime do a pretty good job of sketching out this place. Just add the mud, some raw sewage, and about ten years of garbage.

We make it across town to our delightful new police station, which is pretty much the same as all the other police stations in Iraq. A blue concrete fort, with cement guard towers on the corners—sort of a post-nuclear-war *Beau Geste*. Burned-out hulks of cars rusting in the middle of trash in the front. Wrecked police pickup trucks in the back, one with a corpse lolling around in its truck bed. Guys standing around with AKs and no discernible uniforms. The smell of cheap cigarettes and fake leather. Suspicious looks. Saddam mustaches. Same old same old.

I'm in charge of setting up security, so I put two trucks in the back of the compound, two in the front, and our big ASV blocking the only gate in. The IPLOs, MI guys, translators, and our squad leader go inside to do their thing. I grab two soldiers and take them up to the roof to do counter-sniper watch. It's raining again, and a steel wind blows it into the guard towers. Fogged-over water bottles and the remains of unidentifiable meals lie resentfully in the corners. The place smells like an old castle—crumbling stone, rusting metal, and the thin, unavoidable odor of urine.

The perimeter wall has its own set of guard towers in addition to the ones on top of the station house—flimsy little sheet-metal things, but the IPs here do not seem too concerned about security. And why should they be? They are Shia police in a Shia part of town, right next to the holy Shia capital, Sadr City. No one is going to attack them here. Probably. One of the little towers has an occupant, but he is sitting down, facing the inside of the perimeter, and apparently asleep. Another IP sometimes wanders out to his tower, a big guy wearing a tan jacket and a balaclava. He looks like one of the thugs who led Saddam out to his gallows. They don't fill me with confidence, and it is an unspoken certainty that while they may be safe here, we are not.

I scan the rooftops with my sniper scope and try to keep the soldiers' minds on the task at hand. Nobody is visible, which is hardly surprising given the horrible weather, and it is more likely that we would get hit leaving than while we are in the station. Still, it pays to be vigilant. Just once I would love to find a sniper crouched over his Dragunov in a window . . . first.

After a bit, I trudge downstairs and make my rounds. Check on the guys inside the IP station who are inventorying the police arms room and going through various records with the police chief. Trudge through the mud outside, making sure the gunners are OK in the HMMWVs and still awake. Arrange with the other team leaders to have soldiers relieve the guys on the roof in a little bit; they won't last long in the rain and the wind. Take a break for a few minutes in my truck and read some more of the massive Stephen King book I have been working through for the fourth time. It is eerie to read about the end of the world while in a city that is as postapocalyptic as it gets. Sometimes I look up from the book half expecting to see Randall Flag striding across the rubble-strewn landscape toward me, his dark grin twisting his face. He would feel right at home in this place. After all, he and his cronies created it.

As if the Dark Man heard his name and is answering, I hear gunfire outside—not right outside, but not too far away either, and I head back to the roof to investigate. Nix and Arballo are in one of the corner guard posts, looking toward the northwest. We can hear AK fire, a bunch of it, and then some answering bursts—PKC, by the sound of it—and then the unmistakable crunk-crunk-crunk of a Dashika 12.7 mm, the Soviet version of the .50 caliber. I report it to SSG Huhn over the radio headset and add that I think Checkpoint 4V is getting attacked. Again. Happens almost every day.

This time it sounds like it's a pretty good one. The distant gunfight goes on for a good half hour, as both sides pound away at each other. The fighting doesn't come any closer to us, and no one directs us to go and support them, so the IA must be doing OK. It is interesting, though, since we will be driving through there in just a little while. I go back to my rounds, glancing occasionally at the perimeter wall when a particularly energetic burst catches my attention.

That's when I come across The Dog. I call him "The Dog" since he doesn't seem to have a name, at least not any that he answers to. The Dog has some history with our squad, which he seems to have adopted in a strange, protective way. The other IP station that we go to is four or five miles away. We first started visiting it a month ago, and The Dog was hanging out there with a bunch of other mutts, one of whom was nursing a litter of bumbling puppies.

Baghdad is teeming with dogs, tons of them, most of them half wild, feral, and a fair number infected with rabies. We came across them all the time when we were on the checkpoint missions, particularly at night. A pack would come rushing out of the darkness, barking madly, chasing our HMMWVs, nipping at the tires. We'd swerve at them, and they would back off, and then come charging back in, just behind us.

Supposedly Arabs don't like dogs, but someone must have imported them at one time. There are all sorts: border collies, black labs, golden retrievers, although barely recognizable with their matted pelts and wild eyes. Just more lost souls trying to survive in the broken city.

These dogs at the station didn't seem unusual, except for the fact that the IPs allowed them to hang out in the walled parking lot. With hours to kill and nothing to do but scan for snipers, we would pet them and try to play with them. Our IPLOs started bringing scraps for them from the chow hall, and that got their interest. But they must have been pretty well fed. I've never seen a dog refuse anything, and these guys were pretty picky, occasionally turning their nose up at suspect infidel grub, like corn dogs or egg rolls.

The Dog is not the cutest of them, or the friendliest, but he has personality. The first thing we notice is that he really doesn't like kids. As any soldier who has spent time outside the wire in Iraq will tell you, the kids are everywhere here, and they always cluster around your trucks begging for water or candy or anything. It's cute at first, but it gets annoying after a while, and it's also a security concern. We've seen UAV footage of kids burying IEDs and heard intel stories of kids attaching magnetic IEDs to HMMWVs. But mostly it's just really annoying, since you cannot get them to leave or even just shut up for a minute, except the way the IPs move them, which is by hitting them, and we don't do that.

Anyway, The Dog doesn't dig 'em. He'll bark and charge, driving them out of the police compound, although he will never actually bite them. He'll veer away at the last second, or suddenly stop, turn around, and stalk back to his resting spot, looking carefully over his shoulder at them. I can only imagine what the street urchins here do to dogs, and I assume he has had some bad experiences.

At that IP station there was a funny kid who would bring chai tea for the IPs and eventually for us. A nice lad, with an easy smile, especially when charging you double the going rate for a thimble full of chai. T.D. hated him, too, and would trap him for hours inside the station. At first we were worried that he would bite the poor boy, and had long, earnest conversations with The Dog about his antisocial behavior, shaking our fingers at him. He would just sit there, looking straight ahead, occasionally blinking, but never taking his eyes off of the doorway. As if he was just putting up with our sermon. "Yeah, yeah, I hear ya, Mac." And then he'd charge again as soon as the chai kid emerged. You just can't get through to some people.

The Dog provided some entertainment on particularly boring days but was not really anything that unusual. Just another vaguely golden retriever–ish mutt in a bad part of town. Until last week.

I was on mission with another squad at the time but heard about it later. The guys went to the MP station as usual, and there was The Dog, as usual. But when they left, The Dog decided he was going to come along and left with them, running down the street, zigzagging between the trucks, sometimes falling behind, and then catching up at the intersections. For five miles. All the way to the next IP station.

And he'd been here ever since, waiting for us to come visit him. Facundo hooked him up with an MRE, which he gratefully wolfed down. We all clustered around, scratching his ears, petting him, glad to see a friend in this decidedly unfriendly part of town.

When the IPLOs and MI guys finished up their business inside, it was time for us to go. We had to do a quick assessment of one checkpoint right on the northeastern edge of town, about six miles from the station. So we loaded up the trucks, checked the radios, and lurched out into traffic. And The Dog came with us.

It was exactly as the guys had told me. He kept right up with us, sometimes running point just in front of our lead vehicle, sometimes crisscrossing in front of the other trucks or falling just behind my vehicle, but always somewhere in the convoy.

Apparently he decided to take on the responsibility of providing flank security as well. He would swerve wildly off to the side at the sight of any kid over the age of ten, barking ferociously, and charge them, tail swinging madly in circles, making sure they stayed away from the convoy. I watched one kid jump out of the way at the last possible second, and The Dog, in a failed attempt to adjust fire, face-planted hard in the slick mud. He was not discouraged, though, and quickly regained his footing and returned to his slot in the convoy, a long doggy grin plastered on his face, as if to say, "Yep, meant to do that."

We laughed hysterically, until tears shone in our eyes. The Dog was all right. Soldiers in the trucks started radioing back and forth to each other.

"Is The Dog still with us?"

"Roger that! Still going strong."

"Where's he at?"

"Just on the right rear bumper of CPL Glessner's truck, over."

"Whoa, there he goes again!"

We could hear his barks, muffled, through the armor of the HMMWVs. He was off like a shot, barreling straight for a kid who was walking the other way, oblivious. He homed in like a missile on his target, and we braced ourselves for the impact, holding our breath with that delicious half-giggle you get when something both funny and tense is about to happen. The kid jumped in shock at the last minute, leaping to the side, and The Dog zoomed by him, curving back to us like an F-15 pulling out of a bombing run. It wasn't about hurting anyone. The Dog was just counting coup. Getting some payback.

Then we started watching out for him, the same way he was watching out for us. A couple of times neighborhood dogs, understandably uncool with this intruder on their turf, came charging out of dark alleyways at him, very serious about it. They were going for his legs and no doubt his throat if they could take him down. We'd swerve our trucks at them, scaring them off. The Dog would dig down deep, sprinting forward, glancing at us, that big grin on his face. It was all one big game for him. I called up to SSG Huhn on the radio.

"Can we keep 'im? Take him back to the FOB? Pleeeze?"

SGT French chimed in, "I second that!"

Other voices joined in on the freq, thirding the suggestion, fourthing it. SSG Huhn wasn't too hot on the idea. We all knew the medical advice about strays—diseases, fleas, parasites, etc. Lord only knows what our platoon sergeant would do or say if we showed up with this muddy, dirty, stinking mutt in the back of one of our trucks. I'd gladly put him in my HMMWV, but I had the MI guys taking up space. Hell, given half a chance, I'd dump Fatso and take the pooch instead. The Dog would probably be more useful in a firefight anyway.

"Hey, we could put 'im in the ASV. They have enough room to carry him!" I offered.

"Uhhhh, I dunno, man. The PSG would have my ass."

Then the radio chatter turned to the subject of an appropriate name for The Dog. Since I'm on a Stephen King kick, I tried to think of the name of the junkyard dog that chases the group of boys in one of his novels, but I couldn't remember it, or the short story and subsequent movie that came from it.

"Hey, what's the name of the dog from that movie with the kids, where they get chased, y' know? In a junkyard? And they have to climb a fence to get away from it? Chompers? Gnasher?"

"Oh yeah, yeah, from *The Sandlot*, right?"

"No, that's not it. Stephen King wrote it. Remember, the junkyard guy tells the dog something like, 'Chompers, balls! Sic 'em!' And the dog chases the kids?"

"Hercules. The dog's name is Hercules."

"Hercules, Hercules!"

"No, that's *The Nutty Professor*."

"What movie?"

"The one with River Phoenix. Bunch of young guys, get chased by a dog . . ."

"Oh, yeah, that's . . . that's . . . oh, man, it's right on the tip of my tongue."

As usual, SSG Huhn got it. *Stand by Me*. He and I are the biggest movie buffs in the squad. But neither of us could remember the dog's name.

Meanwhile, we are sloshing our way up a particularly unpleasant side road, coming up to Enduring 7, our checkpoint. We don't like this road, since even in dry weather it is full of festering pools of liquid sewage. Now it's indescribable. We take it because we figure only a really die-hard terrorist would bury a bomb in the middle of this reeking gunk. None of which fazes The Dog, who launches himself into and through the shit pools with the tongue-lolling jubilation that only our canine brethren can enjoy.

We churn through the liquid excrement and lurch up to the checkpoint, reeking of garbage, mud, and Lord knows what. The

Dog is waiting for us as we dismount, sitting patiently, panting as if he is thoroughly delighted with the morning exercise. We crowd around him again, all of us, the civilian IPLOs, the MI guys, and all of us MPs, congratulating him on his hard work. He is absolutely filthy, fur matted down with brown goo, but we don't care. He has affected all of us and is a Good Dog, much the same as you would comment on a stand-up guy in your unit—he is Good People. We gotta take him home.

SGT French and I have a plan. We open up the side doors of the ASV and prepare a spot for him. SGT Nasholts, the ASV team leader, says it's OK with him, as long as SSG Huhn gives us the go-ahead.

"Sure, sure. He said it's OK, thinks it's a great idea."

To hell with orders. Problem is, The Dog won't cooperate. We coax him over to the great hulking armored vehicle, but he just won't get in. It's not that he seems distrustful of us, or unsure of our intentions. He just isn't interested, even with the offer of another MRE. He wanders past us, unconcerned, and pads off across the road to sit on the sidewalk and watch the distant houses. We call to him, trying all of the names we have come up with.

"Hey, Hercules! C'mon, boy, come here!"

"Chompers!"

"Gnasher!"

"Renegade!" Renegade is our platoon name and pretty fitting for him.

The Dog just sits and contemplates the landscape, his back toward us, his head still, facing the *mahallah*. Maybe his English is not that good. Maybe he is meditating on the state of affairs in the war-torn city. Perhaps he is on counter-sniper watch. But he is not getting in the ASV.

I come to the conclusion that The Dog is simply his own master. He does what he wants, with no explanations to anyone. He's not going to trade his independence for "three hots and a cot." You gotta respect that.

Still, when it comes time to leave, he is on point again. This time he has learned some more of our TTPs, as we find out after a bit, when he takes up position just behind my truck. If any civilian cars enter the 100-meter bubble we like to keep around us, he cuts them off. He is as good at rear security as he is at securing our flanks.

After a couple of blocks, though, it starts becoming apparent that the day's exercise is taking its toll. He starts falling farther and farther behind. He almost gets clipped by a car coming through an intersection, as my gunner relays down to me. I tell Coop, in reply, that he is authorized to open fire on any Iraqi vehicle that gets too close to our buddy. And then have to tack on a reluctant, "Just kidding."

By the time we roll up on Checkpoint 4V, about a mile and a half down the road, The Dog is gone. Tuckered out, he has stopped somewhere for a cold drink and a cigarette and is nowhere to be seen. I radio up to SSG Huhn that we need to pull a security halt at the checkpoint so he can catch up with us, but, no joy, we don't have time to stop.

It could be, though, that The Dog knew something we didn't. We roll up the bridge that Checkpoint 4 is on, and past the IA and IP guards, and down into the section of Adhamiyah on the other side. On one side of the bridge it is wall-to-wall traffic, as usual. On the other side, it is a freakin' ghost town. Nothing. Nobody.

That part of MSR Dover is really wide open—four lanes, big median, open sidewalks. It's normally a chaotic crush of cars and trucks. Mayhem. Now, there is absolutely nothing. Bad juju.

Just past the checkpoint, we cross an intersection covered in brass shell casings of all calibers. Obviously there was a pretty big firefight here recently. And then I remember the gun battle we heard from the IP station. A quick check and it is confirmed that this is the place, and that there is still fighting going on in the area. We can't hear any gunfire, but the sudden emptiness of that long space is more than slightly unnerving.

The earlier hilarity is instantly gone. The radio is silent, except for SSG Huhn telling us to watch the rooftops and windows. TCs occasionally relay info to their counterparts—a suspicious box, a lump in the road, a car abandoned by the side of the road. This is the same street that our other squad got hit on, with a car bomb, just a few days before Christmas—with no real injuries, thank God. Still, there are plenty of guys in our convoy who were hit that day, and the memories of that sudden fireball are all too fresh in their minds, in all of our minds.

Nix starts swerving the truck back and forth randomly; a tactic designed to make it harder to target us with rocket-propelled grenades. My eyes flit from side to side, up and down. I'm checking everything; garbage by the side of the road, windows, balconies. Everything. We pass a single small bonfire on the left side of the road and eye the old, kaffiyehed man standing next to it with his grandson. It's a pretty common sight in Baghdad in the wintertime—people trying to stay warm while they sell what few wares they have. These two are the only people along the whole stretch of road.

In my rearview mirror, I see them dart indoors after we pass. Maybe it's because we are rolling six vehicles deep. Maybe it's because we are obviously alert and ready for trouble. Maybe it's because there is nobody bad watching us from the dark windows above us, but whatever it is, nothing happens. We enjoy a few tense minutes, a couple of blocks of holding our collective breath, but there are no sudden BOOOOMS or flares of tracer fire. We finish the last few miles of our patrol without incident, and then we are back in the endless mud sea of the FOB.

My day ends where it began, sitting on our frigid front porch, smoking cigarettes and discussing doghouse construction plans with SGT French. One of our Iraqi interpreters is sitting on the table next to us, playing his guitar. He has come up with an impressive riff, which starts with an acoustic rendition of AC/DC's "Thunderstruck," then segues into a Spanish flamenco piece, followed by occasional forays into Led Zeppelin, the Indigo Girls, and Pink Floyd, all tied together with more classical guitar. Somehow it all works, cohesively, without pause or break, and the sound of it is pure magic in the cold Baghdad night, even with the sound of the fighter jets somewhere overhead, beyond the clouds.

This is Iraq in a nutshell. It varies from boredom, to hardship, to hilarity, to violence, back to boredom, into tension, and occasionally it trips across wonderment along the way. Gotta love it.

Tomorrow we are going out again, same as always. Ostensibly, we have to go back to one of the IP stations for more assessments, but really, we are going to look for The Dog. He's out there somewhere, probably on a recon mission. Probably has a higher body count than us, to boot. They don't like us here, and we have to look out for the few friends we have.

Note: That's The Dog, on the right.

PIECES IN THE SNOW

NAME: **CAPT BENJAMIN TUPPER**
STATIONED IN: **PAKTIKA, AFGHANISTAN**
HOMETOWN: **SYRACUSE, NEW YORK**

The streets, the fields, the market bazaar, everything as far as the eye could see was covered in a coat of pure white. Overnight a snowstorm had passed through our corner of Paktika, dropping just enough snow to cover all the mud and dirt and garbage that paints the landscape of the town.

I stood on the main road of the normally bustling bazaar, in an expanse of pure white, staring at a mysteriously vibrant pink and red object. Around me, there were no footprints disturbing the snow except my own. It appeared as if this strange object had been dropped from the sky. It lay there in simple repose—thin fibrous strands splayed like a peacock's tail feathers along its top. At the base, a stiff stalk of white segments adorned with bright red dollops.

After the initial distraction of marveling at its intricate makeup, I refocused on my original purpose in approaching it. I needed to identify what it was. Having now done so, I turned and walked back to my Humvee.

It was the neck stem of a human spine, blasted 150 meters in the air from the site of a suicide bombing minutes earlier. I had been in the middle of a slow, frustrating meeting with my commander and our ANA counterparts, arguing over attendance numbers, when a very subtle vibration passed through our room. It was gentle and unassuming. With no one even mentioning the distant thud, we continued our conversation until one of my ETT teammates ran into the room and yelled, "We're rolling—there's been an explosion in the bazaar!"

Now I stood amid a chaotic scene. ANA soldiers and ETTs trying to organize a wide cordon around the blast site, with rumors spreading of a VBIED still in play, and the confusion of sorting out who was dead, who was wounded, and who was lucky.

These initial moments were pretty tense. Scattered in the road intersection were seven unoccupied vehicles. Any one could be a secondary explosive device positioned to kill the first responders, a classic enemy tactic. As we went about trying to get a grasp on what had happened and what needed to be done, we all were within the lethal blast radius of even a small car bomb.

I found myself nervous but ironically fighting to contain a smile. I kept expecting a fiery white light to instantly wash me away. BANG! Torn car metal. Flame.

When none of this transpired, I was happy as a kid on Christmas morning. And every second that there was no explosion, my grin continued to grow. I was just happy to have a few more seconds with no Technicolor finish.

This reaction probably seemed out of place, given the random burned and twisted body parts lying around me as I walked through the scene. But no one noticed me. Each of us was in our own little world, trying to process the remaining risks and the results of this suicide blast.

The events up to this point were fairly easy to reconstruct. A lone suicide bomber had walked up to a group of ANA soldiers who had congregated at a street intersection outside of our base. He detonated his explosive vest, which instantly scattered his mortal remains in a truly random pattern. Ground zero was a large blackened circle where he stood, which instantly evaporated the snow and burned the ground below it.

His head flew straight up, landing about 20 meters away on the hood of a white Toyota station wagon. It rolled off onto the ground, leaving a red smudge and streak across the hood. His heart landed about 50 meters in the opposite direction. It sat there, in perfect condition, as if carefully removed from the chest by a surgeon's delicate incisions. An ANA soldier walked by and kicked it like a small soccer ball down the road. A gesture of disgust at this suicide attack.

And in my sector of the cordon, I stumbled across the aforementioned spine segment. Wandering another 20 meters, I found

the rest of the spine, adorned with the remaining ribs, cracked and splayed like old fingernails.

And in this dramatic yet mundane spot, I spent my day. The sun rose, and the sun set. A cold, silent street, randomly speckled with red pieces in the snow, devoid of people, activity, and life, except for the soldiers who remained to secure the scene for the bomb experts. The only other visitors to our grim vigil were gaunt dogs, who, smelling the fresh meat on the wind, came to steal a meal from the bones of the bomber.

The silence of this morbid scene was finally broken at sunset by gunshots and the horrible yelps of a dog caught sniffing around the bomber's head. Shot but not yet dead, the dog was howling as it cursed the irony of locating food, only to die from its lucky find.

Up until this moment, I had spent my day staring at parts of the human body normally hidden from view. I had poked at a large sheet of flesh, covered in goose bumps from lying flat in the cold snow. I had spent 20 minutes within the kill radius of a car that was reported to be loaded with explosives. None of this distressed me in the slightest.

But this dog's continued cries, echoing off the cold and silent marketplace, hit me like an emotional bomb. They were as painful and solemn as any noise I've ever heard. It's what bothered me the most about today.

TWO VERY DIFFERENT CONFLICTS

NAME: **1LT STEFAN C. RALPH (GruntMP)**
STATIONED IN: **SOUTHERN AFGHANISTAN**
HOME STATE: **WESTERN MASSACHUSETTS**

The responses to my post/memorial to my fallen comrade, Scott Lundell, and the responses to others' posts on this blog brought to my attention the fact that many people have a difficult time differentiating between Iraq and Afghanistan and the very different reasons for entering into these two very different conflicts. I implore you to arm yourself with knowledge. Below you will find a reading list that I put together before I came here (to Afghanistan) so I would better understand the land, conflict, history, and people I was about to spend a year of my life involved with. I hope this list will help all those who seek some insight into the complexities of these conflicts.

BOOKS PERTAINING TO AFGHANISTAN
Afghanistan: A Military History from Alexander the Great to the Fall of the Taliban, by Stephen Tanner

This was the first book I read specifically about Afghanistan, and it is probably one of the best history books I have ever read. It's well written and extremely informative. If you only read one book on this list, read this one. But I strongly suggest you read at least two.

Ghost Wars: The Secret History of the CIA, Afghanistan, and Bin Laden, from the Soviet Invasion to September 10, 2001, by Steve Coll

If you only read two books on this list, make this the second. It will give you insight into Afghanistan, our reasons for being here, and the history of our involvement here.

Charlie Wilson's War: The Extraordinary Story of the Largest Covert Operation in History, by George Crile

This reads like a fiction thriller, but it's all true. I can't tell you how much fun it was to read. You won't want to put it down. It's a good-sized book, but you'll fly through it. It's an excellent source of information on how the U.S. supported the Mujahideen during the Soviet incursion into Afghanistan.

Jawbreaker: The Attack on Bin Laden and Al Qaeda: A Personal Account by the CIA's Key Field Commander, by Gary Berntsen and Ralph Pezzullo

This book starts off a little like a chest-pounding, machismo spy thriller, but settles down very quickly and is very informative. For me, what was really amazing was finding out that one of the candidates whom I was a TAC officer for this past January–February, before mobilizing, was on the first Special Forces ODA team.

Not a Good Day to Die: The Untold Story of Operation Anaconda, by Sean Naylor

A very good book about the biggest U.S. engagement in the Afghan war, the strategic mistakes made by higher echelons of the military, and how disconnected they and their civilian counterparts and bosses are from the commanders and troops on the ground. It makes a good argument for the necessity of artillery on today's modern battlefield and describes the extensive problems with joint forces operations that result in military bureaucracy. This book really pissed me off at times, and some things still haven't changed. It has some amazing stories of heroism and tragedy.

This Man's Army: A Soldier's Story from the Front Lines of the War on Terrorism, by Andrew Exum

Not as riveting as some of the other books, but Andy Exum was an infantry platoon leader (2LT) when 9/11 happened, and his platoon was involved in the tail end of Operation Anaconda. What I found very interesting and inspiring is what he chose to do when he left the Army and his feelings toward our generation's commitment to this region in the future.

Taliban: Militant Islam, Oil, and Fundamentalism in Central Asia, by Ahmed Rashid

I started to read this right before leaving for here and have yet to finish it, but I will complete it in the next month or so. I think this is the most informative and honest account of the Taliban and how they came into existence. It has opened my eyes and has given me a clearer picture of my enemy and how we should be fighting them if we really want to win and rebuild Afghanistan.

The Places in Between, by Rory Stewart

Rory Stewart walked across Afghanistan in January 2002. This is his personal account. It's a wonderful story, an easy and enjoyable read. I recommend this as a supplement to these other books because of his cultural and historical knowledge of Afghanistan, which he had prior to his journey.

Jihad: The Rise of Militant Islam in Central Asia, by Ahmed Rashid

Rashid is an amazingly informative writer; his books are probably the most information-dense volumes I have ever read. Although this one is just over 200 pages long, it took me longer to read than any of the others on the list. Being from Pakistan, with regional contacts, he was able to get in and meet people to a degree I think would be impossible for a Western writer. It deals with the five countries north of Afghanistan: Kyrgyzstan, Tajikistan, Uzbekistan, Kazakhstan, and Turkmenistan. It gave me a greater understanding of the reasons for the rise of militant Islam in this region and how it has affected and could affect Afghanistan.

BOOKS ON THE EVENTS THAT LEAD TO 9/11
Against All Enemies: Inside America's War on Terror, by Richard A. Clarke

This is a very well-written explanation of the events/reactions within the White House over the four presidencies that led to 9/11.

Through Our Enemies' Eyes: Osama Bin Laden, Radical Islam, and the Future of America, by Michael Scheuer

You won't find a better or more informed writer when it comes to Osama Bin Laden. I appreciate his honesty and his comparisons, which bring home to the reader what Osama Bin Laden means to so many Muslims and the brutal and multipronged attack the West needs to make if we are going to win this war. It will open your eyes and make you realize on a truly visceral level that we are at war with Al Qaeda and more broadly with militant Islam, and that they fired the first shots long before 9/11. Read this before *Imperial Hubris.*

Imperial Hubris: Why the West Is Losing the War on Terror, by Michael Scheuer

Michael Scheuer was the lead guy on the CIA's Bin Laden unit, and this book is the follow-up to *Through Our Enemies' Eyes.* It changed the way that I view Bin Laden, Al Qaeda, and U.S. Middle Eastern policy. Read *Through Our Enemies' Eyes,* second edition, first, then this.

BOOKS PERTAINING TO IRAQ
No True Glory: A Frontline Account of the Battle for Fallujah, by Bing West

This book will bring you the bloodiest battle of the Iraq War in amazing, heart-wrenching detail. It also does a very good job of tying in the political–higher command missteps that could have headed this off in the spring of 2004. This book made me cry. Semper Fi.

The Last True Story I'll Ever Tell: An Accidental Soldier's Account of the War in Iraq, by John Crawford

My generation's *The Things They Carried.* This book will give you a better understanding of what infantrymen, who are mostly very young men, are like, and what their day-to-day lives in a combat zone are like. I really related to this book on a lot of levels. It also demonstrates how misused and abused the National Guard was in the beginning of the Iraq War, though it has gotten better since. It disgusted me how this kid's unit was treated.

A Book for Growth and Understanding

Fools Rush In: A True Story of Love, War, and Redemption, by Bill Carter

This book is not about Afghanistan. It's about Bill Carter's journey to Sarajevo in the middle of the Bosnian War. This is some of the most amazing writing I have ever read. This book will kick you in the stomach with its honesty and colorfully descriptive writing. I have never read someone who can describe love and loss as well. If it doesn't bring you to tears, or almost bring you to tears, you're not human.

If You're Interested

The Bear Went Over the Mountain: Soviet Combat Tactics in Afghanistan, edited by Lester W. Grau

The Other Side of the Mountain: Mujahideen Tactics in the Soviet-Afghan War, by Ali Ahmad Jalali and Lester W. Grau

These last two books are very dry and repetitive and were both written to give military staff officers a better understanding of the tactics of the Soviets and the Mujahideen. They use short story formats with diagrams. I am a huge military history buff, but I couldn't get through more than two chapters of *The Other Side of the Mountain.* So if you need something to aid you in falling asleep, then these are wonderful companions/tools. But I felt I should include them, just in case there's someone out there with a real craving for the information.

FIRST AID CLASSES

NAME: **SPC IAN WOLFE**
STATIONED IN: **IRAQ**
HOMETOWN: **MINNEAPOLIS, MINNESOTA**

When we were first told we were going to be conducting first aid classes for the local Iraqi civilians we didn't quite know what to expect. We were not sure what they knew, who would be there, or if they would listen. Our team, CAPT Monte Haddix from Cheyenne, Wyoming; SSG Tracy French from Virginia, Minnesota; and myself, started researching and discussing things we could teach that would benefit the people in this area, which is very rural. Although most of the local civilians could go to a hospital in An Nasiriyah, a lot of them don't, and they were getting infections and sicknesses that can be prevented by basic first aid techniques. We got our class together and went on our first mission.

Whether we were being naive or hopeful, we had originally expected women to attend. But for the first few classes, only men showed up. We wanted to try to create a women's class, so we could at least teach them the first aid information we were teaching the men. After all, the women, we found out, do most of the care. One day we were at the house of a sheik teaching a class, and another sheik arrived who was a councilman for the district, so we raised the topic of teaching the women of the village. This particular sheik talked in great length about his plans to open a women's center to teach computers, English, and other subjects to women. We couldn't tell whether he was sincere or not, but we jumped at the opportunity to finally interact with the female population and got to work developing a women's class.

Of course, only females could teach the class, so we enlisted the help of SFC Cassandra Houston, a medic from Charlie Company 134 BSB (Brigade Support Battalion), who is the NCOIC (non-commissioned officer in charge) for our tactical operations center.

She and SSG French decided to take some of what we were teaching the men, such as bleeding control, airway management, and other injury-related issues, and also focus more on care-related issues, such as burns, wound care, fever, hygiene, and illness. They also addressed some female-specific issues such as hygiene, infection, and preventive medicine. In each session they learn different things about what the women do for female-specific health issues, and what kinds of issues they have, and are constantly changing and adapting the classes.

In both men's and women's classes it has been difficult introducing certain topics that we were not sure how to approach. Prevention is very important and not something that is practiced in this culture much. Every year there are many burn victims, mostly children. Trying to teach simple things like keeping the kids away from fire and not using scalding water as a form of punishment is a very tricky task. We don't want to insult them or tell them they are wrong, but these are important things to help prevent major injuries to themselves and their children. One technique that seems to work well is telling them examples of what we see in America, such as home remedies, infections, and so on, and what we tell our American citizens. This makes it less of an accusation, or not as much like we are telling them that their culture is wrong, and gets through to them at the same time.

It has been very important to tell them we are not here to treat them or replace a doctor; we are teaching them tips and techniques they can use as prevention, what to do in an emergency before you get to a hospital, and when to seek higher medical care. The women's class has become a much-talked-about program and has been very well received by the community. Hopefully it will help decrease the amount of preventable injuries and illnesses and improve the stature of women in this society. Both SSG French and SFC Houston are involved in health care back home. They have brought a great deal of knowledge to the classes not only as health-care professionals, but as women and mothers, and being able to teach the women's health class has been a highlight of their deployment. They feel that even if they only reach the younger girls, or only a few of the mothers, then it is all worth it.

DOHA

Name: **CAPT MATT SMENOS**
Stationed in: **AFGHANISTAN**
Hometown: **SANTA MARIA, CALIFORNIA**

---

himmering monoliths of glass and steel towering over the white sands of Qatar reflect in the lenses of my sunglasses as I climb out of tour bus number three. I gaze up at the skyscrapers, so mysterious and conspicuous in the middle of the great desert nation, and I let out a little "Wow." I have seen cities; I was born in one. But this city is unique. The city of Doha is alive tonight. The pent-up energies of 100,000 people buzz in the humid evening air. Great throngs of citizens, dressed in ceremonial finery, are gathered to recognize the last day of Ramadan. EID MUBARAK is sprawled across banners and posters and street signs as far as the eye can see. As the local clock strikes 8 P.M., the city roars with joy. Amid the song and cheer, the night sparkles from all sides with flash photography, glittering confetti, and streaming color ribbons and silk. I am thrown and shoved and trampled by crowds blind to the infidel on this, the first night of Eid, the holiest time of the Muslim year. Though not a Muslim, I can appreciate the release from a month of hardship and am, in my own secular way, celebrating a night of freedom.

As the sun goes down, my companions and I set out from the tour bus to explore the eye-popping diamond capstone of one of the richest nations in the world. This is the first of our four days of pass, an Army R&R program allowed to six-month deployers. We come together from all corners of the Middle Eastern theater of operations, and yet we share a common disconnect from a place that bears so much painful resemblance to home. We recognize the cars, the lights, the decoration and festivity, yet we are the invisible people. We pass like ghosts or shadows through the dancing and parties. We feel like crashers or unwelcome guests. Our drab T-shirts and track pants identify us as military to a wary crowd, who nod cautiously, if they take note at all. Though we have become used to being the relatively rich ones, here the petty contents of our wallets pale in comparison to the wealth doled out by a nation of millionaires unleashed from a month of sacrifice and starvation.

I swear that Benjamin Franklin frowns and looks around nervously as I hand him over to buy a Christmas gift for my daughter Jade. The man receiving him shoves the bill into a cardboard box under his register, apparently where dirty, foreign monies are hidden away until they can be reckoned with and converted. He mouths a quiet "Thank you" in English and flashes me a subtle gold-studded smile. He knows I am using my Western cash to buy a heathen gift for my infidel child and daring to do so on this night of nights. He will keep my secret as long as I move along quietly and promise to keep spending.

The combination—punches of familiar and unfamiliar—continues. We drink Starbucks coffee, seated on huge pillows on the floor. I eat a grilled chicken salad at Applebee's, where a great smiling Mickey Mouse poster points at me and laughs. When the check comes to the black-robed ladies at the next table, they pay it with neat stacks of multicolored Qatari cash from a shared briefcase doubtlessly given them by a shared husband. The stacks of cash fill the case, and it strikes me as not unlike a scene from a gangster picture or a ransom caper with a character waiting to make "the exchange." Is individuality and identity worth a briefcase full of cash? Though their faces are completely veiled, I can sense they have noticed me staring at their allowance. I hastily make an exit.

I hide in a Maserati dealership and quietly stave off the nine attendants who descend upon me. No, I don't want any chai, or a massage, or a cigarette while you sell me a sports car. I head back out to the streets and try to blend. I feel like a giraffe amid the march of the penguins. I see a buddy of mine trying to buy mascara from a street vendor. The vendor keeps grabbing her arm and pulling her back to the mirrored shelves of colorful bottles and jars. He urges her to smell, feel, and sample. He dabs at her cheeks and hair with drops of oils and lotions. She ducks and weaves like a prizefighter before finally pulling away with a polite backpedal and an apologetic nod. She sees me leaning against a kiosk speckled with Dari and Arabic flyers in tatters and rushes to my side. She grabs my hand with an iron grip and smiles in a way that says, "Let's get out of here," and drags me onto the sidewalk.

We walk and share our experiences and the wonderment of being in an alien place for a strange celebration, and we discuss the way that buildings and pavement and glass only make a setting. It's the people that define a life. As we sit on a bench at the bus stop, a final display of cultural variety blows past. A fluttering wave of colorful, translucent robes settles around me like butterflies, along with the smiling faces of a dozen children, boys in ceremonial caps and girls with their first veils, who have discovered a white-skinned giant with yellow hair and mirror-eyes. They pet my skin and knead my shoulders. They poke hesitantly at my lenses and chatter at me with earnest questions I do not understand. They giggle and push each other at me, as if I might swallow one of them. I smile back and tell them my name, and with dark eyes and furrowed eyebrows they stare intently at my lips moving. The boys puff out their chests and jab with their thumbs to inform me of their names. The girls avoid eye contact and just tug at my fingers and sleeves. When I stand to catch my bus, they gasp in unison and giggle and blow away with the warm, evening breeze. "Eid Mubarak!" I call after them. I think I made their Christmas (so to speak).

The rest of our pass was quiet. We stayed on the R&R post, tanning and swimming in the pool. Doha is an amazing place, a random utopia of wealth and progress in a literal desert of starvation and desolation. It's a break in the monotony and a surprisingly rich experience. Some people skip their passes. Don't ever do that. I don't think I'll ever forget mine.

SOUNDS OF WAR

NAME: **CAPT ERIC COULSON** (Badger 6)
STATIONED IN: **RAMADI, IRAQ**
HOMETOWN: **ST. LOUIS, MISSOURI**
MILBLOG URL: **BADGERSFORWARD.BLOGSPOT.COM**

War here in Iraq has generated an entire set of sounds that are unique, whether in origin or presentation. They come from both the mundane and the deadly, and each has its own particular flavor.

The most common sound we all share is the drone of the generator. Every building has its electrical power provided by generators. In Fallujah, large banks of huge CAT diesel generators are so well insulated they are almost quiet. In Ramadi, we have more and smaller generators that are not so well insulated. Inside my barracks they emit a drone. Standing next to them, one is best advised to follow the warnings and wear hearing protection. The sound is a constant companion.

Gunfire is a very common sound. A lifelong firearms enthusiast, I would be dishonest if I said I no longer like it. It is, however, far more contextual for me now. Gunfire to the south is just as likely to be coming from the ranges as any place else. Gunfire to the north is almost certainly a battle being waged. Range fire has more of a predictable rhythm, while gunfire from battle has peaks of intensity, as well as rapid stops and starts. I find myself with a heightened level of awareness of gunfire and its likely ramifications.

Aircraft sounds are not restricted to the battlefield. You experience them in a whole new way here. Helicopters in the civilian world are usually either some sort of Life Flight or your local television or radio station traffic-and-news chopper. Here, helicopters might mean medevac or the arrival of VIPs, or they can be just general transportation. Since I've been here, I have flown on two models of helicopter I never thought I would have the chance to ride.

They fly low, very low. Two days ago I watched a Black Hawk make a tight turn and tilt so far I thought the blades might strike the building it was flying over. Every flight is serious and a combat operation. Helicopters are also inherently dangerous, at least more so than fixed-wing aircraft. I marvel at the skill of the pilots.

Fixed-wing aircraft, at least at low levels, are far less common. In fact, only twice have I experienced low-level flights by fixed-wing air-craft—F-18 Super Hornets on attack runs. If you have ever been to an air show where the Blue Angels have performed, you know what that sounds like. Those two times were moments that I thought my life was about to come to a quick conclusion, as I mistook them for incoming rockets.

Loud explosions are not uncommon. Fortunately, instances of incoming mortar and rocket fire have been few and far between. We have experienced it, but it is not something we are experienced at. Outgoing artillery fire is another matter. Before my current incarna-tion as an engineer, I was a field artillery officer, and I thought I was accustomed to the sound of outgoing artillery. But I think that was because I was giving the order to fire. It is always a surprise and a little disconcerting. Because among other things it can be confused with . . .

High order explosive detonations. We have had two of these in the last two days. AIF hit an IP checkpoint about 2,500 meters from our TOC. It shook the place good, and we could only watch the smoke rise from the scene. Two days ago the fatality was the bomber. Today I don't know what the results were.

I know being here has affected me and has changed me. I am sure these sounds, and maybe others, will always remind me of the war in Iraq.

NOT SURE HOW TO RESPOND

Name: **CAPT BRIAN CASTNER**
Returned from: **IRAQ**
Hometown: **BUFFALO, NEW YORK**

should have had enough practice by now, but I'm still not sure how to respond. I just got off the plane a week ago, finally home again. It was my third trip to the Middle East since 9/11 and my second to Iraq. I know by now how to reunite with my wife and kids. I know not to argue with my wife about chores or bills and to take my place as the outsider in the home for a while. I know how to play with my kids so they become used to me again, and I don't push myself on them too quickly. I know how to have a couple beers without having too many, and I know how to quit smoking again, a habit I always seem to pick up while deployed. Having gotten good at all those things, the thing I still don't know how to do is to respond when a stranger says, "Welcome home. Thank you for serving your country."

I did not have a good tour in Iraq. I did not come home confident in the rightness of our cause. That may be because I have no personal stories of building schools, handing out candy to children, or watching a fledgling democracy take shape. As the commander of a small explosive ordnance disposal unit (the military bomb squad) trying to cover an entire province in northern Iraq, my men and I only saw the worst humanity had to offer. We disarm fewer and fewer roadside bombs. We save fewer and fewer lives. Instead, we do more and more "postblast analysis," where we conduct a crime scene investigation after an attack and try to reconstruct what the bomb was made of and how it was used. That took us daily to car bombings of Iraqi clinics or police stations and attacks on American convoys. We saw far too many Iraqi victims of the indiscriminate violence destroying what's left of the country's infrastructure. And we saw that every day, with seemingly no ability to stop it.

When that suffering is the only thing you see outside the safety of your base while doing your job, you start to develop a different mission. The mission stops being about disarming the bomb and starts being about bringing your troops home safe. We had a saying: "It takes five things to go home in one piece: luck, training, luck, equipment, and luck." My teams would subconsciously develop a catch-22 mentality, counting their missions and playing the numbers game. I would have my team sergeants come up to me and say, "Sir, I've been on 125 missions already, and I haven't gotten hurt yet. But this can't keep up. Do too many missions, and the numbers say you're going to get killed." My team leaders would know; they were disarming the bombs and doing the postblasts on the blown-up HMMWVs. I made the safety of my teams my number one priority and counted the days for them until we could all go home.

So when I get off the plane in Baltimore and am suddenly surrounded by America again, in all of its glittering, excessive glory, what do you say when a complete stranger walks up to you and says thank you? I usually mumbled an inadequate "Thank you for the support," or "I appreciate it," wishing that I had come up with a more sincere or meaningful response. I always think that I should be happy. During Vietnam, soldiers were blamed for the policy decisions of elected officials. Our country learned from that mistake, and I believe most Americans, no matter their feelings on the war, now make it a point to support the average soldier. But instead of warming my heart, when someone says "Welcome home" and "Thank you," I feel embarrassed and guilty. Embarrassed because my service was no greater than others, and only I know our mission was more about survival than success. And guilty because I am coming home to my wife and children, and so many other soldiers are either still there or not coming home at all.

HOPE AND DESPAIR

Name: **CAPT DOUG TRAVERSA**
Stationed in: **KABUL, AFGHANISTAN**
Hometown: **TULLAHOMA, TENNESSEE**
Milblog URL: **TRAVERSA.TYPEPAD.COM**

I work at the Central Movement Agency (CMA), the only transportation unit of the Afghan National Army (ANA). More simply, we are a trucking unit. In addition to running convoys all over the country, we have taken on the additional mission of picking up cargo flow into KAIA, the Kabul International Airport.

Until recently, this cargo was handled by civilians, and having us take it over is a big deal, as CMA grows and takes on more missions. With this growth comes more responsibility and a sense of pride in the troops, both ANA and American. When we got here, everyone

was excited that CMA had moved four artillery pieces to the south. Now they run convoys all the time, and they make me proud.

But life here is a continual series of ups and downs. We are still fighting against an "every man for himself" mind-set, as well as trying to figure out the best ways to motivate the Afghans. Sometimes we'll have a problem that makes us feel like we are hitting ourselves in the head, slowly and repeatedly, with a very heavy hobnailed baseball bat. For instance, a couple of months ago we opened a new recreation room for the soldiers at CMA, which included a Ping-Pong table, dart board, two chess sets, a TV with new rabbit-ear antennas, and some games. This was bought and paid for by our small group of American NCOs, and they also did all the labor.

One day we heard that everything had been trashed in there, so we went to check it out. Sure enough, virtually everything was destroyed. The Ping-Pong table was in pieces, the darts were all broken, one chess set was missing, and the other's granite board was broken. The antenna on the TV was broken. There were soccer ball marks all over the walls.

After this, it was hard to think positive thoughts. We had a chat with the commander and sergeant major about how badly this reflects on the unit. The commander is constantly telling us that the soldiers come from villages, and it will take a long time for them to develop discipline. That may be, but we are at war, and they need to whip these guys into shape a little quicker. To his credit, the commander had the place cleaned up immediately, posted a guard in there, and said he would replace all the broken items himself.

But when something bad happens, it isn't long until something good happens, giving us hope again. While we were loading cargo at the airport one day, a fellow captain came out to watch. He was incredibly impressed by how quickly and eagerly our CMA troops were getting the cargo strapped down and their truck ready to roll. And also envious that we get to work with the Afghans daily. Even though he is assigned to work with the National Police, he rarely ever sees an Afghan. I have to agree that despite the risk of traveling each day, I have a much better job and would not trade with him.

You may have read or seen on the news that Camp Phoenix in Kabul (my home) was attacked recently—a suicide bomber rammed his car into our front gate. But before he could detonate the explosives packed into the vehicle, an Afghan guard and an interpreter pulled him out and subdued him. The guard was a man known affectionately around here as Rambo. He wears an Army uniform, carries a red baton (which he will not hesitate to use), and even has a "Rambo" name tag. Someone had a special rank insignia made up for him that looks like his red baton. He salutes us all when he comes in or goes out, and I always salute him back, even though he isn't technically in the Army.

Now he is probably the most beloved man in this camp. I don't know the interpreter involved, but these two show the outstanding side of some of the people here. Once again Afghans, not NATO or the U.S., risked their lives and thwarted a bombing. When something like this happens, it makes you proud to be here helping to rebuild this country.

But with the good comes the bad. It all started at the airport, when all of our trucks were waiting to enter the flight line and head out to unload a plane. The fourth truck was parked on a slight incline, and instead of going forward, it rolled back and hit the fifth truck. The bumpers touched, and I don't think there was even a scratch, but the driver of truck five (we'll call him "Five") jumped out and started yelling at the driver of truck four (and, of course, we'll call him "Four"). Four got out to look at the damage, and Five got in his face and started yelling.

We all saw that a fight was brewing, and as we started to get out of our vehicles, Five punched Four right in the nose. I ran up to them and started yelling. Meanwhile, a second guy in truck four slid over into the driver's seat and started heading out, leaving his buddy behind. I yelled at Five and pointed at his truck. He promptly threw his half-eaten orange at Four, then we all ran to our vehicle with Four and jumped in. I jumped in too fast and smacked my head against the door jam, giving myself a massive headache for the rest of the day. Four had a nice bloody nose, but we got him cleaned up while heading out to the plane.

Once we get there (yes, I know I've switched from past to present tense; it seems more appropriate), Four climbs out of the vehicle with blood in his eye. I'm following him, yelling "Nay!" because I know he's out for revenge. He motions that he needs to get his helmet and heads back to his truck and does indeed retrieve it. However, he still looks deranged. I'm yelling to Hamid to get the ANA major in charge over here, and Four takes off and finds Five as he is getting out of his truck. Four takes his (very heavy) helmet and whacks Five right on top of the head with it. Five clutches his head and sinks to the ground, and Four jumps on him, swinging the helmet. At this point, six of us are trying to pull them apart. Four swings his helmet back for another blow and hits SMSgt Reynolds in the head, so now we both have headaches. At this point, I've got the ANA major, Hamid (my interpreter), and Four together, and I lambaste Four for his actions. I tell him he is embarrassing Afghanistan, the Army, and CMA. This seems to have some effect, and he promises to stop fighting, at least until he gets back to base. Good grief.

But I refuse to end on a down note. Sometimes the simplest things can bring incredible joy. The same day we were breaking up fights, I gave Hamid my thick winter gloves. I had given him some lighter ones earlier, but he still looked like he was freezing, so I figured he needed them more than I did. He was incredibly happy. "Oh, these are so thick and warm. I have never seen gloves like these. There are not gloves like these in all of Afghanistan."

After lunch we were walking out and he said, "I am so happy today."

"Why is that?"

"I have these wonderful gloves. They are so nice. Thank you so much."

"You are most welcome, my friend."

THINGS I'VE DONE

NAME: **C. MALONEY**
HUSBAND: **DEPLOYED ON FLOAT . . . SOMEWHERE**
HOMETOWN: **SEATTLE, WASHINGTON**
MILBLOG URL: **CORPSDJOUR.BLOGSPOT.COM**

T hings I've done that I might not have if my husband were here:

1) Set up the TV, VCR, amp, and cable
2) Programmed a universal remote
3) Put my clothes in both sides of the dresser instead of squishing them into just half
4) Assembled a table
5) Slept alone for 39 days and counting
6) Watched *Gilmore Girls* every Tuesday without argument (for once!)
7) Ate cereal for breakfast and dinner
8) Used the power drill . . . twice

Being alone provides some unique opportunities and helps you discover new interests. I liked the buzz of the power drill, the burn in my arm from the weight up over my head. I like having ultimate, uninterrupted, guilt-free control of the remote. I like having time to plant a garden, to use the shovel. I decidedly don't like spending nights sitting alone on the couch, but that has pushed me into new activities and more involvement, and there is nothing wrong with more distractions.

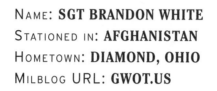

A GLIMPSE

Name: **SGT BRANDON WHITE**
Stationed in: **AFGHANISTAN**
Hometown: **DIAMOND, OHIO**
Milblog URL: **GWOT.US**

Who are these ragtag misfits? They're different things to different people. They are the eyes and ears of any given village in the land and are no doubt exploited by my enemy for intel-gathering purposes. To us troops though, these kids provide a glimpse of hope among ruin and a brief respite from the turmoil of battle. On their little faces shine bright smiles that can only come with youth. No different from American children, they are utterly curious and fascinated by everything, words escaping their lips a mile a minute, regardless of the fact that we cannot understand them.

When I pulled my camera out to take some photos of the surrounding mountains, these guys immediately formed into a group for a portrait. It was the same in Iraq as well. Let it be said: Folks in the Middle East love having their pictures taken.

Afterward, I went and sat back down behind the wheel of my Humvee. Within minutes, all four door windows had faces pressed to the glass, peering in, no doubt fascinated by all the gear and gizmos. One of them spotted the bag of Tootsie Rolls stashed next to a seat. Knocking on glass commenced, as well as finger-pointing to the bag along with "Mista! Mista!" In the interest of silence, I grabbed the bag, gave it to the gunner, and he dispensed the contents. I was then left in peace to scan the horizon for enemy activity.

NAME: **ROB**
STATIONED IN: **IRAQ**
MILBLOG URL: **SNIPEREYE.BLOGSPOT.COM**

It was my downtime, so I was in the palace using the computer when the sergeant major came storming out of the TOC and approached me. "Brian's shot. They got hit on exfil," he said in a nervous and worried tone. "They're on their way back right now with the QRF."

"Fuck" was all I could think as I quickly grabbed my vest and sidearm. I found my boss and told him what had happened, then we both ran out of the palace and to the aid station to wait. Moments later, four Humvees came roaring up the driveway. Brian was on the back of the cargo Humvee lying on his back, pants soaked in blood, a field dressing and a tourniquet wrapped around his leg.

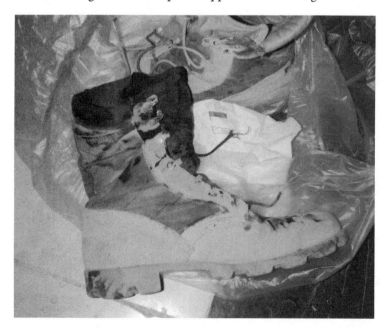

"All right! Let him out slow!" a soldier said, as they lowered my friend out of the Humvee.

My sniper section had gone six months without a single wound. Brian's leg was in bad shape. Nerve damage was obvious.

"What the fuck happened?" I asked Josh, the team leader for this mission, as we walked into the aid station and stood beside Brian's stretcher.

"We were exfiling, then all of a sudden out of nowhere the wall we were walking next to started getting bullet holes in it. It's Ramadan, you know; we had been hearing gunshots all day and night, so we couldn't pin down the location. But Brian caught one in the hand and another straight through the leg. And, before we knew it, fuckin' haji was gone. We never even seen him, Rob."

Ghosts. Ghosts. Ghosts. That's all the insurgents are, goddamn ghosts. The sniper unit that was here before we were told us there was a marksman in the area. He was good. He almost took the head off of one of their men last summer. This had now become a countersniper mission. And we were more than ready.

A few days later, my team and two other teams were loading onto the back of the stripped Humvees. We locked and loaded our weapons, then sped off with the hot sun beating down and the rush of wind upon us. Now was the time. The plan had been laid out and gone over: We were going to bait and kill the insurgent who was responsible for shedding my teammate's blood.

"Matrix 1, Matrix 1, this is Matrix 7. Are you in position, over?" my boss said through the radio. I watched from behind the dirty window as Walter and Billy set up their rifles.

"Roger, over."

"All right, we're getting dropped now and are proceeding to the designated intersection, over."

"Roger, over."

I watched through my binos as Matrix 7's team proceeded to the intersection where they would slowly walk as if they were exfiling. Hopefully the insurgent would see them, present himself, and be eliminated from the face of the earth.

"I see Mike," Billy said, as he looked through the scope of his M24.

"Roger. These kids need to get out of the way," I replied, as Walter and I scanned the area. Some young boys were happily playing a few meters behind Mike's team. The Ramadan fireworks and celebrating were still at their peak. This didn't help the situation.

Mike's team had been walking the area for several minutes now but still no sign of who we were looking for. All of a sudden they stopped.

They stood there on the corner and just waited. If their menacing body language could be translated into words, it would have sounded something like, "Come on, pussy, show yourself. We're here, waiting."

Then "BAM, BAM, BAM!" from down the street.

"Matrix 7! That is only the kids. They just set off their fireworks, over!" I yelled into the radio as I watched the group of boys celebrate their holiday on the wrong street at the wrong time.

Hours passed. And we waited and waited. But nothing. Not a single shot fired. Not a single insurgent out to play. The disappoint-

ment fell on our shoulders like a thousand-pound rucksack as we walked back into the palace with nothing to tell Brian. Sometimes "We tried" just isn't good enough. But the people back home will never understand that. The words "selfless service," "honor," "duty," "courage," and "country" are known to them only as words, with no substance behind them. Only words.

I remember something my sergeant major told us before we deployed. He said, "Men, they'll never understand what it takes to protect and defend this country. Never. You see them every day driving down the I-5 with their Starbucks coffee, going to their desk jobs. And they don't give a shit. They don't know what we go through. But, goddamn, we do it anyways."

People sleep peaceably in their beds at night only because rough men stand ready to do violence on their behalf.
—GEORGE ORWELL

DECENCY AND HONOR

NAME: **CAPT BENJAMIN TUPPER**
STATIONED IN: **GHAZNI, AFGHANISTAN**
HOMETOWN: **SYRACUSE, NEW YORK**

U nfortunately, I was sick with whatever it is that has caused me to lose 25 pounds in less than two months and was unable to go out on our planned mission to our most contested district. But my teammate, Ski, still had to go, so I wished him well.

When he returned that evening, I went over to get debriefed on how things went. As I got close to him, I immediately noticed his uniform was covered in blood, dirt, and gore. His normal upbeat and sunny vulgar disposition was absent, and I knew some heavy stuff had gone down. I made him a quick dinner while he told me about the mission. He was in no mood to cook and could barely manage to light his cigarette. The "thousand-yard stare" was in full effect—he was clearly still out on the battlefield, reliving the various "what ifs" that had played themselves out earlier in the day.

The story started predictably: Taliban ambush, returned fire, RPGs, near misses, etc. As the engagement developed, Ski and the ETT soldiers riding in his Humvee were firing on, and receiving AK and RPG fire from, Taliban soldiers in a small village. The ETTs and ANA soldiers maneuvered into the village and immediately came across a handful of wounded and dead Taliban. Some were dead where they fell, others had crawled into shallow ditches and lay there dying. The fire from the ETT and ANA forces had been so fierce that the Taliban had abandoned their wounded, which is uncommon. We normally find blood trails and no wounded after we engage them.

Now Ski is an infantryman to the core. He chomps at the bit before each mission, hoping we will encounter the enemy. He is not one to wax humanistic. His normal response to most questions about the Taliban is to express a desire to destroy them in combat.

But Ski, upon seeing the wounded Taliban, immediately grabbed his combat lifesaver medical bag and moved to begin treating them. Doing this was at risk to his own life. The enemy was still in the area, and the wounded lay in ditches in an open road. Without hesitation, he used his limited medical supplies on the enemy, in an attempt to give them comfort and aid.

While he ate the food I'd prepared for him, he described how one of the injured Taliban was going into shock. His femoral artery had been hit, and he was bleeding out.

"This guy was looking at me with fear in his eyes, expecting me to finish him off. When he realized I was trying to stop his bleeding, he relaxed and put his hand over his heart." In Afghanistan, it's customary among men to put

their hands over their hearts as a sign of deep respect and thanks.

Here is a Taliban man dying, felled by our bullets, showing a final act of thanks for decent treatment. And there is Ski, the warrior, holding this man in his arms trying to make his final moments as comfortable and painless as possible.

That image of compassion from an unlikely source, in an unlikely place, is stuck in my head. As I sat there and listened to Ski, coated with the enemy's blood, I knew this day would stay with him for the rest of his life. It's a small but tangible example of decency and honor in an environment full of hate and pain.

GOT THEM IP BLUES

NAME: **SGT ROY BATTY**
STATIONED IN: **BAGHDAD, IRAQ**
HOMETOWN: **YELLOW SPRINGS, OHIO**

An old man with a thin white beard is asleep in the back of the pickup truck. He's wearing a terry-cloth sweat suit, brown, dirty, grease-smeared, emblazoned with the name of a Spanish soccer team. He looks pretty comfortable, curled up in a semi-fetal position, his shirt hiked up a bit over his little potbelly. Just taking a snooze in the warm, golden January sunlight, hunkered down beneath the sides of the truck bed to avoid the slight chill beneath the afternoon's breeze. The only problem, of course, is that he is not asleep.

He has a small dent to the right of his forehead, and on the back of his head, just visible, is a very large hole, its edges splayed yellow with a hint of skull matter. Blood, dark red and thickly viscous, has flowed into a long pool that stretches down the entire length of the truck bed. Like all real blood, it looks very different from the red stuff you see by the gallon in the movies and is thus somehow less . . . real? Is that the word? Back in the World, teenagers watch maniacs on silver screens slaughter people for fun. But in this back alley it is irrevocably real and not fun at all.

I'm standing there with Denny, one of our IPLOs. We are remarking on the dead man to each other, using technical terms to dilute the more unsettling aspects of having to look at an executed grandparent lying on a metal floor.

"Can't have happened too long ago—the blood hasn't started to coagulate yet. . . ."

"Yeah, but lividity is already setting in. Look at the purple bruises around his eyes."

"Oh, right. What do you think? Nine mil? Entry wound is pretty small, and the exit wound is not too big."

"Yeah. If it was an AK, the whole back of his head would be gone...."

"Yep, definitely a pistol."

The Iraqi cops hang back, behind us, next to the cement wall around their police station. They don't say much, an occasional word to one another muttered in Arabic. They look like a group of reform school boys waiting to see the principal. There may be a good reason they are so quiet. Perhaps it's because we are fairly damn certain they are the ones that murdered the old man.

Here's the deal. We were at one of our other IP stations, just a few blocks away, and got a call on the radio from "maneuver" that there had been a carjacking in our area. This would be the fourth one in a week, all right here in the *mahallahs* just north of Sadr City. All on Dynacorp trucks—usually car carriers hauling up-armored SUVs to and from the various FOBs around Baghdad.

We had finished up our routine business at that police station and, as planned, came over to this one. As we pulled up, we noticed Grandpa dead in the police truck. The IPs seemed a little surprised to see us. They never know when we are going to show up, which is a good thing.

"What happened?" we ask.

"Oh, well, this is the driver of the car carrier that got jacked," they reply.

"Wow, that was quick."

IPs usually hate picking up dead guys. We've had arguments with them, usually in side alleyways at 2 A.M., about who is going to have to manhandle the newly discovered corpse and take it away. These guys must be really on the ball this time, to jet out to the crime scene and scoop up Mr. Hole-in-the-Head so quickly.

I feel sorry for him in a general sort of way, although that emotion has been hard to come by lately. He is the fifth or sixth dead guy I have come across in the last month or so. Still, he is someone's father, I'm sure; someone's grandfather, probably. Somewhere, a family will soon be wailing with grief. I don't know what possible threat this man could have posed to anyone, or why some scumbag felt inclined to blow his brains out the back of his head on this warm afternoon. I add the muted sorrow I feel for the man, and the undercurrent of resentment at whoever did it, to the dark whispering in the back of my skull.

It looks like he has been shot with a pistol at close range, although there is none of the gunpowder tattooing that would come from a point-blank shot. Still, it's unusual that it would be a 9 mil. AK-47s are ubiquitous here, but pistols are in short supply. Except for the Iraqi Police, who carry and covet the black Glocks that we issue to them.

Grandpa is the second corpse we've come across from a carjacking that occurred in close proximity to Iraqi Police. A couple of weeks ago it was a businessman, lying in the street right outside the Ministry of the Interior. We had just turned the corner and, oops, there's a corpse in the road in front of us. It's disconcerting how quickly you get used to seeing that sight.

This particular street has a whole series of checkpoints on it, designed to keep street traffic away from the government compound. Nevertheless, there he was, his head ventilated and leaking what appeared to be sticky raspberry jam. We stopped and asked the IPs on the checkpoint what had happened. Oh, it was a carjacking. Someone stole his car. Right here? Oh yes, yes. Did you guys

see it? Oh, sure, mistah, it was right in front of us. Did you shoot at the guys who did it? Oh, no, no. So you're telling me that a bunch of bad guys carjacked this dude five feet in front of your checkpoint, in broad daylight, stole his car, and somehow made it 500 meters down the street, past two other checkpoints, and nobody fired a single round at them? In a country where the police will empty a magazine of AK rounds at cars just to stop traffic?

Riiiiight.

Now Denny and I are leaning on the truck bed of the police pickup, looking at Grandpa, then at the IPs behind us. They don't make eye contact with us, suddenly enthralled with their pastel blue police shirts, or with something on the bottom of their shoes. Denny pulls out his digital camera and slowly starts taking pictures of the dead man, for his report to our higher headquarters. When he is finished, the IPs reluctantly move toward us. "We go now." "Ma-sahlam-ah." "Good-bye, mistah." And off they go, driving quickly away. Grandpa lolls around as they bump their way across the potholes, somehow still asleep despite the rough ride.

Denny goes inside the police station, along with my squad leader and the other IPLOs. They have questions for the police chief. I go back to the little cordon of HMMWVs and our huge ASV, sitting at the entrance. We have been increasing our security while out and about these days, after what happened in Karbala the other day.

You probably read about it or saw it on CNN. A group of American soldiers, including at least one MP, were at a provincial meeting in Karbala. Supposedly a number of new SUVs pulled up with what appeared to be American soldiers inside, wearing something like ACU uniforms, flashing American ID cards. They were summarily waved into the compound by the IPs who were guarding the place. These apparent soldiers then threw a number of concussion grenades into the conference room and burst in, shooting everyone present. Then they kidnapped two of the American soldiers, who were found murdered shortly afterward, just down the road, left in the SUVs.

Bottom line: five dead American soldiers, as well as some local ministers and businessmen. That's the story, anyway. Since every American who was there was killed, what really happened is known

only to the IPs that were present, and somehow they all miraculously escaped harm. Personally, I think the IPs just turned on them.

In any case, we are changing things up a lot, in an attempt to make sure that the same thing doesn't happen to us. Just the thing for a paranoid ex-Marine.

I'm searching everyone who comes into the joint. There is a steady stream of civilians coming into the compound for various legal reasons, and, more worrisome, a whole bunch of IPs in civilian clothes. Now, as any Iraqi vet will tell you, there is not really a standard uniform for the Iraqi Police, other than a vaguely blue shirt. That's it. No badge. No nothing. Sometimes just a blue collar peeking out above a jacket. Apparently even that is too stringent a dress code for some of these guys, and we have seen our fair share of dudes in jeans and a kaffiyeh coming around the corner, brandishing an AK. Hey, whaz up, mistah. Just goin' to work.

Amazingly, these guys take umbrage when I stop them and demand some ID and pat them down. You would have thought that with the security situation the way it is in Iraq, at least the police would understand when we set up some basic procedures. But no. Every other guy protests when I go to stop him: "IP, IP, mistah. No, no." Some of the ID cards are ancient versions that are no longer issued. Many are expired. Occasionally they have no police identification at all. The cops tell me they left them at home, or forgot them, or something equally asinine. They are all armed, usually with concealed Glock 9 millimeters.

I've also started searching the civilian cars that come into the compound, and this evokes the same indignant response. Such was the case with Starsky and Hutch.

I come trudging back to our little checkpoint at the entrance, just as a small silver compact car weaves its way through the Haskell barriers. Inside are two Iraqi guys, wearing civilian clothes. The driver is older, with a big Saddam mustache. His passenger is a kid—looks like a teenager. Starsky, the older one, is wearing the tan suit jacket that seems to be the new fashion rage among IPs since Saddam's execution. Hutch is wearing a jogging suit, which is very common for younger Iraqi men.

My driver, already on guard, mentions that they had just come in a few minutes ago, and he had checked the car and found nothing. They had stayed for a few minutes, then left, and now were coming back inside for some reason.

"*Indak heiweyah?*" I ask Starsky. Do you have ID?

Starsky mumbles something in indignant Arabic and finally produces an ancient yellow IP badge, the kind issued a couple of years ago, long since obsolete. Still, not that unusual, for this station anyway.

I am about to let them go when I spot a bit of wire sticking out from a black jacket on the backseat of the little Daewoo Crown sedan. I open the back door, move the jacket, and find two folding-stock AK-47s underneath. All of the Kalashnikovs that belong to the IP station have wooden stocks on them and painted ID numbers on those stocks. These AKs are not standard issue. Not to mention that you are not supposed to have them in a civilian car, while wearing civilian clothes.

I ask Hutch, the young guy, if he has ID. Hutch decides to get mouthy with the big, shaved-head infidel who is blocking his way. It becomes apparent that he doesn't have any ID. I've never seen him before. In fact, I've never seen either of these jokers before, and with the discovery of the AKs, I'm not feeling very charitable.

Get out of the car, asshole.

Starsky gets out easily enough, with a bit of an anxious grin beneath his mustache, but Hutch continues to talk shit, moving slowly. I tell him I am going to search him—"*Taftish!*"—and motion for him to turn around and raise his arms.

Hutch spins around on me as soon as I touch his side. He clearly doesn't want to be searched, and he's not going to cooperate.

Fine with me. I slam his body back around, up against the side of the sedan, and I'm not terribly gentle about it. Grandpa's face is still a sharp image in my head, his grizzled white beard speckled with blood. You guys might be badasses with unarmed senior citizens, but I promise you, it will not be so easy with me. My driver moves behind me, his M4 coming up to cover Starsky in case he gets stupid, too.

Hutch is still not done. I go to pat down his arm, and he brings it back at me, trying to pop me with his elbow. Now, I'm six foot three, I weigh 235 pounds, and I'm wearing an additional 60 pounds worth of assault rifle, grenades, ammo, and body armor. He weighs maybe a buck fifty soaking wet. When I bounce his head off the hood of the car, it sounds like a rifle shot. I slam his arms out to the sides of his head on the hood and kick his legs out wide to the side with the same degree of tact and diplomacy.

Hutch gets the point.

As soon as I frisk his torso, I find out why he doesn't want to get searched. Hidden up underneath his running jacket there is an assault vest filled with loaded AK-47 magazines. He's got four of the damn things under there, 30 rounds apiece in each mag. Call me paranoid, but I'm really curious as to why these guys are trying to sneak in here with over 120 rounds of AK ammo and two hidden assault rifles.

The earpiece to my tactical radio buzzes urgently. It's my squad leader. Apparently he is watching this little piece of drama from somewhere around the station house, probably up on the roof.

"Whoa, whoa, SGT Batty, just search him, don't beat 'im up! Gotta watch that temper, jarhead!"

I turn to my right, facing the IP station, and reach up with one hand to key the mic. The other hand is securely around Hutch's neck. He ain't going nowhere.

"Hey, Sarn't, this guy is trying to come in here in civilian clothes, in a civilian car, with two hidden AKs and an assault vest full of mags under his clothes. And no fuckin' ID card. And then he wants to get stupid about it."

The radio is silent for a minute. Apparently the news has set my squad leader back a bit. Meanwhile, a small crowd of uniformed IPs are swarming out of the front gate of the station and coming toward us.

"Well, what are the numbers on the stock of the AKs? Maybe they are detectives," says SSG H in my ear.

"That's what I'm trying to tell you, Sarn't. They're folding-stock AKs, hidden in the back. Not issued IP weapons."

The crowd of IPs have reached us. The largest one, one of the "officers," is pointing at Starsky and Hutch. "IP! IP!" Some of the guys from our trucks have dismounted and are keeping them back.

"Ummm, OK. I'm coming down. I'll bring a translator; see if we can figure out what is going on." My squad leader clicks off.

Some of the IPLOs join the crowd, and eventually my squad leader and platoon sergeant also join us, along with their translators, and the whole crowd of Iraqi cops starts doing the usual Arab argument act, with stiff-armed gestures and lots of loud gibberish. It's a regular little fiasco.

Eventually, it all boils down to this: Starsky and Hutch are the bodyguards of one of the IP majors, although that major is not here today. They drive him around in a civilian car to blend in. The officers from the IP station vouch for them, so they are allowed in.

As usual, several key questions never get answered. Where did the AKs come from? Why are the guys here in the first place? Why does Hutch not have any form of police ID? And why are they trying to come in here, armed to the teeth, if the major is not even here?

This illustrates a significant problem we have with the police in Iraq. What happens if they do something improper or illegal? Since Iraq is now a sovereign country, we don't have any real authority over them. If Starsky and Hutch did do something illegal, all we could do is detain them and hand them over to their own guys. Who will promptly let them go.

Which is what happens this time. Starsky and Hutch drive off in their silver Daewoo, Hutch glaring resentfully at me in the rearview mirror as they go. I hope, at the very least, that the message has gotten out not to mess around with the Americans, or at least not with the big tattooed one. The LT and my squad leader congratulate me on the catch and tell me that I am definitely the guy for the front door job. You better believe I will continue to be aggressive on the checkpoint.

The next day we are back at the same station, and the saga of the carjacking continues. Word comes from Dynacorp that the vehicles stolen from Grandpa's car carrier were up-armored SUVs, coincidentally the same kind of vehicle that was supposedly used in the hit in Karbala. Seems like the carjackers in this area have been specifically targeting them.

These particular SUVs were being transported back to Kuwait, since they were inoperable for various reasons. As soon as we get to the IP station, lo and behold, we are told that the IPs have located the missing SUVs. They are in the junkyard of a local tow truck company. The same tow truck company that contracts for their station. There is, conveniently, no word on how the SUVs got in the junkyard, or where they were found. Nada.

We mount a quick little raid on the junkyard, in case it is a trap. It's not, and we quickly locate the SUVs, since they are the only torched vehicles in the place. Yep, they're completely gutted, a total loss.

Sounds like someone figured out that they didn't work and decided to torch them to destroy any evidence. And then gave them back to us, so as to reap some kudos for their investigative efforts.

After we leave the IP station, having documented the VIN numbers on the trucks, we get a weird call from our TOC. Somehow they have information that a driver from one of the earlier carjackings is being secretly held in the detention cell of our IP station. Soooo, we go back to our station and try to find the guy. Who isn't there.

So what does it all mean? What's the point of this long story? Well, the administration and the Iraqi government are putting a lot of emphasis on the Iraqi security forces being able to take over and run the country. Prime Minister al-Maliki said last week that, properly equipped, his police forces could assume complete control of the country in the next three months.

Problem is, the type of issues that we are dealing with day to day, as just described, are not uncommon—quite the opposite. They are de rigueur for operating with the Iraqi Police forces. Keep in mind, this is after four years of training and equipping these guys. At best, the Iraqi Police are corrupt and incompetent. At worst, they are one big criminal gang and outright insurgents to boot.

I keep reading news reports that talk about how the Mehdi Army has "infiltrated" the Ministry of the Interior and all of the police agencies. "Infiltrate" is such an evocative word, bringing to mind images of dark-clad guerrillas scaling chain-link fences in the middle of the night. That simply isn't the case. These guys have not surreptitiously snuck into the MOI. They are not hiding or operating clandestinely, whispering quietly to each other in secret meetings after work. They've been outright hired by their buddies, particularly after the Shia gained control of the Iraqi government. Every IP station I have been in has Shia and Mehdi Army propaganda posters openly displayed inside it. They are not working to bring down the system. They are the system.

These are our buddies, our comrades in arms, with whom we are supposed to bring Jeffersonian democracy and security to this wonderful country. This is the hope to which our president is pinning the success of his plans. To tell you the truth, I don't think our IPs know it or are particularly worried.

They are too busy washing Grandpa's brains out of the back of their pickup truck.

SIGNS

NAME: **CAPT MATT SMENOS**
STATIONED IN: **AFGHANISTAN**
HOMETOWN: **SANTA MARIA, CALIFORNIA**

The driver pulled his cab onto the median, checked the mirror for traffic, and stepped out of the vehicle. The honking, blinking stream of vehicles blew cold, gritty wind in his face as he walked carefully to the rear, opened the trunk, and removed his tool bag. The wooden signpost on the median was sturdy, but a bolt needed to be replaced in order to straighten the advertisement for his business. Kneeling between the car and the signpost, he unzipped his tools.

The busy sounds of midday traffic washed over him. He had been a cabby in this little Afghan town for many years. He had seen the Russians and the Taliban. Now the giant U.S. Humvees rumbled down the roads in convoys with the Afghan National Army. Many things changed, but the roots of the town went deep. He knew the watching, waiting eyes of the dissatisfied, the dissolute, and the desperate. He knew the very ground beneath him held the bloody memory of decades of war and faith and sacrifice. He knew that many things had not changed, and that many people would suffer before they did.

He wiped sweat from his brow as the old, rusty, broken bolt finally came free. Dropping it into the bottom of his tool bag, he reached into his pocket for a new one. Out of the corner of his eye, he saw a flash of green and turned to see a group of Afghan soldiers in a pickup truck moving slowly across the traffic circle. A crunch on the gravel road told him someone was behind him. He stood and turned, wiping his hands on a rag. A tanned, skinny fellow in a brown jacket was trudging slowly past the cabby's parked car. The cabby called out a greeting, but the man just walked on, gaze fixed on the horizon, silent and distracted. He could have been any of a dozen pedestrians on the roadside that morning. Nothing about him stood out.

The cabby shrugged and returned to his work, forgetting the walker and the soldiers as he renewed his efforts. The sounds of traffic continued to hum past him, and the crunch of the pedestrian's shoes faded as he moved around the traffic circle. No one saw him reach into his pocket. No one noticed his lips forming silent prayers. No one noticed anything until it was too late.

My intelligence officer finished describing the detainee's statement and sat back down, as memories of the day's events continued to unfold in my mind.

I had been on the phone with my wife. Let me rephrase that. I had been on the phone with my wife for too long. I seldom get the opportunity to call home. Even less frequently do I get the chance to talk with her for more than a minute or two. Now she was filling me in on the details of our annual tax return.

"Our deployed tax-exemption actually lowers the bracket we're in, and when you add it up you get . . ."

BOOM!

The plywood walls echoed and vibrated with the deafening roar. The lightbulbs on the rafters swung and cast wild patterns of shadow as clouds of dust leaped up from the stone floor. A plastic coffee cup detached itself from its hook on the wall and bounced painfully off my head. Everyone stood silent as the dust settled, and suddenly it was too quiet.

I murmured a subdued farewell to my wife, hung up the phone, and got started. We worked tirelessly for the next several hours trying to figure things out, radio receivers pressed to our ears, cradled in our shoulders, and handed back and forth. Every military agency for miles around came up on the net, as word of the totally unforeseen bombing rippled outward and up the chain of command. Radio controllers and operations officers in dozens of ready rooms, communication stations, telephone cubicles, and on cell phones shared map coordinates, manifests, detailed descriptions, rumors, assumptions, misconceptions, and lies. Navigating the buzzing chaos of the command net during a crisis is like panning for gold. An experienced controller learns what to keep and what to throw away.

We didn't get most of our answers until the detainee was questioned. As my initial response force arrived, they reported a terrible bombing had occurred just a few meters outside the gate of our little base. They described overturned cars, burned and dismembered bodies, choking smoke, and the cries of the wounded. Initial reports placed the suicide bomber on the roadside, having exited a taxi cab seen parked on the median. The safest course was to secure the entire area, assume the parked taxi was still a threat, and capture the dizzy, stumbling cab driver as he shook his head and tried to focus his eyes.

Over the last few months, I have read the statements of a number of detainees. I have witnessed their capture and release. This man, though treated the same as any other, acted differently. He was terribly concerned for his car and his wallet. He carefully cataloged the contents of his pockets and asked for receipts to ensure the safe and accurate return of his belongings. Most detainees suspected of collaborating with the enemy don't act like that. Most have a dead stare, like that of a doll's eyes, and a general disregard for themselves or their belongings. Most act caught.

This man did not. He was shocked and panicky. He coughed and choked and rubbed his head. He cried and repeated over and over his story about the sign that needed to be repaired and the man who walked past him and exploded. The Afghan and U.S. intelligence community, when they were able to investigate, discovered that the car was clean. There were no signs of weapons or explosives, and eventually they released the driver. They returned his money and possessions. I think they did the right thing.

In the days that followed, we discussed the bombing, while in the gym, while walking to chow, in the break area, and in bed before falling asleep. In the past we had been rocketed and attacked by small arms fire; our little base had endured numerous blasts and projectiles, but never had such a grisly and totally random act of violence occurred so close to us and made us feel so exposed. Many suspected the driver. They felt his sign-repair story was a sham, and that he was a very talented liar in the employ of the enemy. I had my doubts about this. Not only did his behavior surprise me, but his story gave me hope. Maybe I'm naive, but I really wanted there to be a ruined sign among the wreckage somewhere.

The most common complaint I hear about the Afghan nation is that they don't have a stake in this war. That they lack any sense of nationalism and do not share a vision of making their country better. The driver we detained exhibited another perspective. Like a tomato plant in the desert, here was a guy who most definitely has a stake in what happens in his nation. Here was a man not only striving to make something of himself, to turn an honest dollar, but also a man willing to maintain things and ensure the upkeep of that which he was proud to have built.

I wondered about the driver's sign. I wondered if he would return eventually to replace it, or if this sad moment, yet another display of violence and outrage, would scare him away. Would it sway him to leave town and set up elsewhere? Would he even stay in Afghanistan? Or would the sign become another battered, unclaimed fragment of a nation buried under decades of war? Would there ever be another sign endorsing Afghanistan's people, culture, and services, or would the only sign worth posting read: "Pakistan: 480 mi."?

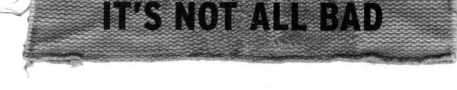

IT'S NOT ALL BAD

NAME: **FC1 (SW) ANTHONY McCLOSKEY (Tadpole)**
STATIONED IN: **AFGHANISTAN**
MILBLOG URL: **ARMYSAILOR.COM**

I have the day off, which is a nice change of pace seeing as I have not had any real downtime in about three weeks. It amazes me how much pressure there still is, this close to the end. But in any case, I took some time today to sit and meditate and reflect on the positive aspects of this deployment, and I have realized that it really isn't all bad.

I have met some fascinating new people and made some terrific new friends. I have been mentored by some truly impressive  NCOs. I have met people who I really hope to keep in touch with, and some I hope to never see again. I have met more Christians here than in my entire life up to now, many of whom seem to take the whole religion thing far too seriously in my opinion, but who are good people nonetheless. I have met some truly impressive reservists, and some truly unimpressive active-duty guys, which has helped break down many stereotypes for me.

I have seen some amazing views. I have seen views of mountains and valleys that most people will never get to see. I have gotten to travel over every type of terrain imaginable, in almost every type of vehicle imaginable. I have lived scenes that most people will only see in movies. I have had experiences that have given me a new appreciation for life and all that I have.

I have had the opportunity to truly help people. I have fed the hungry, clothed the cold, and helped provide medical care for the sick, wounded, and weary. What is amazing, though, is that I think each of these experiences has helped me more than it has helped them.

I have a whole new appreciation for the Navy! I now know, beyond *any* shadow of a doubt, that I joined the right branch for me. The Army is *way* too politically correct and Christian for my taste, the Marines are *way* too serious, the Air Force is *far* too sensitive and squishy. The Navy is the way to go for a fella who likes drinkin', fightin', travelin', and chasin' women!

I will leave the country financially, physically, and spiritually more well off than I came. I will leave debt-free with a nice little savings. It's easy to save money when you have nothing to spend it on, even when you are helping family at home. Despite some serious hearing loss and some scrapes and bruises, I am in better shape than I was when I came. Spending a lot of time in the gym and walking around in full "battle-rattle" will definitely keep you strong. Spiritually, I have had a lot of time to read, think, and meditate while I have been here. I have read much of the Qur'an and the Bible, and I have realized that I don't really buy into either. I have discovered that there is a name for my spiritual beliefs. I discovered that I am a Deist. I have deeply explored and read the teachings of the Dalai Lama, and I have discovered the true value of reason over blind faith. I have learned a new appreciation for my fellow man and the value of striving to do no harm. I have learned the negative aspects of attachment and have worked hard to free myself of them. I have discovered that fear, while natural, need not be debilitating. If handled correctly, it can be empowering.

I have also gained a new appreciation for my mother, who worked so long and so hard to make me the man I am today. And also for my first true mentor, HTCM (RET) Betterton, a man who met me when I was at a truly low point in my career. A man who I didn't know from Joseph, but who saw something in me. He managed to see enough in me that he took the risk of taking me under his wing. He taught me valuable lessons about leadership and life. He taught me how to pick my battles. He taught me many lessons to which I directly attribute my survival in this country.

So indeed, after much reflection, I have realized that I am taking away from this experience far more positive things than negative. If I had to choose whether or not I'd do it all over again, I cannot honestly say yes—after all, I miss my loved ones, good food, a warm body next to mine, and all the other comforts of life at home—but I can't say no either. It would be a tough decision.

TIME IS KING

NAME: **CAPT LEE KELLEY**
STATIONED IN: **IRAQ**
HOMETOWN: **SALT LAKE CITY, UTAH**
MILBLOG URL: **WORDSMITHATWAR.BLOG-CITY.COM**

Out here in the desert, Time is King; the minutes are his minions and the months his sabers by which you are knighted. The King controls all that you do, when you come and go, and how long until you see your children. Every mission and order is based on a strict time schedule. We are deployed for a year, "boots on the ground," so 365 becomes a mystical combination of integers, a mantra, a prayer.

We are nothing more than Australopithecus in a uniform, or a burka, or an expensive tailored suit. From the geographical perspective, humankind's time on this earth is less than the blink of an eye. Plate tectonics dismiss us. Volcanoes are too wise to notice our antics.

We study anthropology even as we live within it. We fly and drive and move around this planet, on these continents; we live and we fight. We are caricatures of ourselves, cartoon nations embroiled in our global struggles. The mountains fold their arms and they watch. We used to fight for food or a mate. Now we fight for freedom or money.

When you find yourself as a soldier in Iraq, holding some of the finest tools in your hands, the modern equivalents to stone and flint, to a rock swung from a stick to snare the hunted, you can't help it—you count the days. It's a reflexive reaction. Hit my knee with a rubber mallet.

You track the hours, the seconds, and the months. X amount of Sundays left. X amount of weeks. I will eat in this chow hall X more times. This many times I will lie in this bed and stare at the cracks in this ceiling. Like the wallpaper in the home you grew up in, you don't even notice it anymore. You just cast your thoughts upon its patterns and let your mind roam free.

And just because you're in the desert and the sights and sounds are so surreal, and you've forgotten what America smells like at nine in the morning as you walk past your neighbor's garden or the bakery on the corner, you act as if the possibility and difficulty of life is a finite thing, while your true path lays spread before you like a virtual chess board. Pawn or king? Bishop or rook? Should I move forward slowly or attack my fate with a flank?

To live is so startling it leaves little time for anything else.
—EMILY DICKINSON

GETTING SHOT AT

Name: **BEAU CLELAND**
Stationed in: **AFGHANISTAN**
Hometown: **PANAMA CITY, FLORIDA**

From an e-mail I sent home:

I'm still at Firebase Snake, which is a cool-sounding name for a small group of ramshackle brick buildings and a Hesco wall tucked in a river valley somewhere in Uruzgan Province. I can't talk specifics, but there aren't a whole lot of Americans here, and our only link to friendly forces is by air, due to the bad roads and worse people who control them. I'm working on month eight of this deployment, and I've been on plenty of patrols, but getting shot at is a relatively new experience for me. Since this is an experience most of you will never have (and I'm thankful for that), I'll do my best to describe the sights, sounds, and feelings of a gunfight for you.

Usually we have some kind of heads-up that the bad guys are around, so things haven't started in a surprise fashion for me, but even when you know it's coming, the first shots are startling. The most prominent thing about a battle is the noise—it is ungodly loud. Think of the loudest war movie sequence you've ever seen, and multiply that until it would make your ears bleed. Literally. One of our interpreter's ears were bleeding after this last one—he wasn't wearing ear protection. I wear a radio headset that also acts as hearing protection, and without it I'd be stone-deaf right now.

Guns make a distinctly different sound when they are pointed at you—sharper and higher pitched. Bullets make a zip noise that's tough to describe, but it isn't like the movies either. You can sort of judge how close they get by the sound and intensity of that noise. Recently, as I was in the open, rear-facing seat of a Humvee, fighting started up at the front of the convoy. We were toward the back and couldn't see the engagement in front of us and weren't taking any fire from the left, where it started from. Within a short time, I start hearing zzziip, zzziip. I look around in confusion, because I didn't hear any shots. The zips continue, and I still don't hear anything, so I yell to the guy up front, "Hey, Larry, I think someone's shooting at me." It sounded so ridiculous I still want to laugh about it, but I didn't at the time because we figured out where it was coming from when the truck behind us got raked down its right side. So everyone swings right and lets loose on some mud compounds and trees just across the river. I never saw the guy or guys, and that's often the case, but the shooting stopped, and we moved on.

Everyone's least favorite noise is that lovable RPG sound. Rocket-propelled grenades suck. There's a whooshing sound and then a terrific BOOM when they hit. Thank God that the Taliban can't shoot worth a damn. Artillery, on the other hand, is such a beautiful noise, since we know it's ours. Of course, I'm partial to it by profession, but it makes a pleasing jet sound or low whistle when it goes over your head, depending on the angle, fuse, etc., etc., etc., and then a satisfying "crump" when it hits. Explosiony goodness and hot-metal action for the bad guys. It must be terrifying for them, but I don't care.

Aerial bombs are incredibly loud—the noise is a lot sharper than an artillery round, and more intense, but it's short. There isn't some multisyllabic "kaboom." It's just every pot and pan in your kitchen hitting the floor simultaneously, and then stopping. The gun from an A-10 is really cool—you hear dozens of almost simultaneous little booms when the rounds hit, and then a few seconds later you actually hear the gunfire with a low-pitched "brrrrrrrrrrp." There's lots of yelling and radio traffic, too. So, mash all of that stuff together and mix it in with the occasional bout of eerie quiet, and you have the sound track to a bad time.

The sights are captured a little better by movies such as *Black Hawk Down* or *Saving Private Ryan*. There aren't huge fireballs from weapon muzzles; it's just a little bit of smoke and dust in the daytime. People in the distance are just little black dots with legs running, or peeking over a ledge at you. Bomb and artillery explosions are mostly dust and smoke as well, and they kick up a haze that lingers in the air with smoke from the inevitable fires. Mud houses don't really burn, but there are hay piles and other flammables aplenty. Airburst munitions provide a little more of a flash, but it's muted in comparison to some TV-show imagining.

You see some crazy things sometimes, like an idiot civilian woman with a herd of kids walking them right across the valley where the enemy is trading fire with us. They're lucky someone took the time to notice they weren't combatants, and we placed ourselves at greater risk by not shooting in their direction despite the enemy. There is the ubiquitous livestock presence, too. I feel bad for those animals; they're tied up and can't run away, and some are inevitably hurt. Somehow this brown cow managed to make it through the cross fire untouched. It was amazing. I wanted to ask it, "How now?"

The feelings involved: I can't speak for anyone else, but mine are usually stark fear, adrenaline, and excitement. Fear is very uncomfortable, like you had lead pancakes for breakfast. Four-letter expressions are quite common. Oddly, there's a good bit of laughter and joking, too, often after a near miss, along the lines of, "Oh shit, that was close. Hahaha." Gotta break the tension, I suppose. When it's over and done (and we're all in one piece), elation: "I am still here, and he is not." Then, bone-weariness and an urgent need to pee. I looked at my watch, and six hours had passed in what seemed like the longest five minutes of my life. I was a little woozy from 3,000 rounds of .50 caliber being fired next to my head, but otherwise fine.

I debated not mentioning this topic at all, to keep you guys from worrying, but I think you're better served by knowing what goes on, and what it feels like, and how truly terrible it is. Hawkish behavior is the realm of people who haven't done this before.

IT WAS MEMORIAL DAY

NAME: **SGT ZACHARY SCOTT-SINGLEY**
RETURNED FROM: **IRAQ**
MILBLOG URL: **MISOLDIERTHOUGHTS.BLOGSPOT.COM**

I cried. It was Memorial Day and it hit me so hard; my first Memorial Day since leaving the Army. My wife watched me and felt helpless as I sat there and quietly broke down in long silent sobs as the memories came flooding back, and the guilt started again. She didn't know exactly what to do. She made sure my son and daughter were still playing together in the other room, and she held me.

She suggested we go to my father's house so that I could talk to him. He had served in Vietnam, and I knew he would know what I was going through. I drove without saying a word as I turned on the radio to NPR and listened to vets talk about those they lost. They had one vet for each war since World War I. I drove with big rolling tears, quietly, so that my children wouldn't know that their father was so weak right then.

I saw my father in his backyard watering the grass, and as I walked up to him, Tara drove off with the kids. I crumpled in a heap when he turned to me, and I couldn't make it stop. Memories I thought I had filed away came flying back hitting me, and without control I finally sobbed aloud as he walked over and extended his hand.

The only thing he said just then was, "You feel guilty, don't you?" He knew without even needing to ask. I was so very grateful for him at that moment. Not to have to talk about it and try to explain, just being able to have someone understand without asking anything was like gold. After a few minutes I calmed down and asked him if it was ever that hard for him. He told me it was. The memories and feeling that guilt for coming back alive while so many others have died, both soldiers and civilians. That was all I could think about that day: Why me? God, why did you let me live

when you took so many others? But it wasn't God; it was us, mankind, that did this.

My father helped me put myself back together piece by piece
until I felt complete again and that it was over. The rest of the day
was uneventful, but in the back of my mind I realize that the guilt is
still there. It always was, I just didn't see it until that day. I love you,
Dad, and I know why you came back alive from Vietnam. You came
back because I needed you.

BUSTING AT THE SEAMS

NAME: **CAPT MATT SMENOS**
STATIONED IN: **AFGHANISTAN**
HOMETOWN: **SANTA MARIA, CALIFORNIA**

It used to be the remoteness of it all. The lean, Spartan efficiency of a forward operating base made us uncomfortable. In July 2006, when we first arrived in Sharana, my team of airmen and I couldn't believe how little there was here. Our huts were simple, four-walled boxes. The occasional dividing wall or curtain within was seen as a decadent extravagance and spurred jealousy and vandalism.

At first glance, the bathroom had a certain tropical, steam-room quality, reminiscent of a barefoot resort or a running-water cabana. We all quickly realized such simulations are just that: simulated, and secret provisions protect resort patrons from that which our little baño had in abundance— bacteria, dry rot, and odor. Our work centers were marvelous fusions of old and new. Plywood rectangles with simple wooden shelves and tabletops were laden with laptops, router cables, IP equipment, fax machines, printers, cell-phone chargers, and wires. Flies and spiders ran a close second in the food chain.

Though things were rough and unfinished, we all tightened our belts and learned to make it work. You discover very quickly what you can live without. We quickly forgot privacy and modesty. A "males only" environment brings out the Cro-Magnon in everyone. Everyone got leaner and became more comfortable with swinging hammers, hauling wood, pounding nails, and cutting PVC pipe. In time we received gym equipment, but few felt the need to use it.

We learned when the hot water heater would die and when the pipes would freeze. Some just stopped showering. Having at one time flinched at every pop, bang, or boom, we now hardly blinked an eye at explosions or smoke. Once treated with reverence and fear-

ful respect, our weapons now hung casually from our shoulders as the creases in our once neatly pressed uniforms faded in our laundry-less universe.

In time, the routines we developed became transparent to any but newcomers. Visiting soldiers would ask, "Why is the Internet down?" and be baffled by the response: "Duh, it's 1345, give it 20 minutes." They'd scratch their heads as they watched me shut off the lights and unplug the freezer in order to microwave a paper cup of oatmeal.

Hanging over it all was an aura of displacement. No major roads, no crowded sidewalks, no sounds or lights could be seen or heard. Here was true darkness at night, like summer camp in the woods. Standing on the wall, looking out past the wire, one could see the cook-fire smoke from distant *qalats*. Occasional herds of goats mingled with stray dogs, baying and trotting about, sniffing at piles of offal and ash. Beyond were great brown stretches of war-torn waste and distant, unfamiliar mountains. It felt like living on another planet.

We were all very vocal with our complaints. Our oft-repeated outcries for better food and more equipment became an almost cathartic theme for daily reflection and mealtime conversations. But even as we hated it, we subconsciously conditioned ourselves to live in, and eventually find contentment in, our strange little home. We would have been the last to guess that the very improvements we claimed to desperately desire would be seen as unwelcome waves of painful change when they finally arrived.

As uncomfortable as we were at first, we had learned to adapt and had hit our stride amid difficult conditions. "Different" and "difficult" are relative terms, and our perceptions of each had changed over the months. The next adaptation would actually be a movement toward what we had originally wanted.

It all started with a security force assigned to our FOB. This was terrific. Up until their arrival, information managers, network administrators, and radio operators were standing nightly rotating security watches. Though we had all been trained to do so, it was nice to have a force specifically dedicated to base security. They

settled right in. Around the FOB, we noticed a few more people in the chow hall, a few more people using the shower, a few more in the gym. No big deal, right? Wrong.

Another infantry team and a group of IT experts were assigned here. Word from our highers suggested that larger numbers were being pushed down range, and preparations needed to be made. Construction ramped up to erect more living quarters and a larger chow hall for our growing FOB. I began to notice that the gym was full by 0630, and I needed to be in by 0530 if I didn't want to wait on equipment. The chow hours expanded, and certain items were now being rationed. A new team of interpreters, Romanian soldiers, replacement U.S. soldiers to overlap and train with current soldiers—they just kept coming.

For me personally, the real moment of realization occurred when an interpreter walked up and "borrowed" my shower shoes while I was shaving. When I asked him what he thought he was doing, he told me that since he'd arrived, there had never been a shortage of shower shoes, towels, and sundries strewn around the bathroom. He didn't think anyone would notice. That makes sense in an Afghan sort of way. My brothers and sisters in arms can attest to that. The real issue was that we were drowning in sweating, hungry, loud, uncomfortable people.

Evidently, it was no better in the northern part of the country. Word of the some 3,200 soldiers from the 10th Mountain Division being extended (along with the Fort Drum wives' riot—let's give it up for the wives, they're awesome!) and being redeployed around Afghanistan along with the 82nd Airborne had reached us, along with an order not to send any overnight supply or R&R convoys to Kabul or Bagram. I heard the tents were busting at the seams, and the chow halls couldn't feed people fast enough.

You can imagine the new breed of bitching that began. In e-mails from coworkers, peers at other FOBs, instructions from commanders at meetings, arguments in the showers, and everywhere else you could hear it. Space was tight, and the pressure was on. Memories of our lonely, rustic, emaciated little war camp seemed sweeter by the day. What we wouldn't trade to be alone in the dark as we had been before.

This too shall pass. New FOBs will shoot up, and hopefully my replacements will be here soon. They'll never know that this place was once a scattered camp of rickety plywood huts and tents. They'll miss out on the quiet, moonlit security watches and the howling of the dogs, long since run off by the booming "progress" in the area. They'll probably have a brand-name coffee shop soon and never even fathom what it was like making filters out of paper towels.

Don't get me wrong—I'm not bitter, and I wish those that follow us safety and success to see them through to the end of this place. I only write this to commemorate my time at the beginning.

NAME: **CAPT DOUG TEMPLETON**
STATIONED IN: **AFGHANISTAN**
HOMETOWN: **KANSAS CITY, MISSOURI**

I write this post from the safety of my office back in the States. I am here on 30 days emergency leave. My father died after a four-year battle with cancer. Never in that time did he ever complain about the pain or worry me about his suffering. When the end came, it was a shock to me because he seemed to be doing well. I know it was his way of keeping me from being distracted. He believed in what I am doing and would not have wanted to bother me with things I couldn't control. He was a trooper, and I will miss him terribly.

Since this site is for passing along the events and feelings of service members, I thought I would try to explain what has been going through my mind the last few days.

I was notified of my father's death through an e-mail from my mother. She had sent it two minutes earlier, and something compelled me to check my e-mail as I went about my many daily tasks. I notified my leadership that a Red Cross message was coming, and they started to make the arrangements for my travel.

I had to convoy to my point of embarkation, and when I arrived the following morning, I was met by the First Shirt, who had everything I needed as far as leave paperwork and such, complete and waiting. I left Afghanistan that day on the first thing smoking back to the States. It took about 32 hours to get to my home in Texas, to collect my wife and daughter before heading out the next day on a ten-hour drive north to Kansas City.

Here is where the odd feelings started to weigh on my mind. I miss and loved my father as did the rest of my family, and the funeral was a tough time for all of us. We used one another for comfort and strength to get through the event. After that, I spent a few days with my mother to help her through the transition of no longer having someone around the house.

The similarities between being with my family at home and my family in Afghanistan began to cause me to feel a little out of place. You see, we have a responsibility to each other for safety and comfort and to help each other through difficult events. It is the same in both locations, and that is why I feel like I have to get back.

My family here is safe and sound and is beginning to move forward without Dad. My family in Afghanistan is still in harm's way, and I am part of that team. No matter what, I have a responsibility to uphold and a mission to complete.

For those not in the military, this may seem strange, but those who serve will understand. I am a sixth-generation military officer, and these principles have been instilled in me from birth. This is what my father would have wanted, for me to get back to work and to make a difference and to complete my mission.

TOMATO PLANTS

NAME: **SPC JAMI GIBBS**
RETURNED FROM: **IRAQ**
MILBLOG URL: **AMERICANBABBLE.COM**

I think my mind has definitely hit the "rough patch." I've never been one to know what depression is. Yes, I have always been moody. But I have generally been a very pro-life person. I've always been able to see bad experiences as just something along life's journey. Lately, though, I've been starting to feel this very dark, sinking dread. Not having any prior experience with the feeling, I suppose I can only associate it with depression.

I hate feeling sorry for myself. I've been letting myself get into a cycle of feeling self-pity, then getting mad at myself for feeling pity, then getting upset that I'm angry that I'm feeling self-pity, etc., etc., etc. I think after a week or so, I realized that many other people in my unit are feeling the exact same way as I am. They are feeling trapped. They don't know what more to talk about. They can't find anything that will make them truly smile anymore. It's hard for me to describe the stir-crazy feeling because it tends to be so overwhelming.

A couple of weeks ago, I noticed a little miracle. Underneath a bench surrounded by sand and concrete was a tomato plant. It was growing in seemingly barren ground. I was astounded. It was over a foot tall and had three little white blooms. I picked a leaf and smelled it, as if my eyes were deceiving me. The telltale aroma of tomato plant was overpowering. I pointed it out to my roommate later, and we stared at it for a minute together in awe.

The next week it wasn't there anymore. Some Iraqi laborers had come by and chopped it down. They were hired to come around our area and pick up trash and pick weeds and such. For some reason I felt a profound sadness for this stupid little plant. I told myself that it didn't really belong there in the first place. It had no place flourishing in this wasteland. And I convinced myself that it wouldn't have survived long in the 100 degree heat anyway. But as it turned out, it had a better chance of surviving Mother Nature than the hands of a laborer.

Sometimes it's all the little things adding up that have the biggest effect on us. But I'm still grateful that all I'm mourning are tomato plants. I hope it stays that way.

CHILDREN

NAME: **CAPT DOUG TRAVERSA**
STATIONED IN: **KABUL, AFGHANISTAN**
HOMETOWN: **TULLAHOMA, TENNESSEE**
MILBLOG URL: **TRAVERSA.TYPEPAD.COM**

Today Hamid (my interpreter) came with me to lunch, and I stopped by the hut to drop off my armor and rifle.

"Hey, you've never seen my blog, have you? Come in and I'll show it to you."

I pulled up my front page and showed him the recent archives so he could see how much I am writing. As we walked to chow, he said, "You really do write a lot. What do you say?"

"I write about anything that happens to me. People love to read about our friendship, because it gives them hope that we can have peace in the world, even if we come from different worlds. For instance, I wrote about our discussion the other day concerning friendship."

He laughed. "I bet you write about how much I eat."

Now I laughed. "Ohhhh, yeeesss," I said, dragging out each word. "You can bet I wrote about that. You are famous around the world for your massive appetite. I told people how you eat four plates of food and store it like a camel."

At this point we are both laughing very loud. We do that often. Hamid loves to laugh, and I love an audience, so we laugh a great deal indeed.

"But that's not true!" he complained, still laughing.

"Well, they don't really think you are a camel." But as for the four plates of food, it has been known to happen. "You can bet if we've had a good talk, I've written about it."

Once we sat down to eat, I waited for the conversation to take one of the unexpected twists I've come to expect. (Can you really

225

expect an unexpected twist?). Interestingly enough, it was the *Stars and Stripes* that provided us some great stuff. I usually have a copy open and glance through it while we eat. The actual conversations start after we stuff our faces.

I saw a photo of the world's smallest prematurely born baby that survived. She was 10 ounces when born. I showed the picture to Hamid, and we discussed just how young (22 weeks) and tiny the baby was. I ended up discussing the miracles of modern medicine that allowed us to save such a tiny baby, and somehow we got to artificial insemination. Hamid was amazed that such a thing was possible. He had never heard of it, and I would soon learn how important this option would be in Afghanistan.

To Hamid, you get married in order to have children. In fact, he says that if a married couple does not have children, it is a great shame to them, and they withdraw from society. The man is assumed to be impotent and is mocked and called a woman or a she-male. This disgrace is so onerous, Hamid says, if it is the woman who can't conceive, the man will usually marry a second wife so he can have children.

"Well, in America, we can only have one wife. Suppose I had gotten married, and my wife could not have children. What should I do?"

Hamid answered easily and quickly. "You should divorce her and marry someone else. What is a marriage without children?"

The cultural gulf exploded in my face. The utter casualness with which he said this was as shocking as when Wali told me gays and apostates should be executed.

"I married my wife because I love her. Why in the world would I leave her if she couldn't have children? I want to be with her."

Hamid seemed as baffled as I was. "But a marriage is nothing without children."

"Why?" I demanded.

"Who will take care of you when you are older? Who will pray for you when you die?" he explained.

"That sounds incredibly selfish. You only want kids to take care of you when you are old?" I countered.

"So when you get old, you don't want your children to take care of you?" he asked.

"Of course, I would like them to, but that's not why I had children. I wanted children to share the love and joy of raising a family. As I told you, my family means everything to me. I loved having children, but I did not have them so I could have little workers to take care of me all the time."

Hamid and I paused; no doubt my thoughts were as alien to him as his were to me.

"Let me tell you about my aunt," he began. "When she got married, she could not have children. At first her husband loved her and treated her nicely. But as time went on, and she never had children, he started getting angry with her. Whenever people with children came over to visit, he would yell at her after they left. He blamed her and even told her he would never have married her if he had known she could not bear children.

"However, after 12 years of this, she was able to get some medical treatment and was finally able to have a child. Once this happened, he started treating her nicely again and loving her."

I was saddened but not surprised. "I find this hard to understand. How can men be so cruel? Why would they blame a woman for a medical problem that isn't her fault?"

Hamid shrugged. "As I said, a marriage without children is nothing. Why even get married?"

I had had enough. Cultural tolerance only goes so far. I got as stern as I've ever gotten with Hamid. My wife can tell you about the look. It melts steel and has made teachers and ROTC cadets cry. Really.

"I love my wife. She is the most important thing in the world to me. Why in the world would I want to hurt her, divorce her, or shame her if she couldn't have children? That is the most stupid thing I have ever heard. I would never want anything to do with a religion that taught such a thing. It is absolutely hateful and pure evil!" I have no doubt that Hamid felt like a little bunny looking into the barrel of a gun held by a very angry hunter.

"No, no, no," he waved his hands. "It is not Islam, it is Afghanistan that teaches this. It is our country."

I turned off my glare, sat back in my chair, and pulled my hair back with my hands as I tend to do when faced with a dilemma. "We really do come from different worlds. I can't understand why you treat women so badly. To me, marriage is a partnership and a friendship. I cannot imagine deliberately hurting my wife, as your men do."

"It is our culture."

"Well, I can't change your culture, but I hope what I say can change you. I am concerned about you. I don't want you to be like that. When you get married, I hope you will treat your wife better than that."

"I actually believe as you do. But I was telling you how most men think here." Hamid looked sad. "In fact, I have bad news to tell you. You know the girl I wanted to marry, the one my mother was going to look into in the spring?"

"Yes, of course." I waited for the bad news. It was written clearly on his face.

"Her father has a business in Russia. I found out last night that he is taking his family to live there. I will never see her again."

Sometimes I want to cry. In fact, as I write this, I do.

THE DRUG FRONT

NAME: **SGT BRANDON WHITE**
STATIONED IN: **AFGHANISTAN**
HOMETOWN: **DIAMOND, OHIO**
MILBLOG URL: **GWOT.US**

J ust got back from a three-day mission down south. While I can't go into operational specifics, I will list the keywords: Taliban, weapons, poppy.

This photo shows someone's little "backyard garden" of *papaver somniferum*, a.k.a. opium poppy. These guys look to be no more than a few weeks old but would have grown to produce thousands of dollars for the key players of the opium trade. Sadly, the cultivators who are trying to put food on the table would get hardly enough to do just that. Why is that sad, you ask? Well, come on over here and see how they're livin', and you'll get the gist.

The growers aren't the bad guys. It's the local Taliban "underlords," who are exploiting them, selling the stuff for a premium, and pocketing the money, who are the bad guys. Sure, it would be great

to end the whole dern drug cycle here, but what do we replace that poppy with for the farmers? What could be exported in mass quantities that can grow easily in these arid lands? Those are questions that I sincerely hope someone, somewhere (besides myself) is thinking about. Otherwise, we are doing nothing but breeding more terrorists by eliminating this crop. Mark my words on that one.

Here is a zoomed-out view of the same backyard garden. This little plot is pretty small in comparison to the ginormous fields that surround this village.

ALIVE IN YOUR MIND

NAME: **CAPT BENJAMIN TUPPER**
STATIONED IN: **GHAZNI, AFGHANISTAN**
HOMETOWN: **SYRACUSE, NEW YORK**

This is a story about two men. Both are brave, committed soldiers. Each has a long and distinguished military record. Both
are likeable, selfless, and humorous. They are the kind of guys
you'd want as a neighbor, a drinking buddy, a teammate on a sports
team, or a brother. Both are stubborn in their onset of middle age. It
would be dishonest to say they are perfect. We all have our character
flaws, and these two are no exception. But the balance sheet on their
personal and moral fiber weighs heavily in their favor.

They are good men pretty much every day, all day.

One is American, and the other is Afghan.

And unfortunately, at the end of this story, one man lives and
the other man dies.

Ali Raza makes his own introduction. At first glance, he appears
like a large bear walking on hind legs. Gruff, barrel-chested, a hulking man ruggedly assembled from head to toe. His face is like a map
of old battlefields, with a network of scars weaving through his black
beard. Ali Raza is a veteran of nine years of intense fighting during the Soviet-Afghan War and now four more years against the
Taliban. Some of his war stories from the 1980s may be a little far-
fetched, but one cannot deny the scars on his body and the hardness
of his warrior eyes.

The first time I met Ali Raza, he literally pulled me off the
ground with the strength of his handshake. Startled by this power,
I composed myself and said the first thing that came to mind: "This
man is a bear!" Once this was translated into Pashto by my interpreter, Ali Raza let out a laugh that shook the mountains.

While I may have painted a picture here of a hardened veteran,

I must add that Ali Raza is not a cold or cruel man. His heavy arms are equally suited for hugging his small children and for giving them a sense of security and protection in this violent environment. And so this bear of a man goes about his military duties with all the energy and force he needs to accomplish them. Sometimes this force may be a bit overboard, but Ali Raza is honest enough to admit he is not perfect. Although he is a devout Muslim, he still fancies vodka and beer, an acquired taste developed during years fighting with the Russians. Before you judge him for this religious infraction, Ali Raza will happily show you a doctor's prescription recommending alcohol for "medicinal purposes."

In the realm of tactics, there is no ambiguity with Ali Raza. He unabashedly prefers the Russian approach to clearing enemy villages: "Bomb everyone with airplanes and artillery, and then let them rebuild a new, friendly village." (How we guarantee the future friendliness of a village we just destroyed is a simple technicality to Ali Raza, a technicality I'm still waiting to hear him explain.) Suffice to say, if you ever met Ali Raza, your immediate reaction would be simple: "I'm glad he is on our side!" One could only assume that if he hasn't been killed yet in decades of warfare, he's never going to be.

In some ways, MSG Scotland shares many similarities with Ali Raza. Both are above average in size and demeanor. MSG Scotland is perhaps one of the tallest ETTs ever to come in-country. Both men have a long record of service, although Scotland is a senior NCO, while Ali Raza is an officer.

MSG Scotland comes from the Midwest and volunteered for the yearlong ETT mission in order to do his part as a soldier. With his rank and time in service, he could have easily hidden under some rock back home and avoided a deployment into harm's way. But he didn't shirk his sense of duty, and he ended up here as a volunteer combatant, on the same FOB that Ali Raza and myself call home.

Scotland never shirks the dangerous aspects of the ETT mission. He embraces the risks as if they were free of all possible negative consequences. He even goes so far as to tempt fate with his humor and sarcasm. Before missions, he jokingly tosses his cell phone to the Afghan interpreters and urges them to use it: "Here, call your Taliban friends. Tell them I'm coming for them."

Every day, MSG Scotland volunteers for every mission. When he is not selected to go, he works back channels to get on one of the up-armored Humvee gun-truck crews. A day with no mission for Scotland is a day of lost chances to engage and destroy the enemy.

And like Ali Raza, he has a family and children back home. No one doubts a happy homecoming in the future for this loving and patriotic father.

Many bullets were fired that hot July day. All anonymously passed through time and space and disappeared into oblivion. All except one, which struck its mark. It dove into the shadow of a soft, ticklish armpit. A split second later, it passed completely through the body, came out the other side, and was gone.

Where it landed no one knows. But for that split second, this bullet left a wound that no medic or bandage could fix. The injury was gentle enough to let the wounded man sit back and realize he had been hit, but violent enough to impress upon him the fact he would likely die.

Had he been an average-sized man, the high-velocity round would have passed harmlessly above his shoulder and smashed into nothing but air and empty space. The harm inflicted by this bullet on someone smaller would have been purely psychological. A simple cracking noise, a reminder to keep one's head down.

For his comrades, who tried unsuccessfully to stop the bleeding, it must have seemed like furious seconds passing, and then he was gone. And for the dying man, time might have passed slowly, like sand through an hourglass.

Miles away, at the exact moment of his death, I sat listening to the morbid codes and phrase words being passed over the radio. Like you, I was only aware that a man was dead. His identity remained a mystery.

This story's end is not a surprise. One of these two men is dead. In fact, he's been dead now for months. Only today did chance events transpire to weave these two lives together into this story. And as I prepared to craft the ending to this sad tale and to reveal the identity of the fallen man, I realized that it wasn't something I wanted to do. I realized that his death is only as real as I make it for you.

Both of these men are alive in your mind until I tell you one isn't. Can't you see Ali Raza hulking over his men on this chilly Afghan winter day, the steam rising from his mouth as he yells fiery insults to motivate his sluggish soldiers? And look at Scotland, standing before the desk of our commander, pleading his case about why he should be on today's combat patrol into a tough, nearby village.

Don't they both still feel alive to you?

So as I write this, I find myself in a unique position to grant what I think is the "universal soldier's wish," that upon our death in combat, we are not forgotten.

That we can live on in the minds of our comrades, our families, our friends, and even strangers. That we can be seen much like you envision my two comrades in this story—still active, still engaged, still alive. If we can live on in the memories of those we touched, then we can cheat the bullet's bite. And so I'm going to grant my fallen comrade this simple soldier's wish and let him cheat the death that claimed him. I feel some solace in knowing that right here, right now, he is still alive in your mind's eye.

Note: "Ali Raza" and "Scotland" are modifications of the true last names of these men.

THE LITTLE THINGS

NAME: **MAJ MICHAEL IRWIN**
STATIONED IN: **IRAQ**
MILBLOG URL: **CYBIRR.BLOGSPOT.COM**

t's the little things that get our attention—in this case, five cents.

At overseas locations, the base economy is penny-less. AAFES (Army and Air Force Exchange Service) does not use pennies; all prices are rounded to the nearest nickel. The cost of shipping pennies is more than the value of the pennies themselves.

Here in Iraq they take it further; no coins at all. But they don't round to the nearest dollar. Instead, they issue "pogs." These mini–gift certificates are used in place of coins. On one side is the AAFES logo and some suitably patriotic image, and on the other a 5 cent, 10 cent, or 25 cent notation. AAFES makes it clear that pogs are cash value as depicted and can be redeemed at any AAFES worldwide for the full value. And really, I don't want to carry a bunch of loose change in a combat environment. This program makes sense.

So I have not seen a real coin in several months.

While shopping at the local BX to get something or other, I handed the cashier some dollar bills and put my hand out, expecting a few pogs. An odd weight settled in my hand. I looked down and, lo, there in my hand was a nickel! My two colleagues and I stopped talking and all gazed in wonder at the coin. It was as if there was an angelic chorus in the background, and the image of Jefferson seemed to glow. It was a real nickel. A tangible piece of home! A no-kidding bit of America!! It was a remarkable moment. . . .

To us, but not to the cashier. She looked at the slack-jawed idiot aircrew standing in front of her, staring, then looked at the coin in my hand for a moment, then looked at the three dummies again.

"Hey, it's a nickel. Get over it! *Next!*"

THE REALITY OF WAR

NAME: **SGT BRANDON WHITE**
STATIONED IN: **AFGHANISTAN**
HOMETOWN: **DIAMOND, OHIO**
MILBLOG URL: **GWOT.US**

He was that tiny baby, who stared in bright-eyed wonder;
into his mother's eyes, the blanket of security that he was
under.
He was that three-foot toddler, who let you have it;
when he asked his daddy, if you were pregnant.
He was that neighbor boy, who was always into something;
he pulled your flowers and sent your hubcaps sailing.
He was that kid, who threw gum in your hair because he secretly
liked you;
what he never knew, is that you liked him, too.
He was the one, who sped through your neighborhood;
a new license and Mustang, life was too good.
He was that boy, whose name you can't recall;
who helped you at the grocery, carried your bags and all.
He was that son, who made his parents cry;
when off to war he went, little time for good-byes.
He was that young man, who always made you smile;
you wonder what became of him, you haven't seen him in a while.
He was that boy, who became that man;
in a distant battlefield, that was full of sand.
He was that guy, whose letters came less and less;
the images too horrific, pen to paper he could not press.
He was one of those, that you heard on the news;
who was patrolling downtown Baghdad, when the enemy
lit the fuse.
That boy you used to know, whose face you can't remember;

THE REALITY OF WAR

bled out on a dirty street, this past May or maybe it was
    September.
That kid who meant so little to many, yet so much to a few;
his life was cut short, and it was still very new.
That boy who used to be in your life, and whose fate you
    will not allow;
Oh, him, that guy. He's gone now.

When I wrote this poem I was in a mood that I have yet to
identify. I was having a range of emotions—from happiness to anger
to sorrow and everything in between— because of this war. I have
little doubt that readers will have a similar reaction to it. I did not
post it to offend anyone. The message in the poem is clear to me but
may not be to others:
    Many of my fellow Americans feel that this war is distant, that it
concerns them none. Heck, they don't even know anyone in the service or haven't even had a family member in the service in all of the
generations. This poem shows them that they have known someone
in the service, whether they realize it or not.
    It's also about the sacrifices that troops and their families are
making on a daily basis, for which we need to hold them in the
upmost respect at all times. The reality of war is ugly, and I've always
been a direct kind of guy, so there you have it. Have faith in the mission and in your troops.

THE ROADBLOCK

NAME: **1LT ADAM TIFFEN**
STATIONED IN: **IRAQ**
MILBLOG URL: **THEREPLACEMENTS.BLOGSPOT.COM**

The sky has turned a striking shade of purple and red as the sun begins to set in the west. To the east of the Alamo, the tall blue and green minaret of the Shia mosque is lit up with a single string of white lights. The mosque, standing alone in "no-man's-land," has only been partially completed, and the unfinished sections of brick wall look ominously down over the crumbling city in the fading light.

Across from the mosque, in a small woodworking shop, a man has just been murdered. An hour ago, three insurgents entered his shop and shot him in the head. The weapon was held so close that the muzzle blast burned and blackened his ear. Only 300 meters from the Alamo, he was left to die, four AK-47 shell casings lying next to his body. He is the second man to be executed within sight of the Alamo in as many days. The city is restless tonight.

In front of the Alamo, in the falling darkness, a squad of soldiers works to improve the fixed defenses. A single HMMWV sits on the road, its hood stacked high with concertina wire, a soldier crouched low in the turret, scanning the surrounding darkness with his night vision. The soldiers work quietly. Triple strands of razor-sharp wire are stretched across the road and weighed down with sandbags. Concrete barriers are maneuvered into place. Spike strips are laid across avenues of approach. All designed to stop a suicide car bomb.

As I walk out from between the concrete barriers and onto the main street in front of the Alamo, I can see a soldier with a flashlight waving at oncoming traffic. As his squad erects the barrier, he is signaling cars to turn off onto a side street. Every one of those cars is a threat.

Farther out in the dark, a blue van stops for a second, its driver confused by the roadblock. The soldier with the flashlight tenses and raises his rifle up to cover the driver.

On the corner sits a white and orange taxi, its lights turned off. The taxicab driver shouts helpful directions at the driver of the blue van, and the blue van pulls down the side street. I can see the soldier relax, his shoulders slumping beneath his heavy body armor.

It is a Thursday night, and this type of traffic is normal. In the twilight, the local men walk from house to house for a cigarette or a cup of tea with their neighbors. Cheap tobacco smoke permeates the air as they cluster on doorsteps smoking French Gauloises.

Across from the Alamo, a small convenience shop is doing a brisk business, and a crowd of men has gathered outside. Signaling two soldiers to accompany me, I walk across the street and up to the group. One of the men is older, with a careworn face and a full, white beard. He is wearing a flowing white robe, which contrasts sharply with the darkness of his skin. His eyes are dark and shadowed in the harsh light of the fluorescent bulb hanging from the wall of the shop.

Touching my hand to my chest, I give him the traditional greeting. "Salaam aleichem." The old man returns the greeting with a slight smile.

Beside him, a young man gets up from a worn wooden bench. He is strangely pale and overweight, and his hand nervously grips plastic prayer beads. The small red beads click together quietly as he methodically counts them.

The old man begins to speak in Arabic, and my interpreter, Tornado, listens to him politely before turning to me to translate.

"He is asking about the Hurricane Katrina." This was the last thing that I had expected to hear.

"Really? What does he know about Katrina?"

The old man's face grows solemn.

"We heard that 10,000 people have been killed, and that the city is destroyed. We have heard that there is disease and fighting." Behind him, the younger man smiles at me. In the shop behind him, I can hear the muted sound of a strident Arabic voice on the radio.

"And how did you hear about this?"

"We have a satellite. It told us all about the Hurricane Katrina."

"Do you have such hurricanes here in Iraq?"

The younger man's smile widens. It seems that he wants to tell me something, and as he leans forward, his hands briefly touch as he makes a dusting motion. "No, we do not have such things as hurricanes in Iraq. We do not have them because we are protected by Allah. We have the shrines of the prophet, and Allah does not permit such tragedies here."

He leans back as if he has gotten something important off of his chest. He has made his point. It sounds like a theory out of the Dark Ages. As if on cue, the sound of automatic weapons fire erupts in the northern sector of town. It is a series of sharp reports, one after the other. In response, another automatic weapon opens up, its higher-pitched whine audible over the lower, more guttural single shots.

Turning around, I scan the low hulking shadows of the houses across no-man's- land for any sudden muzzle flashes that would indicate the shooter's position. There is a gun battle going on, no more than 400 meters from the Alamo. The sky and the buildings to the north remain dark. To my left, one of the soldiers, a young private, flips down his night vision and scans the darkness of an alleyway for movement. He is fidgeting nervously from foot to foot. Anybody could be out there tonight.

Turning back, I face the younger man. "Are you saying that America had a hurricane because there are no shrines in America to the prophet? Because most Americans do not follow Islam?"

He nods his head, pleased that I understand him. "Yes, it is God's will. In America there are no shrines, so Allah does not protect Americans. Here there are no tornadoes, earthquakes, volcanoes, or hurricanes. If there were more of Islam in America, such things as hurricanes would not happen."

The gunfire in the north sounds as if it has doubled in intensity. This man is telling me that Iraqis are protected by God because of their faith in Allah, and that America, because of a lack of faith, deserves to be hit by a hurricane. With the gunfire in the background, the irony of his statement has not escaped me. The comment has also pissed me off.

I take a step forward.

He takes a step back.

"So God protects Iraqis from hurricanes? What about the violence? The fighting? The murders and executions? The poverty? Look around you! A man was murdered a few hundred meters away tonight! If God is protecting Iraq, why does God permit such violence here?"

Tornado hears the passion and anger in my voice, and he echoes my harsh language in his translation. The young man goes pale in the fluorescent light. He begins to speak, falters, and then goes quiet. He looks as if he has swallowed something unpleasant.

To the north, the gunfire has tapered quickly off. The stillness is only broken by single, sporadic shots in the distance. We stare at each other in the darkness.

The old man, pulling contemplatively on his white beard, takes a hesitant step forward and gently pushes the younger man back. Then he turns toward me and smiles apologetically: "Insh'Allah. All of that is in God's hands. It is for Allah to know who lives and who dies. It is not for us to question or explain the will of Allah. He gives help to those that ask, but in the end all of our fate is in his hands."

He touches his right hand to his chest, turns, and without looking back, quickly ushers the younger man, still pale, prayer beads clicking in his hand, into the shop.

Taking a deep breath, I turn and stand quietly in the darkness, watching the armored HMMWV slowly roll past in the shadowed street. I need a second to cool down.

The hood of the HMMWV has been emptied of concertina wire, and the two soldiers escorting it are taking off their tough, rawhide gloves. To the west, I can see that the wire roadblock has been stacked three strands high and tied tightly into the rusted steel bars of a power line. Any vehicle trying to drive through that is going to come to a sudden stop, tangled up in a mass of steel razor wire.

At least it is something.

Turning away from the now-quiet shop, I walk over to the roadblock to finish inspecting the reinforced obstacles. A few feet behind me, I hear the young private that was pulling security during my conversation mutter quietly under his breath. "Well, I'll take his help if he is offering it, but I am not leaving anything that I don't have to in Allah's hands."

Pulling on the concertina wire and checking for any gaps in the defenses, I can't help but smile. Those are my thoughts exactly.

![WHY I'M IN](image of worn fabric patch reading "WHY I'M IN")

NAME: **ARMY GIRL**
STATIONED IN: **AFGHANISTAN**
MILBLOG URL: **DESERTPHOENIX.BLOGSPOT.COM**

W hy do you stay in the military?" my friends and family ask me, and I look at them, dumbfounded. I have to pause and stop myself from saying something really hurtful and sarcastic. There's a war going on. Two, in fact. There are people being buried in mass graves, children starving, and women so desperate that they'll come up to you on the street and beg you to take their baby girls home with you to America. They single me out because I'm a woman. And despite my weapons, my uniform, and everything we use for protection and intimidation, they know, they think, they want to believe, that their daughters would have a better life with me than they themselves can give them. They must sense that my heart breaks every single time I think about it.

I serve so that these women have the hope of bringing their daughters up without subjecting them to the kind of life they have had to live. Americans have it so great and don't get it. Any one of those women could have been my grandmother, 50 or so years ago, in Korea, trying to give away her daughters—a burden on the family, another mouth to feed, another dowry to come up with. I know that my amazing, generous, self-sacrificing, and beautiful grandmother could never have imagined that she would have a daughter like my mom, whose strength and pride brought her through so many hardships, successes, and struggles. Or granddaughters like my sisters—giving, intelligent, and the world theirs to conquer. Or me, someone who despite everything and no matter how hard I try, will never be even one one-hundredth of the person she was. All I can do is hope to honor her memory by living my life to the fullest, whatever that entails, and holding on to that. Being true to myself, my heart, my dreams, and what makes me tick.

It just occurred to me that of the girls that I'm close to here, one was born to Iranian parents (and she's served several more years than I have and really cares), another was born to Filipino parents (and she's dedicated herself to this mission completely), and another is of Mexican heritage (and she's outside the wire as I write this). All of these girls are trying to bring to Afghanistan something more than what they have. I can't speak for them all, but I know that's why I'm in, and will stay in, this fight in one capacity or another until my time is up, and I've given all that I have to give.

WHEN THIS THING IS OVER

NAME: **CAPT LEE KELLEY**
STATIONED IN: **IRAQ**
HOMETOWN: **SALT LAKE CITY, UTAH**
MILBLOG URL: **WORDSMITHATWAR.BLOG-CITY.COM**

When this thing is over . . .

Just drop me off on any Arizona or Utah highway, where the buttes and the red rock canyons create optical illusions in the distance and across the horizon—I'll walk home.

Place me right at the top of a hill; I'll let gravity help me down.

Leave me on a back road in rural America, it doesn't matter where, so long as the leaves crunch under my feet and it is dusk, and as I walk, the shadows deepen and every so often I can see the lights from someone's house, and smell their cooking, and see families together on their couches watching movies, and hear their laughter.

Airlift me directly into a canoe in the middle of Black Creek in Missoula, Montana. It's fine, just leave me right there. I'll wet a hook for a while, then paddle to shore at dusk, enjoying the sound of the oar splashing in the clear, cold water. I'll clean the fish right there on the bank and cook it fresh over a small fire. Then I'll find the nearest road and hitchhike home.

Believe me, it's no inconvenience.

Instead of transporting me directly to my home of record, according to my official military personnel file, do something spontaneous for me. When I get back to the States, blindfold me, and then leave me in a pearl-white Corvette Stingray or a rebuilt '77 Jeep Cherokee that has a three-inch lift, with a full tank of gas, a sleeping bag in the backseat, a compass, and a map. Don't tell me where I am. Just leave me with my release papers and pat me on the back for my service to God and country. I'll remove the blindfold, crank the engine, turn on the radio, and start driving.

It doesn't matter what state or what city you leave me in—pick one. I'll have a grand adventure getting home.

Better yet, ask me where I'd like to be dropped off. I'll hop out right in front of my daughter's school. It's only 9 A.M. you say? That's just fine. I'll sit here on this nice wooden bench under this tree for a while. Leave me that newspaper, will you? Thanks. A little later I'll stroll up the street to where all the fast-food places are. I'll get a large fries at McDonald's, and I'll put lots of salt on them. Then I'll get a Frosty at Wendy's. And I'll pick up a Whopper with cheese, extra onion, from Burger King. Perhaps I'll browse the shelves of the local Barnes & Noble after lunch and finish up with a cup of Starbucks Irish Cream coffee. By the time I get back to the school, it will be just about time for the bell, and I'll surprise my daughter and hold her tiny hand all the way home.

My son's day care would be a fine place to drop me off, too. I'll go in and check him out early. It may take him a minute to realize that Daddy's back because he's only three, but I know he'll be very excited to see me. Then I'll take him with me to lunch and the bookstore, and to his sister's school. I'll walk all the way there with him on my shoulders. I'll buy him a Happy Meal with a toy.

Just get me on American soil.

Get me to New Orleans, and then put me in a taxi. I'll have the driver tune to a classic rock station that plays a lot of Queen and Styx and the Eagles and Steve Miller, or a nice jazz station, and bring me straight to my parents' house to surprise them. They'll be very pleased. I'll bring Mom a dozen roses and Dad the American flag I flew for him in Iraq.

I don't sit around all day dreaming of home. We are too busy, and there is a lot of important work to get done. It's when I sit down to write, and I'm trying not to bore readers with the little everyday mundane things that I do, that I get really nostalgic like this. I can't help it.

I honestly live an inspired life, and I am perfectly content to be here fighting in a war in Iraq if this is God's plan for me right now, but that's because I know this, too, is transitory. I wouldn't want to stay here. It's not my home.

It is not America.

My children are young enough that they won't realize I was gone for so long until they're older. One day when they are teenagers, it will dawn on them, and we'll be sitting around after a barbecue or something like that, and I'll get a faraway look in my eyes and realize that they're growing up too fast and that I am having an adult conversation with my children, who were just starting kindergarten when I went to Iraq.

And they'll say, "Wow, Dad, you were really gone for a year and a half? I don't remember it being so long."

In fact, they're young enough that one more day won't matter. I know, I know, their mother will probably pull her hair out if I wait any longer than I have to.

But still, I mean it.

Open a road map of the United States of America, pick a cozy little town like Kinston, North Carolina, or Gig Harbor, Washington, or Lafayette, Louisiana, or Moab, Utah, and just leave me there. It can be rock, asphalt, water, or sand; a busy college campus in New York or an abandoned park in Savannah, Georgia; the noise of a large highly populated metropolis or the silence of the Appalachian Trail. Put me next to an interstate or next to a campfire; in a library or at a rock concert; in California or Maine. Leave me in a nameless park, on a darkened street, or in a snowy canyon.

Don't ask me why. I don't want to explain it, and I can't explain it. But it will be fun and completely unplanned, and I like the idea of that very much. I'll have time to be utterly alone and think about a few things as I journey the last leg home to the life I left behind. And I'll have a lot to think about.

So just drop me off and let me drive out of the past, through the present, and into the unimaginable future of this crazy life.

THE KEEP

NAME: **SGT ROY BATTY**
STATIONED IN: **BAGHDAD, IRAQ**
HOMETOWN: **YELLOW SPRINGS, OHIO**

It was beautiful, once, in that brief, halcyon era of aggressive building, fueled by rising oil prices and the limitless credit of the newest despot on the block, in a yesterday where the Americans were friends, Arab-on-Persian warfare was still a few years away, and the power of Tikrit's favorite son ran unchecked. In that gleaming age, this building was a shopping mall, tall, white, and new, filled with fresh Western products, thanks to the hardworking folks over at the Ministry of Trade. An artificial waterfall cascaded down through the central interior courtyard, its clear raindrops illuminated by colored recessed lights, and children played in the eternal rain as it landed in the wading pool below. Escalators purred quietly, smoothly lifting suburban women up to the shops above, languid in their thin black robes, their dark eyes flashing in the crisp air-conditioning as they chatted to each other, excited at the prospects of a day's shopping. In the middle of the night, when the soldiers are sleeping, I fancy that I can still hear the whispers of their robes, edged with gold filigree, brushing against the tiled floors, somewhere back in the Stygian darkness.

Inside the human pipeline between Kuwait and Iraq, returning from R&R to the strange planet that is Baghdad, I ran into some fellow soldiers from my unit and heard the rumor for the first time. The Great Surge is on, and we are destined to be a part of it. The 82nd is in town, ready to bring the smackdown to the various militia groups that have held this city in their grip for so long. I am excited to be a part of it, even if it means leaving our little Mayberry of an FOB next to the Ministry of the Interior. FOB Shield had become a comfortable home, with its excellent chow hall, the friendly Pakistani guys at KBR, and the cool civilian cops of the IPLOs. By the time I got boots on ground at the Thunderdome, I was greeted with a hearty hand-shake and a directive: "Don't bother unpacking. We leave tomorrow. Oh, and your soldiers already packed the rest of your gear for you." At least that trial was taken care of; nowadays the worst part of a move is figuring out how to squeeze all of my junk into a couple of duffle bags and a ruck.

The initial rumors had been varied and interesting, which is how initial rumors usually sound. We're moving to a palace here, a hotel there, maybe an Iraqi Army FOB there. How bad can it be? I nursed a secret hope that they were going to put us up in one of those great five-star hotels that the reporters all stay in—maybe the Palestine Hotel, or the Al-Rasheed, downtown near the Green Zone. It was not to be, however, and instead we ended up in this bombed-out, half-torched, abandoned hulk of a building, somewhere on the far east side of Baghdad. The place is completely gutted and lacks every single amenity you need to work and live properly for three months. No electricity. No running water. No showers. No hot food. Not even a rickety bed to sleep in.

Nothing.

When I stepped out of my HMMWV and looked on its bul-let-riddled, RPG-spalled edifice for the first time, my dream of mimosas with Christiane Amanpour disappeared with a quiet, stom-ach-churning POP.

Our translators tell us that it was an Iraqi Ministry of Trade shopping mall, built in the '80s by Saddam Hussein. It is of strange, crenellated design, with a sawtoothed exterior in which each suc-cessive floor juts out above the one beneath it. With the concentric rings of T-walls that we have added around it, the entire complex now resembles some brutal, Vulcan castle. I think of the place as "The Keep." At some point, either during the first Gulf War or during our invasion in 2003, the mall was looted by the local Shia people. Every single possibly useful item was stripped and hauled away, and then the first floor was set on fire. There are black-charred smoke marks above the windows. The escalators look like the skeletons of long-dead reptiles, nothing but steel ribs and the lolling plastic tongues of the handrails. The Iraqi Army used the structure for a while as a machine-gun post, which explains why the fourth floor is filled with human excrement. We moved in four days ago and have been shoveling it out ever since, as well as trying to improve the place in other, slightly more advanced, ways.

But really, it's not that bad. Part of me has wanted a rougher experience. The surrealism of eating Alaskan king crab every single day for three months at Shield was not exactly what I had in mind when I first envisioned coming to this war-torn city. This is more of a "real" experience, as if we are getting a little taste of what it was like back in OIF I, during the invasion, when food was scarce but America was winning, and who cared if you only got one MRE a day when you were allowed to actually shoot back at the bad guys?

Our new home combines all the best aspects of living in a coal mine, a bunker, and a ruined city, in one convenient package. We've boarded up and sandbagged all of the windows, since the locals still like to take occasional potshots at us, so except for the gray light that filters down from the central skylight, the interior of the structure is perpetually dark. They handed out cool little LED lights for everyone the other day, which strap right onto your forehead. At any one time there are several hundred multicolored spheres of light bobbing around in the gloom, and out of that gloom lurch lumbering, hunchbacked troglodytes, bent low beneath the weight of their black weapons and gear; soldiers in body armor moving back and forth on their missions. I'm reminded simultaneously of H. G. Wells and Pogo— "We have met the Morlocks, and they are us."

Without electricity, there isn't a whole lot to do when you're not out on mission. Books have enjoyed a sudden rise in popularity, along with chess sets and cards. You start keeping farmers' hours, which means once it gets dark, everyone who's not on mission goes to sleep, as if on cue. It's interesting to think that the entire Western world is one flick of a switch away from the Middle Ages.

Sometimes we wander outside to enjoy the thrill of watching the local day laborers dig trenches in the mud for our plumbing. At one point I count ten soldiers standing around, smoking cigarettes, watching five old men and one teenage kid waist-deep in the muck. It smacks a little bit too much of colonialism for me, and after a while I amble off to enjoy the only other available spectacle: that of watching the trash fire. It's a massive steaming hump of coagulated plastic and scorched metal, but if you throw on a couple old MRE boxes full of trash, you can get a pretty good bonfire going in no time. Living fire in the middle of a dark night is always hypnotic, but when you add the bullet-scarred concrete looming overhead, and the stark, empty faces of the tactical vehicles clustered around, the effect is even more powerful. Nothing quite says "apocalypse" with the same intensity, and the mingled taste of burnt plastic and tobacco in your mouth can't help but add an extra dimension to one's cinematic memories of combat hell, born of Francis Ford Coppola and Joseph Conrad.

There are times, though, when the place still has a strange sort of timeless beauty to it. I woke up the other morning and swam my way out of the nylon folds of my sleeping bag. It was somewhere before six in the morning, and most of the soldiers were still asleep. A still, silver light was shining down the central courtyard, and the shaft was quietly full of birdsong. The little brown birds were flitting back and forth across the long-dead face of Saddam's waterfall, and my buddy, Phil, was standing there, out by the rails, alone, watching them with his head cocked to the side, peering up at them, that usual quizzical look on his face. The concrete stairs, once encased in marble, were salmon pink in the early morning light, looking more like ancient sandstone than raw cement. For that moment, it didn't look like just another bombed-out building in Iraq, but rather like something from the last Indiana Jones movie—the lost city of Petra, a rose-colored ruin forgotten in the desert, a relic full of whispered secrets. In that moment, before the cacophony of the Baghdad rush hour burst over us like a wave, anything was possible—perhaps even rebuilding this monument to suburban glory and mass consumerism.

Maybe then I could get that ice-cold Pepsi I've been dreaming of for the past ten days.

ON THE HOME FRONT

NAME: **SHARON SWANKE**
HUSBAND STATIONED IN: **KUWAIT**
HOMETOWN: **BLOOMINGTON, ILLINOIS**

O n the home front ...

1:30 A.M. The smoke detector on the main floor starts intermittently beeping, loud enough to wake me but not the kids. It is running low on batteries.

1:45 A.M. A thorough search of the house reveals that all batteries that fit the beeping smoke detector went overseas with deployed husband.

1:50 A.M. Shop for batteries at the local 24-hour store. Outside temperature is 17 degrees. My bed was a whole lot warmer than this.

2:10 A.M. Stand on chair and struggle with smoke detector reinstallation.

2:25 A.M. Check e-mail just once more. . . . No message from my spouse. Six days without a message and counting. Prior to his deployment, we had daily contact for 20 years. It is a big adjustment to go without: his message, his voice, his touch.

4:00 A.M. Eyes wide open, no sleep tonight.

Still, it is better than being shot at. Remind self: Next time husband deploys, check his bags for basic household items that are going with him, then restock said items.

A CLEAR SHOT

NAME: **CAPT BENJAMIN TUPPER**
STATIONED IN: **GHAZNI, AFGHANISTAN**
HOMETOWN: **SYRACUSE, NEW YORK**

O n 26 June 2006, CPL Polanski, our Afghan National Army (ANA) company, and I spent almost four hours surrounded and under fire from a very tenacious and determined Taliban group in Andar District, Ghazni Province. It was only one of three separate combat engagements that we weathered that day.

After nearly eight hours of ambush, counterambush, ineffective maneuvering, and a Black Ammo status, we took our cue from the setting sun and returned to our ANA FOB. Temperatures were still in the high nineties, and most of us were beyond dehydration. I remember stumbling into the TOC office and tossing my rifle, body armor, and helmet on the ground. Then I pretty much collapsed right there in the middle of the meeting room, spread-eagle on the floor.

Even though it was highly abnormal for someone to be laid out in the busy TOC, no one asked me what I was doing or why I was there. I alternated between mindlessly staring at the ceiling and rolling over and marveling at my hands. I felt like after 37 years of life, I had just discovered they were attached to my body.

After about 30 minutes of this mental escapism, I mustered the emotional and physical energy for a phone call home. I crawled over to the table that held the satellite phone, reached up, and called my wife. I remember trying to impress on her how lucky I was to be alive. I should have died in that long ordeal of being surrounded, and the more I told her this, the further I got from getting the point across. An RPG had me dead to rights, but by some manufacturing defect, the tail fin stabilizer didn't deploy, and it nose-dived into the ground in front of me instead of hitting me with a fatal kidney punch.

This war story carousel went round and round, until she finally told me to go to bed. I don't remember anything else about my conversation with her, or even how I made it from the TOC to my room.

The next morning started like every other one. Our adversaries in Andar permitted no rest for our weary bodies and shaky psyches. We had our regular team meeting and went over the day's planned mission. There was another patrol scheduled into the same area in which we had been ambushed three times the day before. The same undermanned and poorly planned mission into Andar was laid on for us.

Fortunately, I wouldn't have to endure the bloodbath that was only hours from occurring. I was physically sick, with an extreme case of diarrhea and dehydration, and mentally I was still rattled by the previous day's combat triple-header. Given my condition, my commander said I was in no shape to go out on mission that day. But I felt a sense of guilt that I was being a pussy and was sure all saw me as ducking my duty as an infantry officer.

So CPL Polanski, CAPT Krow, and CAPT Castro were selected as the crew for the sole up-armored Humvee going out on patrol that day. Within the hour, they linked up with the ANA company that would accompany them and made their way down Ring Road toward Andar District.

CPL Polanski had a habit of placing his digital camera in the windshield of the vehicle when he was the driver. He would put it on movie mode and let it run when he anticipated trouble. His two-gig memory card allowed for a good 45 minutes of footage. Because of this practice, he captured some memorable moments and great audio of our combat engagements.

The transcript you are about to read is the audio, as recorded on his camera, from the final assault on a small Andar village, on 27 June 2006. In this attack, one ANA soldier was killed by an RPG, and four Taliban were KIA. Most were shot by CAPT Krow. Both sides sustained numerous wounded.

Setting up the scene is simple: Ski is the driver, CAPT Krow is in the turret manning the M240 Bravo machine gun, and CAPT Castro is commanding the vehicle, trying to manage the fight as best he can. Janis, the Afghan combat interpreter, sits in the backseat, communicating with the ANA on a handheld radio.

On the audio, the noises of the incoming and outgoing fires are deafening at times. Add to this the clunky hum of the Humvee engine and the radio traffic squawking, and you can appreciate the confusion and perhaps understand the amount of repetition of orders and comments passed among the crew of the Humvee.

CPL Polanski is driving the Humvee out of a narrow alley on the outskirts of the village, and CAPT Krow is engaging some Taliban who are attempting to cross an open road. Ahead, about 50 meters, is an opening where ANA and ANP (Afghan National Police) have set up a supporting fire position. . . .

Audio starts:
>   (Heavy gunfire from the 240.)
KROW: "He went down!"
SKI: "Nice, you want me to go forward?"
KROW: "Fuck!" (The 240 Bravo machine gun jams.)
CASTRO: "Yeah, yeah, go forward, see if we can go to an open field."
KROW: "He had a fucking weapon!"
CASTRO: "OK, get to a fucking open field!"
KROW: "He went down, that's all I know."
SKI: "That's what's up!"
CASTRO: "You shot someone, you saw someone go down?!"
KROW: "Yeah, I seen somebody fall down."
CASTRO: "OK, then we gonna search in a minute over there."
>   (The vehicle starts moving forward toward the opening and the ANA and ANP soldiers.)
>   (Incoming gunfire is heard.)
>   (Vehicle stops near the opening.)
KROW: "Goddammit, I don't have a shot here!"
SKI: "Back up?"
CASTRO: "Do you have a shot?"
KROW: "The wall's too high!"
>   (The vehicle creeps forward.)
CASTRO: "Can you see anything?"

KROW: "Trees are in my way!"

CASTRO: "The wall finishes over here. Once the wall finishes you should have a clear shot."

CASTRO: "The ANP are calling us. Go, go, go!"

CASTRO: "Do you have a clear shot now?"

CASTRO: "Get ready for it, get ready for it . . ."

CASTRO: "Here, you have a clear shot?"

KROW: "No, I don't have a clear shot!"

(ANP soldiers yelling in background.)

KROW: "What is he saying?"

JANIS: "He is saying they [Taliban] are in the corner of that hill."

CASTRO: "Lets get over there then."

SKI: "Huh?"

CASTRO: "Go forward, and then turn to your left."

JANIS: "One of the ANA is wounded."

CASTRO: "One is wounded?"

SKI: "Where?"

KROW: "Right there!"

SKI: "Want me to give him first aid?"

CASTRO: "Yeah, fuck the risk."

JANIS: "Don't go out there, they [Taliban] are in front of us there!"

KROW: "He's right behind us!"

CASTRO: "Wounded—"

(Audio is disrupted by a large near-miss explosion of an RPG aimed at the Humvee.)

KROW: "Goddammit!"

SKI: "Yo, I'm getting the fuck out of here!"

SKI: "You want me to go forward?"

KROW: "You need to either go backward or forward!"

(Vehicle starts moving forward.)

CASTRO: "Right here."

KROW: "STOP!"

CASTRO: "You got a clear shot? Go for it!"

(Long bursts of 240 machine-gun fire.)

KROW: "I'm out!"

(Reloading noises—ammo cans clanking. Continued 240 Bravo fire, as well as incoming shots.)

CASTRO: "The ANA is moving. Fire! Fire!"

(Audio disrupted from another RPG explosion near the Humvee.)

KROW: "See that wall? They are right in there!"

SKI: "I wish I had a fucking 203 [grenade launcher]!"

(Incoming enemy AK-47 and RPK machine-gun fire.)

KROW: "Where the fuck did that come from?"

CASTRO: "Where is the guy that's wounded?"

KROW: "He's right back there, he's sitting there on the side of the road!"

SKI: "Get me the [medical aid] bag quick. I'm gonna run!"

SKI: "Get me the bag!"

CASTRO: "Hang on, I'll cover you!"

SKI: "Start shooting!"

(Extensive incoming/outgoing fire as Ski exits the vehicle and runs back to treat the wounded ANA soldier.)

(Gunfire.)

(Gunfire.)

(RPG explosion.)

(Gunfire.)

Audio ends.

Postscript: CAPT Krow was severely injured by an RPG weeks later, within kilometers of the site of this 27 June 2006 engagement. He was in Afghanistan for only six weeks before he was evacuated back to Walter Reed for extensive surgeries and rehabilitation.

The names Krow and Castro are modifications of their real last names, in order to respect their desire for anonymity.

FEBRUARY 27TH

Name: **AMERICAN SOLDIER**
Returned from: **IRAQ**
Milblog URL: **SOLDIERLIFE.COM**

M ost soldiers will tell you that the things they see during the war stay in the war. They experience it and deal with it at a later time. Well that time has come for me. February 27th.

Let me take you back to a year ago. An irrelevant city, a nameless street, and a small home where a little girl and her mother lived. I never did see the father during my many trips past this home. I often wondered where he was—dead, divorced, who knows. I'd have my gunner hand out extra candy whenever we'd pass. The child looked like my own daughter. Dark, wavy hair, charcoal eyes, and tan skin. She always had a smile and waved, while the boys tried to look tough. She would giggle and laugh at us. It brought a piece of home to me during the long nights on patrol or the early morning stroll.

We all had ways to deal with our tour. For me it came to be about seeing the future of Iraq. These children loved us, and we appreciated it. However, this was not meant to be a happy story. This is reality in a war. And for me reality came crashing down.

We were heading out for a patrol and were doing our morning checks in different parts of the city, always keeping on a different path and being random, to avoid any trouble. This doesn't always work because someone can just wait, and sooner or later they will hit you. We all get blown up. That is just the fact of war and patrolling outside the wire.

As we neared the house of the little girl, we saw a bleak front yard. A few pottery planters, a metal grate door, and a white stone fence, and, of course, dirt. There was a makeshift soccer field adjacent—not a soccer field by Western standards, but these local kids would kick balls on it and play tag. I looked across and saw the little girl running back to her house. I was in the lead vehicle and radioed back to my trail vehicle to look out for kids running across the road. Watching the side of the roads for IEDs is tough enough, let alone when you have children running, without warning, in front of you.

She was running and waving and had that beautiful smile. Just like any child happy in their own little world. A smile came across my rough face, and I blinked my eyes and looked forward again. Our vehicle is passing by. The sun reveals itself in my window, and I squint. The stinging of sweat in my eyes irritates them. I rub my eyes and look in my rearview mirror, and I lean forward.

The spiraling trail smoke from a rocket. It is flying toward where my vehicle has just passed. With a thunderous boom it explodes. My face, half-smile fading, goes into war mode. My trail vehicle takes evasive action, going around where the rocket had impacted. My driver speeds up, and we get ourselves in a better fighting posture. We drive around a corner to try and identify the culprit, but like most times, he fades into the shadows. We go back to check out the area and my heart stops. The smiling face, the peaceful bliss, and the innocent child, now on the ground.

Her mother had run to her and was now crouched down beside her. She lifted her up and was crying at us, damning us with a language I could not understand. As we approached the house, we came under small arms fire and had to move out of the area fast. We could not go back to check on her, but we found out the result later on. That area became empty to me. No more smiling face, no more innocence. It was taken away, and I was a part of that. A burden I live with to this day.

I look back at it, and it really hurts me inside. Something in my heart died that day. I can deal with seeing bad guys blown apart or hurt but not children. It breaks me and goes deeper than any other pain.

Later that day I was involved in a situation that earned me a Purple Heart. But the date is not seared into my brain due to the medal but due to the loss of a child. I look at the medal, and that is what I remember. The grind of battle wears on the toughest of men. The experience is stored away until various anniversary days come and go. February 27th is one of my dates.

WAR COCAINE

NAME: **SPC GORDON ALANKO (Teflon Don)**
STATIONED IN: **RAMADI, IRAQ**
MILBLOG URL: **ACUTEPOLITICS.BLOGSPOT.COM**

There's a rush that comes on the heels of a significant event here. After the IED explodes, or the RPG whistles overhead, or the shot cracks past, there's a moment of panic as you process the fact that you are still alive—that this time, they missed you. After that second's hesitation, the rush hits.

No one really knows what it is, exactly, but we all feel it. It's physical. It's emotional. For some, it's spiritual. Some say it's endorphins or adrenaline; some say it's rage, or hate, or joy. Some say it's safety—the knowledge that someone is watching out for you. It's different for everyone, but it's always there.

For me, the rush is mostly exhilaration. It's a feeling of invulnerability. I've heard the unforgettable sound of an RPG somewhere very, very near my little sector of space and stood a little taller, yelling, "Missed me, you bastards!" as I spun the turret and looked for the shooter.

The first time I got blown up, I had to remind myself to get up and look around for the trigger man or possible gunmen, set to take advantage of the confusion. I felt like I was floating through a world where time stood still. There's something about looking directly at an artillery shell and seeing it vanish with a sharp crack and rush of dust and debris that changes you. My brain was yelling at me: "This isn't normal! You shouldn't be alive and thinking right now!" And my body was yelling back: "Well, I'm definitely alive, so hoist your doubting ass up into the turret!"

I've never felt more alive than I do in the moments after a near miss. I feel the same way after a big jump skiing or after jumping off a bridge, but here the feeling is magnified a hundredfold. It's incredible when you do something that you shouldn't live through but do.

Some might call me sick or crazy. I assure you that I am sane and very much alive.

LOST INNOCENCE

NAME: **1SG TROY STEWARD (Bouhammer)**
STATIONED IN: **SHARANA, AFGHANISTAN**
HOMETOWN: **AMHERST, NEW YORK**
MILBLOG URL: **BOUHAMMER.COM**

It was a new day, and time for more village patrols, where we pull in, talk to the locals and elders, and let them know about the upcoming *Shura*. We press them on Taliban presence and safety in the village, blah, blah, blah—all the same stuff. The adults may or may not tell you anything. Kids are still the best source of information. They will tell the truth as long as they don't think they will get in trouble for it.

Jawed has a good eye for who to talk to and through many missions has repeatedly picked the right man or boy out of a crowd and been able to get some type of intel from them. On this day, we went through about five villages. Somewhere along the way, Face pulled me into the shade of a tree, which was a nice relief, and we just hung back and let the ANA and the 10th Mountain work most of the people for intel. Jawed spotted this one little boy who was about 10 to 12 years old. Jawed told me later he was just not acting the same as the other boys, and we soon found out why.

Through Jawed talking to him, we found out that the boy's father had been murdered by Taliban just 12 days earlier. Apparently the boy's father worked for the government of the province and was home one night when the Taliban came into the village. I guess it did not take long for the locals to tell the Taliban that he was a government employee. They busted into his house and started beating him and questioning him in front of his family. They made the whole family, including the boy, watch him get beaten like a dog. After they beat him really badly, he admitted that he worked for the governor of the province, and they took him out to the field behind the house.

According to the boy's words, they hit his father with something in the head and split it in two pieces. The boy was quite descriptive about this, so it made us think they must have hit him in the top of the head with an ax.

The boy was somber and not begging us for things like other boys did—we ran the rest of them off repeatedly while talking to him. He also told us that none of the local men would help the family with retrieving his father's body from the field, and even the mullah of the mosque we were sitting right next to refused to give funeral rites or hold a funeral procession because the man worked for the government. This means the whole town is dirty, or the whole town is scared to death of having the same happen to them. Either way, it just pisses you off to think you are trying to help these people, give them winter food and supplies, and take care of them, when they won't even help a man's family out after he was just brutally murdered.

I almost never personally give out food or water when we are stopped because I don't want all the kids begging me. But this time I made it a point to give the kid some snacks and some bottled water. Not because he gave us the info, but because for one of the first times since I have been here, I felt sorry for a local person that is not in the ANA. Normally, they are all just in the way and always considered a threat. This time I felt bad for the kid, truly bad for him, and it just made me think what a sucky start to a life he has had. I figured the least we could do is give him some good water and the tasty treats that we take for granted, hoping maybe they would put a smile on his face.

In countries like this where the people are destined for poverty, sickness, and possibly early death just by being born here, you have to block out all your emotions, or it will eat you up. Each of these people has a sob story, but not one you can listen to. The enemy on the battlefield is just a target of opportunity and not someone's father, son, or brother. They are a target that must be eliminated, and when you see them drop, you just mark that as another one that can't kill you.

I am not a liberal, bleeding-heart type of person (in case you haven't figured that out yet), but I am a human being that has a family back home and people I love and care about, both family and not family. I am not a coldhearted killer, but I am a soldier. The only way a soldier makes it through the places and events that we must walk through is to remove the emotion and spirit from the people that are around us. It is easy with adults—actually very easy—but with kids, it is not. When you hear a little boy laugh or a girl giggle, you are reminded of the innocence these kids deserve but will never realize. They are destined to a life one-tenth of which would drive a kid in our country to years of Prozac and therapy. It makes the kids hard mentally. They are not allowed to enjoy being kids.

When you are in a field trying to drag your father's split-head body to a burial spot because nobody else will help you, your innocence is left in the field with your father's soul.

THE CHASM

NAME: **C. MALONEY**
HUSBAND: **ON HIS WAY HOME!**
MILBLOG URL: **CORPSDJOUR.BLOGSPOT.COM**

I've been away from *The Sandbox*. It was just too much. I am so thankful that this resource is here for the world to get a glimpse into the experiences of our military members, but it was a little too close and too personal and just too scary. But I am very happy to say that my husband is out. He is somewhere between there and home, and I'm ecstatic. Having him out of harm's way has afforded me the luxury of peace of mind, and the mental capacity to put my thoughts into words. And here they are: I support our troops, I'm conflicted on the war, but mostly I'm frustrated by the isolation.

I know I shouldn't complain that I get a call from my husband only twice a month, when my grandmother heard from her husband by letter only a handful of times a year during WWII. It's terrifying that death is a possibility, but I know the numbers pale in comparison to Vietnam. Watching your husband go off to war is as old as time—think of the Spartan saying: "Come home with your shield or on it." But for this war, it seems different. . . . It's just that now I feel like it's only me.

I'm one of the few wives that have the opportunity to live on base but work in a professional capacity at a leading company, and I can't tell you the echoing depth of the chasm that separates my two worlds. I walk into the office to talk of stock options, tax cuts, weekend parties, laissez-faire political debates. If I hear about the war at all, it's typically someone priming me to say that it's awful, that they should all come home—don't they know that can be offensive when my husband is risking his life to be there? I'll never forget the day that Al Zarqawi died and I mentioned the news to a college-educated coworker at my Fortune 500 company, and the response was, "Who?" Or when a war-age-eligible man asked me if my husband would be coming home for Christmas. "Nope, unfortunately Iraq doesn't close shop for the holidays." It's not that they don't care, it's that it just doesn't affect them.

Then I hop the train back to my other life. When I come home, I pass through the guarded gates of my Marine Corps life into this parallel dimension. Back here the streets are full of women taking out the trash and climbing on roofs to put up the Christmas lights because Daddy isn't home to do it. Back on base I always have a friend that is about to come home and another that is about to leave. Back home, women are crying because they're afraid that their children won't remember their fathers. On my street, there is a rotation of "Welcome Home, Daddy" signs that fill me with pride and smiles, but also make me want to cry because I want it to be my turn. Back home I know not to knock on a friend's door without calling first, lest she think that that knock is CACO on the other side telling her that her husband didn't make it. Back home, I have to close my front door, because hearing car doors shut brings up images of men in blue walking up to my door and delivering the bad news.

I don't want to complain; I have loved many experiences I've had with the MC life; it's fast and furious and always entertaining. My friends on the perpetual cycle of deployments do not feel sorry for themselves, and neither do I. But still, I'm left with a feeling of frustration, and it comes down to this: The burden is just too big to be borne by so few.

COPING

NAME: **SPC J. R. SALZMAN**
RETURNED FROM: **IRAQ**
MILBLOG URL: **JRSALZMAN.COM/WEBLOG**

I'm doing the best that I can, considering. I spend a lot of time really pissed off or really upset. I know I am getting better at a pretty good rate, but still. In Iraq I was the go-to guy for anything that could go wrong with my CET's (convoy escort team) Humvees. I was the guy that could build or fix anything. Heck, I even built the door and a bench for the building our company stages in for convoys, simply because I was bored and had a little extra time before I went on R&R in November. There was nothing I couldn't fix, build, or do.

Now I'm struggling with the mentality that I'm just a one-armed, four-fingered gimp. I have sharp memories of the accident that haunt me every day: the sudden explosion, the taste of blood in my mouth, realizing the bottom half of my arm was missing with nothing left but a couple of fingers and part of my hand hanging off by some skin and tendons, and then realizing how much pain I was in. All I could do was hold the end of my blown-off right arm with my shrapnel-filled left hand and wait for the medic to arrive and put a tourniquet on. The most terrifying part of the memories is constantly remembering my gunner screaming and then looking down and realizing my arm was nothing more than some ragged meat and two bones sticking out.

I realize there are a lot of other people out there who are worse off than me. I am not asking for sympathy here. All I am trying to do is let you know what it is like to experience this. I have constant phantom pain in my arm where it feels like my hand is still there, and someone is sawing on it with a knife. The nerves are still trying to tell my brain that something is wrong. The phantom pain is there every moment of the day and hurts like hell. My left hand is barely functional since the surgery. What really pisses me off the most is that my left hand feels like it isn't put together right. The doctors removed my ring finger all the way down into my hand, and then pulled my pinky next to my middle finger and tied the tendons together. When I bend my fingers, it feels like the bones are at different lengths and just don't line up right. I was really hoping I would at least have one completely functioning hand since I lost an arm. Unfortunately, because of my wedding ring stripping the skin down to the bone, and multiple pieces of shrapnel that entered my hand and severed my nerves, and the shrapnel that completely shattered my ring finger's knuckle, this wasn't to be.

I am happy that I am finally rid of all the tubes, IVs, nerve blocks, and catheters sticking out of my body. Today is the first time in over a month I haven't had an IV or some other tube sticking out of my body. I am finally to the point where I can go to the bathroom by myself without any help. What is really sad to me when I think about it is how lucky I am compared to a lot of the other people here at Walter Reed. I think of the pain and frustration I am experiencing, and I realize how it is multiplied for them. My pain is always there, and I'm told it will be for months to come. I can only imagine what it is like for the others here. There are soldiers here with injuries that I cannot even describe. Some are missing both legs. Some are missing both legs and both arms. When I think of this, I can't help but feel a little selfish for my own grief.

I spend a lot of time crying, and I don't know why. Sometimes I look at my hand or I look at my arm, and I just start crying. I think of when my hand used to be there, or when my arm used to be there, and what it was like. The arm that was there for the last 27 years is suddenly gone. All the little blemishes, all the little battle wounds, all the little scars from being a carpenter, everything is gone. The ring finger that held my wedding ring that was put on by my loving wife is gone. The last time I saw my wedding ring it was being snipped off with a pair of bolt cutters at the hospital in the Green Zone in Baghdad. It was also in the Green Zone that I got to look at my arm and see that it had been sheared off by shrapnel. It was a gruesome sight, but I couldn't help but look. It's an image that will forever be burned in my mind. Sometimes the loss feels overwhelming for me, and I just start crying. Other times I'm very positive and look forward to getting out of here and getting on with my life. Other times I just don't know what to think.

Please remember this when you think about freedom. This isn't a dream; this isn't some fictional story about patriotism; this isn't some story I'm writing to be a hero. This is my life here at Walter Reed. I am the true cost of freedom. Welcome to my life.

CALLING DR. RUTH

NAME: **CAPT DOUG TRAVERSA**
STATIONED IN: **KABUL, AFGHANISTAN**
HOMETOWN: **TULLAHOMA, TENNESSEE**
MILBLOG URL: **TRAVERSA.TYPEPAD.COM**

I n ongoing conversations with my translator, Hamid, I continue to learn more and more, not all of it good. Despite this, Hamid is my friend. His world is stunningly different from mine, and sometimes the realization is jarring. Some people are wondering why we are over here supporting a government made up of people with such beliefs. The political and security issues aside, simply working with Afghans and sharing ideas is a good thing. No, they aren't all going to suddenly change overnight, but perhaps Hamid will treat his wife more humanely (once he gets married) due to our conversations. Ideas and free thought are fantastic. That's why the Taliban shut off all communication with the outside world. They didn't want their people exposed to other ideas. Anyhow, here's how the rest of our conversation went.

After our discussion about marriage, I was pretty worn out. I looked back down at the *Stars and Stripes* and saw an article about raids on a bunch of drinking establishments in Kabul. I asked Hamid if he had heard about this.

"Oh, yes, they are usually Chinese restaurants."

"So the Chinese restaurants serve alcohol?"

Hamid nodded. "Oh, yes, and they have prostitutes, too."

"What?" I exclaimed.

"Yes, they come over here with Chinese women, and have food, but you can also spend time with the woman. It costs $60 for a half hour."

Hamid is full of surprises. "How would you know that?" I asked.

"The soldiers talk about this all the time. Many of them go."

"You're kidding. Isn't it bad for them to go to a prostitute?"

"Oh, no, it's fine," he assured me.

I was incredulous. "So Islam allows them to go to prostitutes?"

"No, Islam does not," he corrected me. "I mean the government doesn't care."

This, of course, didn't jive with the newspaper article. As best as I can figure it, once in a while the government raids the houses of ill repute to keep the hardliners happy. But apparently it's not a big deal to get into these places. Where soldiers get the money is another question. Sixty dollars is a lot of dough. But Hamid has an apparently encyclopedic knowledge of the dark underbelly of Kabul. I will spare you the details.

I went back to the paper and turned the page. There was a large in-profile photo of an older black man with a beard. Hamid asked me who he was. I scanned quickly and explained: "This is an article about gays and lesbians in the movie business. It says that audiences don't seem to care so much whether actors are homosexuals, but the movie industry doesn't like to use them in movies."

I might as well have lit the fuse to a barrel of TNT. Hamid did not disappoint me.

"But he is old," he exclaimed, looking confused.

"So what?" I said, just as confused.

"When people get old, they turn to God, because they know they will die soon."

"So what?" I asked again, doing my best impersonation of a broken record.

"But he should not be gay if he is old. He should be turning to God."

"Hamid, he doesn't think he is sinning or doing anything wrong. He just likes men rather than women."

"So he doesn't believe in God?" Hamid asked, trying to grasp the concept of an older gay man.

"I don't know if he does or not. Plenty of homosexuals believe in God. They just don't believe in your God." I could tell his brain was turning into Jell-O.

"So are there gay Muslims in America?"

"I have no idea. I know there are many gays that call themselves Christians, even though conservative Christians who take the Bible literally say homosexuality is a sin and God hates it. Yet, there are many people who believe that older parts of the Bible don't apply today, so the verses that forbid homosexuality don't apply now. There may be Muslims in America who believe that about the Qu'ran, too."

Hamid shook his head. "No, that's not right. Men should not be gay. Now when they are young, they don't take their religion seriously, and they may try this, but when they get older, they reject it and turn to God."

Now I was pulling my hair out. "Hamid, that is what you believe, but many people believe very different things. You know that is what America is like."

"But still," he protested, "they should change when they get older."

"Hamid, when you get older, do you think you could suddenly decide you liked men rather than women?"

"Oh, no, of course not."

"So why do you think others can change? I'm not an expert on why some people are gay, but I doubt they just decide to be gay. Even though it is not illegal in America, there are many people who hate gays and even more who think it is a sin against God. Sometimes people beat gays up, just because they are gay. Sometimes they are murdered for it. Just like you and I are attracted to women, others are attracted to people of the same sex. Yet they certainly don't think they need to change, and they don't think they are sinning. It would be like saying you should become a woman because it's a sin to be a man. Would you wish to become a woman? Could you?"

He heard the words, but I don't think they made any sense to him.

"I've heard that in Canada gays can get married. Is this true?" he inquired.

"Yes, I think so."

"Why would they want to get married? They can't have children."

Here we go again. Hamid believed the only purpose of marriage was to have as many kids as possible. Did I mention that Afghanistan has the highest birthrate per capita in the world? I think I now know why.

I explained that if two people love each other, even two gay people, they would naturally want to get married. I also explained that spouses got other benefits, like medical coverage, and that was another reason for wanting to get married.

"But they can't have kids," he protested again.

"Look, I keep telling you that in America, people don't get married just to have kids. Many couples choose to never have kids, because they just want to be together, just the two of them. Besides, they could adopt children if they wanted to."

"But they would not really be your children. . . ."

I gave him the stern look again. "My brother was adopted. Are you saying he wasn't really my brother?" Oh, what an awkward silence ensued. He finally looked down at the table. "Of course, he is your brother."

I eased up a bit. "I know what you are trying to say, but there are many children without parents, and many people adopt. Don't ever say they aren't really their children. It's not the blood relation that matters; it's the love given that makes them your children."

"But I don't understand how a woman can make another woman happy in bed. Or a man make a man happy."

Terrific. How did I know we'd end up here? "Hamid, you don't know anything about sex, do you?"

"No."

"Do you want me to explain it to you?"

"Yes."

"Right here? Right now?" I looked around to make sure no one would be listening in.

"Yes, please."

So I had to explain, in detail (with tactfulness, of course), the intricacies of lovemaking to a 27-year-old whose total knowledge came from the snickering coarse talk of the soldiers, not to mention the Marines he used to work for. I wasn't at all embarrassed by this, as he certainly needed to know what was what. He really knew next to nothing. I guess it's not that important when you look at women as nothing but baby factories. I'm fairly certain you can't go down to the bookstore and buy *The Joy of Sex* translated into Dari. I do know that sex counselor wasn't in my job description.

TIME

Name: **CAPT MIKE TOOMER**
Stationed in: **KABUL, AFGHANISTAN**
Hometown: **SACO, MAINE**

I have been in-country for over nine months, spending just about every day with Afghans, either the ANA or interpreters. I spent six weeks "down range" in the Gardez area training the ANA on logistics and had the opportunity to interact with other ANA soldiers and mentors. I shared my observations with them and listened to them, and from this experience (purely anecdotal, this isn't a research article) I have come to the conclusion that Afghanistan is eerily similar to medieval Europe.

A majority of the population—about 60 percent overall—is illiterate. Once you get out of the bigger cities (Kabul, Mazar-e Sharif, Harat), the percentage is significantly higher. Afghan society is very simple. Out in the hinterland, most people are subsistence farmers, and even the vast majority of those living in the cities spend their days just trying to survive. The simplicity of the society, along with little to no education, results in a society of people who, for the most part, cannot think abstractly.

As in medieval Europe, the most literate and sophisticated segment of society is the clergy, and they use this to their advantage. Because most of the population is merely attempting to survive, with little comfort, religion plays a central part in their lives. It is necessary that there be a reward at the end for all the suffering people are going through. The problem is that the Qu'ran is written in Arabic, a language that the vast majority does not understand, let alone read. And the services here, which really consist of a recitation of the Qu'ran, are also in Arabic. In medieval Europe, services were given in Latin, which the masses could not understand. In both cases, the only thing most people know about the religion so central to their lives is what the clergy tells them—what the clergy wants them to know. This gives the clergy an incredible amount of power, and it is they, not the government, who control the people. In Europe, kings derived their authority from God, supported by the clergy. It isn't much different here, in that Afghanistan is an "Islamic" republic, based on the religion and Islamic law.

All this is a way of explaining why people support the Taliban and Osama bin Laden and are willing to strap explosive vests to their bodies in order to kill Americans. It also gives us an idea about how to proceed in an attempt to moderate this part of the world (not just Afghanistan). If your life sucks and the clergy tells you that the surest way to heaven is to kill infidels, chances are you will take that course. Why would the clergy send so many to death? Power. I am sure they believe that the Qu'ran reads the way they preach it, but also, if there is an Islamic state, who runs it? The clergy becomes the ruling class.

Another factor in all this, as I said, is the lack of education and the inability to think abstractly. They can't take the principles of a 1,300-year-old religion and apply them to a modern society. The vast majority of Afghans think concretely, in black and white, and are unable to determine the principles that underlie the religion. What the Qu'ran says, or what the mullah tells them, must be taken literally and applied the same way. If the interpretation of Islam is that everyone other then Muslims are infidels and must be converted or killed, then this is what the majority will believe. If the mullah says that the Americans and Coalition Forces are occupiers, here to wage war against Islam, then the call to jihad is believed and acted on—despite the fact that most of those who end up being killed in the name of jihad are Muslims. Instead of taking the principles that underlie the religion and applying them to a modern society, they are attempting to make a modern society fit a 1,300-year-old religion. Examples are the burka (yes, most women still wear them), women as second-class citizens, and a strong suspicion of all things not Muslim—like our assistance and attempts to bring them into the 21st century.

The $64,000 question: What will it take to moderate this religion and bring some sanity to this part of the world? The answer: time. Yes, time is the most important element, and we need to face this fact and understand that we are going to need to be here a long time, a generation at least. We need to educate the population, as we are currently doing. We are opening many schools, and the number of people receiving an education is up dramatically. But it will take time before those we are currently educating are able to rise to positions in which they can make a difference. Understand, too, that just about 40 percent of the population here is under the age of 15, which means that if we concentrate our efforts on them, the timeline for change shrinks. Time and commerce will bring sophistication to the society in general, which will help the population in their ability to adapt to the modern world.

Well, I have come to the end of this lecture. It may have been simplistic, but I've been working with the Afghans for nine months, and perhaps they are rubbing off on me as much as I am on them. It is what it is—my attempt to explain what I have seen and experienced. My hope is that you find it helpful in trying to understand why this part of the world is as crazy as it seems.

THE ROOT(S) OF ALL EVIL

NAME: **MAJ MICHAEL IRWIN**
RETURNED FROM: **IRAQ**
MILBLOG URL: **CYBIRR.BLOGSPOT.COM**

For the last few days I have been traveling around Iraq visiting several Iraqi headquarters and its Ministry of Defense. My job has been to get some profiles on the various personalities and processes the Iraqi Air Force has to work with. My impressions, along with those of other advisers, are being consolidated as a report on Iraqi military fitness.

That is not important. What is important is that I have faced the root (or roots, there are three) of all that is evil: broccoli, cauliflower, and tomatoes.

While visiting one of the offices in the Ministry of Defense, I was invited to have a light meal with the deputy for the operations division. A nice colonel named Amir politely ushered me into the office and offered me tea. Arabic tea is one of the bright spots in my day, as it is quite good and makes for a starting point for a conversation. As we sipped our tea, we exchanged some pleasantries (via an interpreter—the colonel's English required occasional support, typical in my dealings and not a criticism by any means) and discussed what we would be talking about.

Then the orderly (colonels get orderlies) brought in a plate of food.

On this plate was what I took to be Iraqi focaccia. You have probably had focaccia at an Italian restaurant, of course—thick bread with cheese and sometimes vegetables, mostly tomatoes. I tend to avoid it unless I can have it my way, without tomatoes. This particular piece of bread was covered with chopped broccoli, cauliflower, and tomatoes. Covered is such an inadequate word . . . it was heaped on. You couldn't have added another particle on top. I was simply aghast!

We were taught, in our Arabic sensitivity classes (me sensitive, *ha!*), that when offered food, we must be absolutely thrilled at the presentation, and consume it with relish, and comment on the exquisite taste and generosity of our host.

It was at this point that General Q, chief of Iraqi Air Force operations, strode in, along with his entourage. He was going to snack with us.

I was doomed.

The colonel cut me a huge slice of this thing. And with a sense of great pride at his staff kitchen's accomplishment, put it on a plate and placed it before me—even before serving General Q. At this point I was thinking, "I've got 30 rounds. I'd probably be able to get to the door and maybe make it to the Humvee. . . ."

The general (obviously sensing my discomfiture) spoke in a deep basso voice via the interpreter: "Ah, this is my favorite. Please, go ahead and eat, Major."

The things I do for my country . . .

After my nightmarish meal, our conversation turned to business. The members of the general's entourage were all talking at once, and it was difficult for me to hear the interpreter. In an attempt to lighten the mood (and get my mind off the churning in my stomach), I joked to the general that we were both follicly challenged, and clearly our intelligence and knowledge on the matters at hand is what had caused us to be so hair-negative. "Perhaps it would be best if we were the only ones speaking right now."

The interpreter passed my comment on to Q, and several people laughed at the joke. It was not a very good joke, but the Iraqis are nothing if not polite. Q didn't smile at all, but spoke in his deep voice. Suddenly all other talking stopped.

"The general," my interpreter explained, "he says, 'Yes, only the bald men may speak.'"

DRIVING IN AFGHANISTAN

NAME: **CAPT DOUG TEMPLETON**
STATIONED IN: **AFGHANISTAN**
HOMETOWN: **KANSAS CITY, MISSOURI**

As near as I can tell, there are no such things as traffic laws here. You are supposed to have a license, but I'm told that with the right bribe you can skip the test and be on your merry way—and from what I've seen, I have no doubt this is true.

I am told there is a traffic light in Afghanistan. One. And it doesn't work. I have yet to find a speed limit sign except in the NATO camps. Stop signs? Well, "stop" is regarded as a suggestion, not a requirement. So it's pretty much a free-for-all.

Just getting to work each day is exciting. Everywhere you look there are cars, trucks, horses and carts, and donkeys, all sharing the same semipaved, pothole-riddled, dirty roads. People dart out from side streets and never look. They just stick their nose out and hope it's still there when they complete their turn. The mud has been pretty bad, so the trucks no longer park on the shoulders. They just park on the road, taking up the lane. Since there are usually vehicles on both sides, this only leaves you a small passage to navigate through, while avoiding oncoming traffic doing the same thing. More than once during a near miss, the air has been sucked out of our vehicle by a collective gasp. I won't even mention where the seat cushion went.

Then there is the factor of who gets to be designated driver of the day. Some days it's a Mario Andretti wannabe; on others it may be someone who reminds you of your grandmother. I won't mention names, but there are some people who, as we leave  the gate, make me glad my will has been updated. All this at the same time we are looking for bad guys who are trying to activate that will. Fortunately, there have been very few accidents for us, and none of them causing injury to any of our group. Every time I make it through another day without incident I knock on wood. It's easy, as everything in my hooch is made of it.

Being home on leave made for some interesting moments. A couple of times I inspired my wife to say, "Don't even think about it." I guess driving on the other side of the road is a problem for her.

BACK TO WORK

NAME: **RN CLARA HART**
STATIONED IN: **A MILITARY HOSPITAL**
HOME STATE: **ILLINOIS**

I went back to work today after taking a few months off for some much-needed "rest and recovery." I decided to try two days a week and strictly on a temporary basis. As I walked down the hallway, my footsteps echoing, I wondered what the day would bring. My hand tapped the silver button on the wall, and the pneumatic doors opened with a quiet swish. It was still too early for any patients to have made it out of the OR, and the recovery room was eerily quiet. I wandered into the staff lounge, opened my locker, and stowed my things. Then, like my Marine and soldier counterparts readying for a mission, I loaded up with the tools of my trade. Pens, Sharpie marker, and index cards in one pocket; penlight, clamps/hemostats, trauma scissors in another; stethoscope draped over my shoulder—I was ready to start my day.

Walking to the nursing station, I picked up the schedule, scanning it to get a feel for how many patients were lined up and what types of surgeries they would have. Looking at the assignment board, I saw the bays I had been given and headed over to make sure all the equipment was in working order and I had all the necessary supplies. Once that task was completed, I sat down to wait.

As the patients began arriving, I quickly acclimated to being back in a military hospital—being called "ma'am" and "Ms. Hart" instead of plain ole "Clara." It was wonderful to once again have patients who were respectful, polite, and genuinely appreciated the care they received! Having spent the better part of my career working trauma/ER and flying medevacs, not always caring for the nicest, most law-abiding people, this behavior was not the norm, and returning from my hiatus, I appreciated how nice it is.

My day flew by, patients arriving, recovering, and then heading out the door. Pretty soon, one of the float nurses came over to relieve me for lunch, and I gave her a report on my patients and headed off in search of food. Returning from lunch, I watched as yet another patient was wheeled into one of my bays. I hurried over to take a report and sent the float nurse off to relieve some other starving caregiver. As I listened to the anesthesiologist, I learned my patient was a 33-year-old man, OIF, injured when an IED exploded under his vehicle. I did my assessment, noting his dressings, carefully making note of his injuries and his previous surgeries. I looked at his face, arms, and hands, peppered with shrapnel and cloaked in white gauze. I studied his chart and orders and set about finishing the post-op tasks. As I worked, I paid close attention to him and the monitors, watching his vital signs, gauging how quickly the anesthesia was wearing off and if he was in pain.

I called his name and saw his one unbandaged eye struggle to open. I told him his surgery was over, and he was in the recovery room. I asked him if he was in pain, and he said no. As I waited for the last vestiges of anesthesia to wear off and for him to emerge from his slumber, I spent a few brief moments completing the infernal paperwork that makes the nursing world go round.

I glanced up at the monitor and then over at my patient and was shocked to see tears silently streaming down his face. Moving closer to the bed I asked him if he was in pain, already thinking what pain medications he had ordered, but he only shook his head no. I quickly moved even closer and, grabbing a Kleenex in one hand and placing the other on his chest, I started to dry his tears. He looked up at me and in response to my silent questions said, "Ma'am, I'm not crying, I just got something in my eye." I nodded my head somberly and placed the hand holding the Kleenex on top of his head, lightly touching the stubble military guys call "hair." In a choked voice, he said to me, "Marines don't cry, ma'am, and I'm not crying." As I continued to dry his tears, I took one of his hands in mine. He grabbed on tightly, as if I was his lifeline, and I felt him taking strength from my quiet unquestioning presence. I went back to my charting, ignoring the sorrow draining down his face, all the while keeping my hand securely tucked in his. Minutes passed, and I felt him regain his composure, and the grasp on my hand loosed. I slid my hand out from his and walked over to the phone, my back to him, to call a report to the floor nurse.

As I talked with the receiving nurse, I glanced over my shoulder to see him wiping his face with his bandaged arms, looking around to make sure no one else had witnessed his private anguish. I quickly turned my back to him again, finishing my report. Striding back to his bedside, I readied him for transport, and as I did, he once again looked at me and implored, "Ma'am, I really wasn't crying. Please don't tell anyone I was." I looked at him and with a smile responded, "Can't talk about something I didn't see." He smiled back at me, relief evident in his face, and I asked him to do me a favor. "Anything, ma'am, just name it," came his speedy, earnest reply. "Please don't call me 'ma'am,'" I said. "It makes me feel old and decrepit. You can call me 'Clara,' OK?" "Clara?" he asked me. "Yep," I replied. "No more 'ma'am.' Got it?" "Got it, Clara," he said. We shared a smile, and then he was whisked away on his journey toward healing.

A LIFT TO THE AIRPORT

NAME: **CAPT ERIC COULSON (Badger 6)**
STATIONED IN: **RAMADI, IRAQ**
HOMETOWN: **ST. LOUIS, MISSOURI**
MILBLOG URL: **BADGERSFORWARD.BLOGSPOT.COM**

C an you give me a lift to the airport?" Back in Boise that gesture of assistance involves nothing more than a quick jaunt south on I-184, then west on I-84 to the airport exit, a right turn, south a block, then another right around the Chevron station, and then the long turn to the left before you make the decision to go to departing flights on the upper deck or arriving flights on the lower deck. A ten-minute trip, assuming no traffic.

In Iraq, though, getting a lift to the airport is a bit more complex.

Many if not most of us are in places where  fixed-wing aircraft do not land. Our options are to either drive or do the fancy-Manhattan-like thing and grab a rotary-wing bird to the airport. That is what I was scheduled to do when I went on leave last month.

Time was counting down for us to head to the helipad. It had been a beautiful day, a good day for flying, but now the weather was turning bad. We generally fly out a few days early so that people will be sure to hit their leave date, but because of then-recent events, this is the last day of my "window" to leave. If I don't get out now, the whole leave schedule will fall behind. I have promised Mrs. Badger 6 that I will be home by our anniversary on Tuesday, and it is Thursday night.

As I watch the rain roll in, the first sergeant of another company comes up to me.

"Hey, sir, I know you are supposed to leave tonight. We have a route clearance mission going to that same base. You want to ride along?"

Hmmmmm. A ride could be relatively short—a couple of hours—and in before midnight with the chance to get some sleep. On the other hand, I could get stuck sitting on two or three events and not get there till sunup. Still, if I ride with them, I am certain of getting there. I could wait on the flight line till 0300 and then still not leave. The patrol leaves in 15 minutes.

"Thanks, First Sergeant. Where are they lining up?"

I grab the other two soldiers I am traveling with, and we pick up our gear and head down to the patrol. Looking at the route, all we really need to do is get through the city of Ar Ramadi. Sure, anything can happen here, but there is a certain predictability to the war as well.

Patrol prep done, we are out the gate. It has been some time since I have been through the city, as we've been doing operations in other areas, and I am pleasantly surprised at the difference that has been made. A great deal of the debris, rubble, and garbage has been cleared away. People are starting to make this city inhabitable again.

Driving past Saddam's mosque, an area known for trouble, we keep a sharp lookout. We investigate a few things but find nothing. We are closing in on the far side of the city when all of a sudden a brilliant flame appears and then immediately disappears.

"Did you see that?"

"Yeah. What was it? A bomb?"

"I don't know. That was really weird."

We pull up and start looking.

"It was really too far from the road to be a bomb. Why would some idiot place a bomb over there?"

But that's what it was. Whoever set this event up had evidently been unable or unwilling to get very close to the road and placed the device way off to the side. Additionally, when it detonated, it only yielded a low-order blast. Some of the explosive did not go off. Good thing, right?

Wrong. Now we need to have the experts come out and dispose of the remainder, so some AIF character does not come along and try to reuse the stuff.

My thoughts at this point are purely selfish. This never happens when I am on patrols with my guys. I am going to be here all night! To make matters worse, the "experts" want to sit on their little base and have us bring the stuff to them. That's a no-go. We have to have a discussion on the radio for 30 minutes before they will even come out. Finally, they do, and we are rolling again.

All of a sudden we see red tracer fire to our south. The IPs and the AIF are having a little gunfight. Again: I never see this stuff, but now that I really need to get somewhere, it's coming out of the woodwork.

Finally, though, we are past that and on the edge of the city. Now we are passing the Al Anbar Law College; I so want a low-profile baseball hat that says Al Anbar Law to go along with my SIU Law, Duke Law, and Wisconsin Law hats. But I digress.

Back in the countryside we pick up the pace a little. And there are no more events. Dropped off by the patrol, my soldiers and I check in with the manifest people. We are told to be back at 0700. We wander over to billeting to get a bed for a few hours. By 0100 we are asleep.

Rotary wing did fly that night, but the other people coming from Ramadi got in at 0300 and got no sleep. So we made a good choice.

And I will never begrudge a friend a lift to the airport.

WALKING ON HISTORY

NAME: **SPC GORDON ALANKO** (Teflon Don)
STATIONED IN: **RAMADI, IRAQ**
MILBLOG URL: **ACUTEPOLITICS.BLOGSPOT.COM**

I am a shameless romantic, a slightly better than average student of history, and there is a current of idealism under my skin that has not yet been dulled by reality. Sometimes these qualities come together and leave me thinking to myself of times long gone and stories all but forgotten. Lately I've been thinking of the paradoxical enormity and insignificance of my presence here.

Here I stand, in modern-day Iraq. I have come farther to fight here than any soldier of any nation before me, and I fight with weapons and equipment that lay pale the panoply of earlier armies. I represent the pinnacle of force projection and decisive battle, and yet I fight here, where unnumbered young warriors have fought and died through time stretching out of memory. It was on this land that the Babylonian Empire arose out of those first Sumerian agrarians, only to be conquered by the Assyrians, and still later throw off the foreign chains. It was here that Alexander's phalanxes swept through, trailing Hellenism in their wake. The Romans, and later the Byzantines, drew their border with Persia at the Euphrates River. At that river was where the Sassanids made their stand against the spread of Arabian Islam. The khans of the Mongols laid this land waste, sometimes killing only to build their towers of bones higher.

This region is steeped in history. We walk on it; we breathe it in. Eons of history surround us, infiltrate us, and turn to dust beneath our feet. The ashes of countless cultures, civilizations, and rulers' dreams are in this earth. With each breath, I inhale a few molecules of the dying gasp of Cyrus II, the Persian "Constantine of the East." In the howling wind, I can almost hear the cries of a multitude, dying on killing grounds across the ages. The same wind carries the red dust that might yet hold a few drops of blood from the battle at Carrhae—the first, crushing defeat for Rome's red-blooded legions. Under my heel, a speck grinds into dust: the last grain of sand that remains of the Hanging Gardens of Babylon, which are now known only in legend. Some of the world's oldest religions tell us that somewhere in this ancient Cradle of Life, God himself breathed on this dust, and it became man, the father of us all. Whatever path we take here, we walk on history.

I walk softly, for I tread on the ghosts of years.

CLEANLINESS AND GODLINESS

NAME: **CAPT DOUG TRAVERSA**
STATIONED IN: **KABUL, AFGHANISTAN**
HOMETOWN: **TULLAHOMA, TENNESSEE**
MILBLOG URL: **TRAVERSA.TYPEPAD.COM**

Hamid swung by the hut today to get me for lunch after he had hitched a ride back to Phoenix. I was just finishing up some writing, so I had him come in.

"Remember our conversation about the Snickers bar yesterday?" (Drew and I had spent a great deal of effort trying to figure out what Hamid's favorite candy bar was.)

"Yes," he replied.

"Would you believe I wrote about that in my blog yesterday?" I laughed.

"No. Why would you want to write about that?" he exclaimed disbelievingly.

"Wait. I'll pull it up and read it to you." After a minute I had the blog up and started reading the section where Drew and I were trying to figure out what candy bar he wanted. As I read, Hamid stared at me in amazement.

"No, you didn't write that."

"Yes I did. I told you I write about our conversations. Let me finish reading."

As I continued, using proper tonal inflections, Hamid started laughing uncontrollably. I actually had to stop reading so he could recover and hear what I was saying.

Once I was finished, and he stopped laughing, he still seemed stunned.

"But who would want to read that? Are people really interested?"

I turned off the computer. "Yes, people really do read this stuff. They love to see what your lives are like, and our interactions with

CLEANLINESS AND GODLINESS

Afghans are interesting, even if we are trying to figure out what kind of candy bar you like. Most blogs are about combat, or at least being in a combat unit. But many of us don't see any combat. Some people enjoy reading about our lives, too."

I put on my weapon, and we headed off to chow. "Not only are you famous, but someone has already said they are going to send Snickers just for you."

"But doesn't it make me look bad if I am always asking for things?" I guess my lessons have been taking hold.

"I've also told them that you only ask because I am your friend, and it's OK in your culture to ask friends for things. It's just another way for people to learn about your way of doing things. Plus, I tell them how I like to give you a hard time when you ask for things. I have fun and get a laugh out of it."

After we got our food and sat down, I expected to eat in silence as usual, then talk. But Hamid was in a very talkative mood and launched right into questions. Today he wanted to talk about religion. He wanted to know where our religious leaders live, what they wear, and how we pray. I did my best to explain it all, considering how many different religions there are in America. He seemed very surprised that we only bow our heads to pray. Muslims must do ritual cleansings, and when they pray, they touch their foreheads to the ground.

Hamid began an explanation of the importance of cleanliness when praying. "As you know, we must wash ourselves before praying. In fact, if a man has had sex or a wet dream, he must not only do the usual cleaning, he must inhale water to clean inside his nose."

"What? You inhale water?" This was a new one on me. I'd never heard this before.

"Yes. You must cup water in your hand and inhale water until it goes up into your nose, where your eyes are. Then you blow it out. Sometimes it makes your eyes water."

I was still in shock. "Yes, I imagine it would."

"You must also shave at least every other week." He saw I was puzzled, since many Muslims have beards and a full head of hair. "Not your face—I mean your groin."

I don't know what comes after stunned, but whatever it is, I was there.

"You shave your groin?" I asked weakly.

"Yes, and our ass and armpits too."

What comes after the thing that comes after being stunned? Is there a word for it?

"You shave your armpits, groin, and ass? Every two weeks?" Clearly I was being punked. Where were the hidden cameras?

"Actually, I do it every week. I do it every Friday morning, since that is our best day [he meant holy day]. Don't you shave there?"

"No." Still reeling from too much information.

"You never shave your armpits? Never?" Hamid looked skeptical.

"No, never!" I pulled my T-shirt sleeve down to show him my hairy armpit. He actually recoiled a little bit.

"In America, women shave their armpits, but it's for looks, not for religious beliefs."

Hamid needed a little time to digest this. Clearly he had not realized just how unclean we were. He continued after a bit.

"I have heard that people from India do not bathe every day, and they can smell very bad."

Nonplussed, that's the word. I was nonplussed, as in "puzzled or perplexed." As a rule, Afghans aren't very fragrant. Of course, some are better than others, but there are some that clearly don't take their cleaning ritual very seriously.

"Hamid, I've not been around many Indians, so I couldn't say. But you realize that there are many Afghans who don't smell very good, don't you?"

"Well, some do not clean like they should. It is very important to be clean for God. As I said, I always get very clean on Fridays. We know the world will end on a Friday."

I give up. I thought I knew a great deal about Islam, but Hamid is showing me what a rank amateur I am.

"Friday?" I managed to utter.

"Yes, God will return and destroy the world on a Friday. It is written."

"In the Qu'ran?"

"Yes, our mullah tells us. There is something I've been meaning to ask my mullah."

I can hardly wait for the next bombshell. Hamid is in good form today.

"You know that a woman should cover most of her body. Only her face and her hands should show. Also a woman should not work outside the home."

I nodded. "I know that's what you believe."

"Women should also not talk to men outside of the family, but I have heard some say that a wife may only see her husband and her own brothers and father, no one else."

"But," I said, and felt like saying it several times, "your sister-in-law lives with you, and you see her. Are you saying that is wrong?"

"Some people think so. I need to ask my mullah."

I stared at him. I said one word. "Why?"

"What do you mean?"

"Why would you do this to a woman?"

"If I see a woman, I might have thoughts about her, or she about me," he replied.

"It sounds to me like you don't trust women."

"Oh, we trust them. But they might have thoughts to have sex with others."

"Hamid, I understand why you have these rules and what you hope to achieve, but basically you put women in a prison. They can't work, and they have to cover most of their body up, just to prevent bad thoughts. Why not make the men stay home and cover up, and let the women go out and run things."

Hamid really seemed to be thinking this over.

"No matter how much you say you love and respect your women, you essentially put them in prisons once they get married," I continued. "What if they want to go to work?"

"The man must provide a home and make the money." This is no different from the view of many fundamentalist Christians back home.

"Yes, I agree the man should work, but what if the woman wants to work?"

"You mean like a hobby?" he asked.

"Or just so she isn't bored."

"But she must keep up the house!" he protested.

"Look, my wife works three days a week. She'd be bored if she didn't go out and work. She likes making a little extra money, and she can quit if she wants to."

"If she is bored, she can watch TV." Hamid had it all figured out.

I decided to change tack a bit. "Doesn't it bother you to be working around our women? They don't dress the way you think they should."

"No, you have your own religion, so you worship God in your way. Is it true that all Americans believe in God?"

Don't you love the way our conversations bounce around?

"No, not all Americans believe in God, but probably a good majority do, though as I keep saying, there are many different religions."

"But they all believe in one God, right?"

"No. After all, we have Hindus in America, and they believe in many gods, just like the Hindus in India."

Hamid was the one who looked shocked this time.

I looked closely at him. "You do realize the Hindus worship many gods, don't you? You watch TV shows from India all the time."

He really seemed taken aback. "Yes, of course I knew this."

"Well, you certainly looked surprised when I said it. Have you heard of Mormons?"

"No."

"Well, they also believe in many gods, though they only worship one God. They also believe that one day they can become gods."

Now Hamid was at that point that comes after being stunned. He put down his silverware (OK, plasticware) and looked at me to see if I was joking.

"I'm serious," I stated firmly.

He threw up his hands and shook his head. "That is crazy. To think you can become a god."

With that, we finished cleaning up and headed out of the chow hall. We had both learned some surprising facts and, despite the vast gulf in our culture and beliefs, parted as good friends once again. I guess that's the bottom line here. No matter how bizarre the information that we relate to one another, nothing has weakened our friendship. Hopefully it is one of many seeds being planted in this country that will allow our peoples to grow closer.

ON BEING HOME

Name: **SGT DEREK McGEE**
Returned from: **IRAQ**
Hometown: **RHINEBECK, NEW YORK**

I am home now; it's nice I guess. Things are different. So am I. It is hard to get excited about things, anything really. Food is all right; I get sort of excited about that, and women—well, one anyway. Maybe I'm more mature now; maybe I'm just bored, I don't know.

I gave up hunting. I regret this because I love venison. I never was very good at hunting, and now I just don't want to do it anymore. I never actually killed a deer, but I scared the hell out of a few. What is the point? They don't even shoot back. Part of me wants to never touch a gun again, and part of me wants to wrap my hands tightly on my old 16, get the scope dead-on, lovingly reapply the camouflage tape, strap two magazines together, throw a round in the chamber, use the meaty-tip of my thumb to flirt with the safety, and go home to Fallujah.

It's not that loud noises terrify me. It's just that I don't respond appropriately to them. My heart goes off like a Led Zeppelin drum solo, my diaphragm sprints, pulling in far more oxygen than I need, and I want to fight back. But there is no one to fight, there is nowhere to go, nothing to do. I'm supposed to just go on normally, but my body doesn't know that, and though I tell it, sometimes it takes a while for it to listen. There was a time when if a noise that didn't belong was heard, people looked at me for some leadership, they wanted me to tell them where to go, and what to do; now they just look and think: Who is the weirdo hyperventilating at the bar because a waitress dropped a tray? This woman I see at the vet center said that the body can reabsorb adrenaline in five to ten minutes. She said to control my breathing and concentrate on something else and remind myself that I really am normal. It works. She is a very smart lady.

I don't sleep that much at all. Unless, of course, I'm drunk. It gets tedious though, to start drinking nightcaps at seven so that sleep will come at two. It's actually worse than just tedious; it's harmful. You think that drinking will make things better, but it doesn't. It lets the bad thoughts in. It lets the irrational thoughts in. I spent 20 minutes at a bar the other night, pretending to play a golf video game even though I didn't have any quarters, and I hate video games, and I don't play golf. I watched this little jerky computer-generated guy in funny clothes drive a few white pixels toward a flag. He never got the ball there, but I wasn't thinking about him; I was thinking that if I had taken the vehicles and checked up on the foot patrol instead of deciding to give my worn-out men a break—I wanted them to get a chance to take their gear off for a minute, the patrol was almost back anyway—if I had checked their route for them, maybe, just maybe . . . who knows. So, this stupid fucker in plaid pants sucks at golf, and now Mike and John are gone, and when I said good-bye, they couldn't hear me because there were holes in their heads that maybe wouldn't be there if I had decided to check up on the damn patrol. Drinking doesn't help.

The smart woman at the vet center explained it to me. She is very smart. You see, for seven months I ran around every day wearing 80 pounds of armor plates, ammunition, grenades, water, maps, little cards telling me how to say, "Where are the weapons hidden?" bandages and tourniquets and this powder that burns the skin to stop the bleeding, radios, and little cards that say, "Sorry we destroyed your house—go here and we'll give you money." It was hot, and we carried all this stuff, and when we took it off, we lifted weights and ran and did all these things. Now I am home. I just had an operation, and I sit around and do nothing except take Vicodin, which kills pain that I don't really feel anyway. I don't follow the directions; no, I save it up for special occasions. What the hell are special occasions?

Well, she tells me (the smart lady) my body is just not used to inactivity. She says that if I exercise, my body will feel normal again, and I won't wake up five to six times a night. I suppose she is right. I want to tell her that I don't mind waking up every 45 minutes or so—it is a nice break from the dreams—but I'm afraid she'll think I'm crazy. She is a shrink and has to deal with crazy people all day, so I don't want to burden her any further. Tomorrow I will start running, or maybe the day after. I should stop smoking and drinking tomorrow, or the day after, as well. I tell her this. She smiles and nods and hands me a card where she has written the time I'm supposed to see her next week. This is good. I'll come back next week and tell her that I should stop smoking and drinking tomorrow—or the next day.

I wake up early and feel compelled to get stuff done, like all good motivated people. I can't get back to sleep; there is too much to do. I'm ready to hit the ground running and get everything accomplished. I'm so overcome with energy, even though I only got three hours of sleep, that it is hard not to flop around and wake up the beautiful girl next to me. I have so much I want to do, I can't go back to sleep now. I should be studying maps and intelligence reports. There has to be a pattern to these ambushes. What if we put a sniper team in over Route Fran? They might see something. Fuck it, let me bring my team in there overnight; we'll shoot something. Are we carrying enough ammo? Are the vehicles ready? What can I do to keep the next patrol from taking casualties? I don't actually think about any of those things. What I think is that I should be doing something important now, but I'm not. Eventually, the beautiful girl next to me will wake up, look over and see me staring at the ceiling, and most likely think: I wish he would get motivated enough to clean his room and do his laundry.

I miss all the guys. If they were all around me, piled into bunk beds, I would be laughing right now. We always laughed, no matter how lousy things were. You didn't think about the bad stuff—well, you thought about it just enough to make jokes about it. One day—there were many, actually—I was fairly certain I wasn't going to make it. Not just me—we all thought like that when things got bad. It wasn't paranoia; three Marines had burned into nothing, and one was found walking around alive but still on fire two days earlier, and we were going to the same spot to show the world we weren't scared. Don't tell anyone, but we were. "Elwell," I said to my driver, "I have no clean laundry."

"Me neither; where are we going with this?"

"Well, I don't want my parents to get a box of dirty underwear and socks."

"All right, I see where you're going. You're saying that today isn't a good time for us to die."

"Well," I said, "I don't want to be a pain in the ass. But if it's all the same to you, why don't we just die some other day."

"Fine," he said, "I guess I'll just stay away from the roadside bombs today. But, Sergeant," he continued, paternally, "you really should stay on top of your laundry; you're a sergeant for Christ's sake."

Somewhere around then my girlfriend left me, or I pushed her away—I don't blame her, love happens sometimes, that's all. I found out that she was gone from an e-mail she forwarded to me, which had come to her from her new boyfriend. She sent me this joke—I don't even remember what it was—because she wanted to make me laugh. She didn't realize that the e-mail also contained a week's worth of replies to replies between them. They seemed good for each other. It hit me in the face like a two-by-four.

Everyone said that they were disgusted because it was the worst time for someone to have to deal with a breakup. They were so wrong.

It was the most thoughtful thing she ever did for me. When else can you say: "Well, my girlfriend is banging some other dude. Who cares? At least I'm not on fire. When does the next patrol leave?" If she had waited until I got home, when I would have had time to think and dwell on things, well, that would have been bad timing.

The next day, when we were leaving the wire, I told everyone in my vehicle, "Don't worry, boys. Nothing can happen to us. I'm invincible right now."

"What the fuck are you talking about?"

"Well, think about it. There is no way God would let my ex-girlfriend and her lousy new boyfriend get my life insurance money."

"It's still in her name, you moron? Why don't you change it?"

"Because," I said, shocked at their ignorance, "then I wouldn't be invincible."

It was always like that—always jokes. But they're off living their lives somewhere else now, and it just isn't as funny anymore. I see some of them from time to time. I talk to them as well.

I've seen a lot of bad behavior from my friends, since being home. I watched them beat the bejesus out of a guy at a bar for not really doing anything at all—except maybe not backing down convincingly enough. Since then I've heard that two broke their hands on faces, and one had his jaw broken for him; those are just the ones I know about. When we talk on the phone, they tell me, in a light sort of way, about the bender they're on and about the many wild fights that just seem to find them. Me too. We pretend it's funny. Once I blurted into the phone, "Loud noises make me act, well, you know, a little odd."

"You're fine," my friend said. "Just thinking about loud noises makes me act odd. I almost passed out in Best Buy the other day because of anxiety. You should talk to someone at the vet center. They're giving me these antianxiety pills."

"I don't want pills," I said.

"But you want to talk. Go see them. They're smart."

After September 11, I became addicted to CNN. I kept it on 24/7, even when I was sleeping. That lasted for years. I don't watch the news anymore. Every time I see a clip of those in Iraq, I feel a guilt that makes me squirm. Why am I here on a couch with a beer and this girl, who I really like, and everything is so great for me, and they are doing my job for me? I don't belong here. I should be there. I don't watch the news anymore.

I have been punched on two different occasions since being home. Both times I froze and didn't do anything about it. I was afraid. It's not that I didn't know what to do. I do. I can. It wasn't that I was afraid of whomever it was that was punching me. I was afraid that if I started punching back, I wouldn't stop. The last time I punched back, I stood in the turret of a Humvee and sent 400 rounds of 7.62-mm, belt-fed ammunition into a residential neighborhood, into houses, people's houses, and there was a mosque there, too. I didn't ever want to stop. Partway through, I stopped shooting for a moment, ducked into the vehicle, opened the rear left door, and kicked a cooler and everything else out. Then I sat on the roof of the Humvee, lifted my legs up to my chest, eased my finger back onto the trigger, and the soothing "bup-bup-bup-bup-bup-bup-bup-bup" began again. Below me, where my feet had been so firmly planted seconds before, they shoved the body of CAPT John McKenna. I didn't know at the time that it was my platoon commander. I didn't know anything that wasn't in my gun sights. We sped off to the nearest base, and I threw bandages down to the guys in the vehicle, pulled the radio receiver up from below—everyone else was too busy to talk on the radio—and it was then that I heard, from Gallagher, who was holding John's head, "Hang in there, sir."

I prayed for the first time in a decade. I thought I had forgotten how. It comes right back. I suppose it is comforting to know that the next time I need to pray it will come back again. I tried to think of something profound to say. Something that would penetrate the unconsciousness and revive the man below me.

"Don't give up, you tough Irish fuck."

That is what I said. It was ridiculous and crass, but if anything would have worked, that might have been it. It didn't matter. He was dead even before his knees had given out and left him pouring his life onto the filthy streets of Fallujah. We didn't know that. He was gurgling and twitching, and we wanted him to live, so I said it again.

"Don't give up, you tough Irish fuck."

I don't want to talk about it anymore.

So, I forget what my point was, but I think it has something to do with this: If you get a deer this year, I would love some of the meat.

Note: This post appears in Derek McGee's beautifully produced small press book When I Wished I Was Here: Dispatches from Fallujah, *which can be ordered directly from crumpledpress.org.*

GLOSSARY

1LT—First lieutenant

2LT—Second lieutenant

1SG—First sergeant

A-10—A-10 Thunderbolt II, used for close air support of ground forces; also known as "the Warthog"

AAFES—Army and Air Force Exchange Service

ACM—Anti-Coalition militia

ACU—Army combat uniform

AIF—Anti-Iraqi Forces

AK-47, AK—Automatic rifle that fires a 7.62-mm round; most commonly made by Russia and China. AK are the initials of Alexander Kalashnikov, the designer of the weapon; 47 refers to the year in which it was first built.

ANA—Afghan National Army

ANP—Afghan National Police

AO—Area of operations

ASR—Alternate supply route

ASV—Armored security vehicle

Black ammo status—Running out of ammunition. The Army uses Green, Red, and Black as symbols when sending up status reports, which gives a quick sitrep to the commanders on a unit's mission capabilities in terms of food, ammo, water, and fuel. Green means they are good to go. Red means they will be in need of a resupply soon, because they are running low. Black means that they are either very close or completely out of whatever it is they are reporting on.

BSB—Brigade support battalion

BX—Base exchange

C-5—The Galaxy cargo plane, the largest cargo aircraft in the U.S. military service.

C-130—The Hercules, a four-prop U.S. Air Force cargo plane; its frame is one of the most versatile in the U.S. fleet.

CAPT—Captain

CAT—Caterpillar, a leading manufacturer of engines and construction and mining equipment

CET—Convoy escort team

CH—Chaplain

CLS bag—Combat lifesaver bag; contains emergency medical supplies for soldiers

CMA—The ANA's Central Movement Agency, which provides supplies to ANA units

CO—Commanding officer

Commo blackout—Communications blackout

CP—Checkpoint

CPL—Corporal

DFAC—Dining facility or mess hall. DFACs are run by civilian contractors. Mess or chow halls are run by soldiers.

Dragunov—Russian-made semiautomatic sniper rifle. The SVD, or Dragunov, was actually designed as a designated marksman's weapon to be used at a squad level. It can be used as a sniper rifle, but its accuracy seriously diminishes after 800 meters.

Eid—The Islamic holiday that marks the end of Ramadan, the month of fasting

EOD—Explosive ordnance disposal: the military's bomb squad

ETT—Embedded training teams

Evac—Medical evacuation, usually by helicopter. Usually the term "medevac" is used.

Exfil—Exfiltration; snipers coming back out of position

FC1 (SW)—Fire controlman first class, enlisted surface warfare specialist

FOB—Forward operating base

Fort Drum wives' riot—Many men of the 10th Mountain Division had already made it halfway home before being informed they had been extended. During a debriefing session explaining the change in travel plans for their almost-home husbands, angry wives shouted at colonels and (according to lore) threw food at them. A cadence written about this and other difficult moments in mil spouse life has been performed by Fort Drum wives:

> I don't know what you've been told,
> The Army spouse is brave and bold.
> We pay the bills and fix the car,
> Then they go and raise the bar.
> Mowing lawns and hauling trash,
> And always feeling strapped for cash,
> We try to hold our heads up high,
> Can't we just throw a fit and cry?

Glock—Austrian-manufactured handgun

HQ—Headquarters

HS—Home station

HTCM (RET)—Master chief hull maintenance technician (retired)

Humvee / HMMWV / Hummer—High-mobility, multipurpose wheeled vehicle: the light tactical vehicle for our armed forces. Now we use the 1114s and the 1151s; new up-armored variants are also called UAHs, short for up-armored Humvee.

IA—Iraqi Army

IBA—Interceptor body armor

ID—Infantry division

IED—Improvised explosive device: a homemade bomb

Infil—Infiltrate; snipers moving into position

IP—Iraqi Police

IPLO—International police liaison officer

IR—Infrared light

IT—Information technology

KBR—Contractor providing many services in Iraq; formerly known as Kellogg Brown and Root

Kevlar—The brand name for the synthetic Aramid fiber used by the U.S. military in body armor and helmets. Commonly used as the mil slang for "helmet."

KIA—Killed in action

Klicks—Slang for kilometers

LANs—Local area networks

LED—Light-emitting diode

LT—Lieutenant; when used without a name, pronounced "el-tee."

LZ—Landing zone

M4—The carbine (shorter barrel) version of the M16 rifle

Mahallah—Neighborhood; commonly used by U.S. soldiers in Iraq when speaking of being outside the wire

MAJ—Major

MAV—Modular assault vest

MG—Machine gun

MI—Military intelligence

MILES—Multiple Integrated Laser Engagement System

MOI—Ministry of the Interior

MP—Military police

MRE—Meal, ready to eat, pronounced "M-R-E"; a self-contained individual field ration

MSG—Master sergeant

MSR—Main supply route

MWO—Either a reinforcing steel plate that is bolted onto both sides of an HMMWV gear box in order to strengthen it, or a mythical component created by sadistic Army mechanics for the express purpose of inspiring fellow soldiers to spend many hours working in the intense Baghdad heat taking a whole wheel off an HMMWV with no power tools.

MWR—Morale, welfare, and recreation

NCO—Noncommissioned officer

NCOIC—Noncommissioned officer in charge

NTC—National training center

ODA—Operational detachment alpha; small, highly trained Special Forces teams

OEF—Operation Enduring Freedom; in common usage refers to the war in Afghanistan. It is the official name for the U.S. response to 9/11, which comprises operations in Afghanistan, the Philippines, the Horn of Africa, Trans-Sahara, and Pankisi Gorge.

OIF—Operation Iraqi Freedom

OP—Observation post

Operation Anaconda—March 2002 operation by U.S. and Afghan forces against Taliban and Al Qaeda forces in the Shahi-kot Valley and Arma Mountains southeast of Zormat.

OPORD—Operation order, which states how a unit is organized for an operation.

OPS—Operations

Outside the wire—Off the base of operations

PA—Public address

Pashtun—Afghanistan's dominant ethnic and linguistic group, which is organized tribally and comprises just over half the country's population; the main ethnic contingent in the Taliban movement

PFC—Private first class

PID—Positive identification

PKC—Soviet-designed light machine gun. The most common light/medium machine guns are the RPK (an AK variant) and the PKM.

PQ2—Infrared aiming devices used with night-vision goggles; pronounced "peck two"

PSG—Platoon sergeant

PSP—PlayStation Portable

PT—Physical training

PX—Post exchange

Qalat—Arabic word for a mud-walled fortress around a village

QRF—Quick reaction force

Ramadan—The ninth month of the Islamic calendar, a month of fasting, charity, prayers, and self-accountability

R&R—Rest and recovery

RN—Registered nurse

RPG—Rocket-propelled grenade

ROTC—Reserve Officers' Training Corps

RPK—Light machine gun made in Russia; fires 7.62-mm rounds

Rustimayah—A forward operating base (FOB) in Baghdad

Sarn—Used in conversation for "sergeant"

SAW—Squad automatic weapon. The M249 light machine gun, which fires 5.56-mm rounds

SFC—Sergeant first class

SGT—Sergeant

Shura—Arabic word for consultation or council

SIM—Subscriber identity module, a removable smart card for cell phones

SINCGARS—Single Channel Ground and Airborne Radio System

SMSgt—Senior master sergeant

SP—Start point

SPC—Specialist

SSG—Staff sergeant

SUV—Sport utility vehicle

T wall—Precast concrete barriers; called Jersey barriers on the East Coast

TAC—Tactical officer; the company commander of a cadet company at the United States Military Academy

TC—Truck commander

TOC—Tactical operations center

TTPs—Tactics, techniques, and procedures

UAV—Unmanned aerial vehicle

USO—United Services Organization, a private nonprofit whose mission is to provide morale, welfare, and recreation services to our men and women in uniform

VBIED— Vehicle-borne improvised explosive device; a car bomb

VCD—Video compact disc

VIN—Vehicle identification number

VS-17—Brightly colored marker panel used to signal to friendly aircraft

XO—Executive officer, the number two in command of any element, right behind the unit commander

FISHER HOUSE
because A Family's Love Is Good Medicine

www.fisherhouse.org

A Fisher House is a "home away from home" for families of patients receiving medical care at major military and VA medical centers. As of this printing, there are thirty-eight Fisher Houses located on eighteen military installations and eight VA medical centers, with another five houses under construction or in design. The program began in 1990 and has offered nearly 2.5 million days of lodging to more than one hundred thousand families.

The Fisher House Foundation donates Fisher Houses to the U.S. government. They have full-time salaried managers but depend on volunteers and voluntary support to enhance daily operations and program expansion.

Through the generosity of the American public, the foundation has expanded its programs to meet the needs of our servicemen and -women who have been wounded. The foundation uses donated frequent-flier miles to provide airline travel to reunite families of the wounded and to enable our wounded heroes to go home to convalesce. They also help cover the cost of alternative lodging when the Fisher Houses are full.

For further information about these programs, to find out about volunteering, or to make a tax-deductible gift, go to their Web site at

www.fisherhouse.org.

You can also obtain information by writing them at

Fisher House Foundation, Inc.
1401 Rockville Pike, Suite 600
Rockville, MD 20852

Phone: (888) 294-8560
E-mail: info@fisherhouse.org